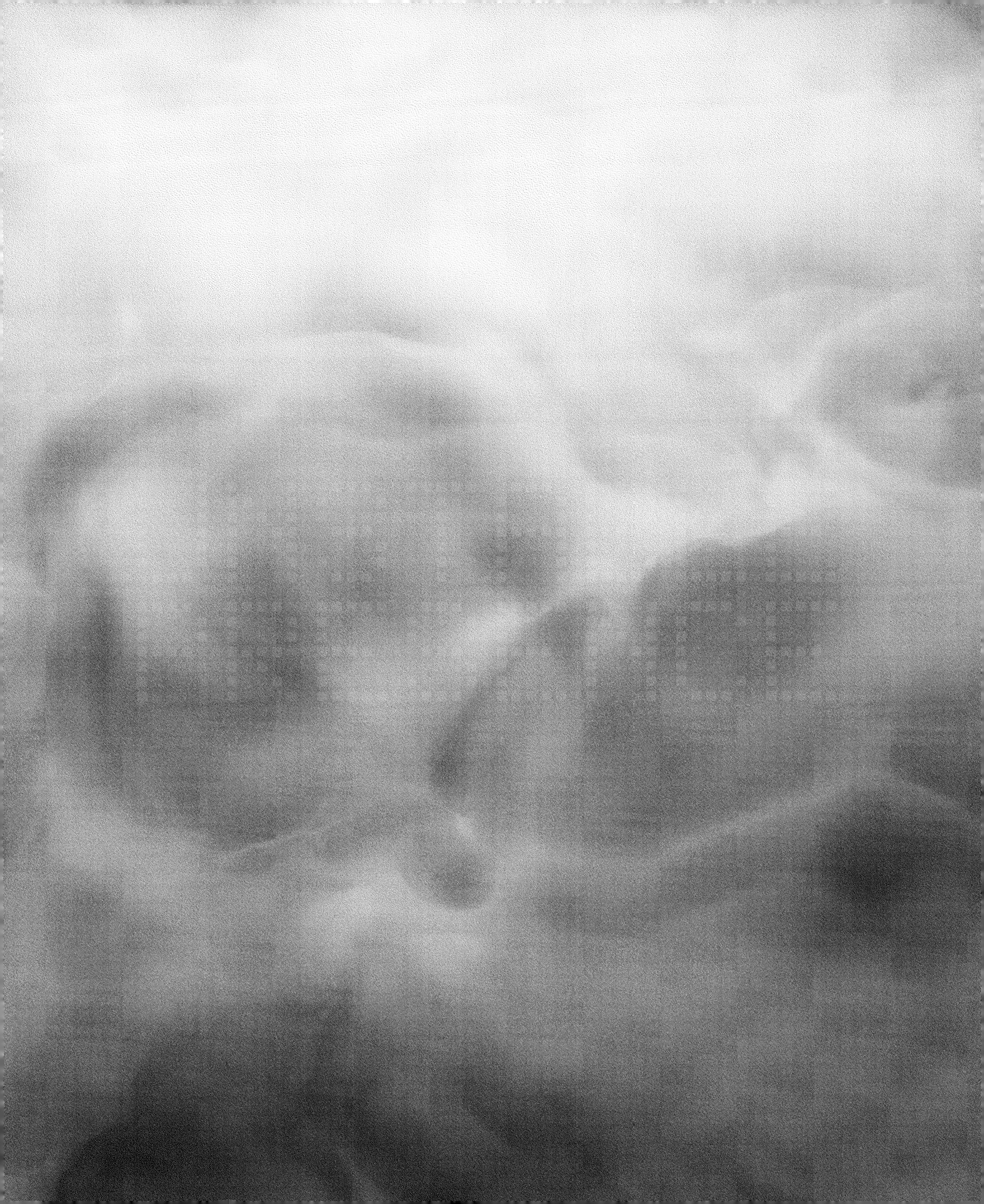

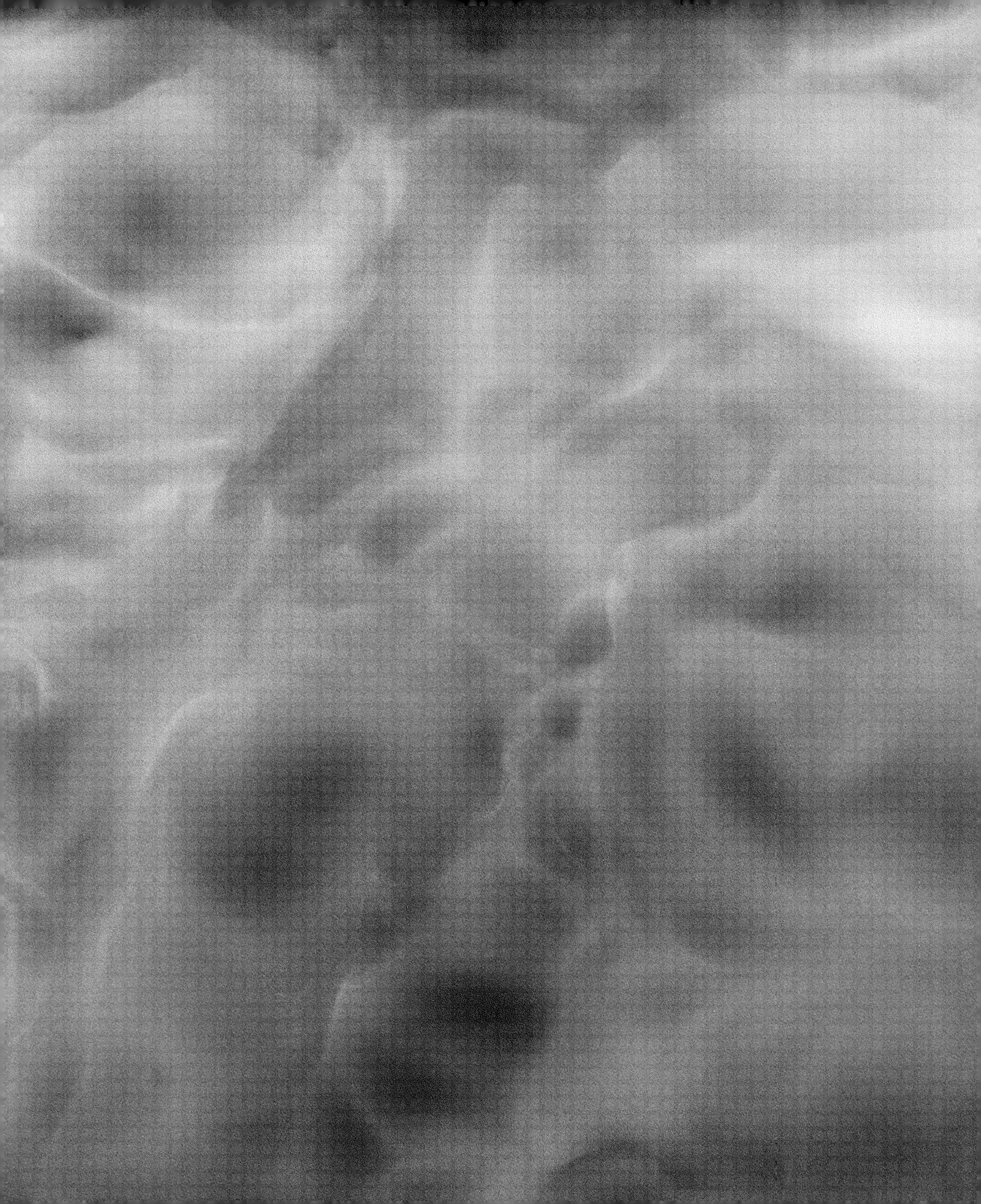

RAFAEL LOZANO-HEMMER

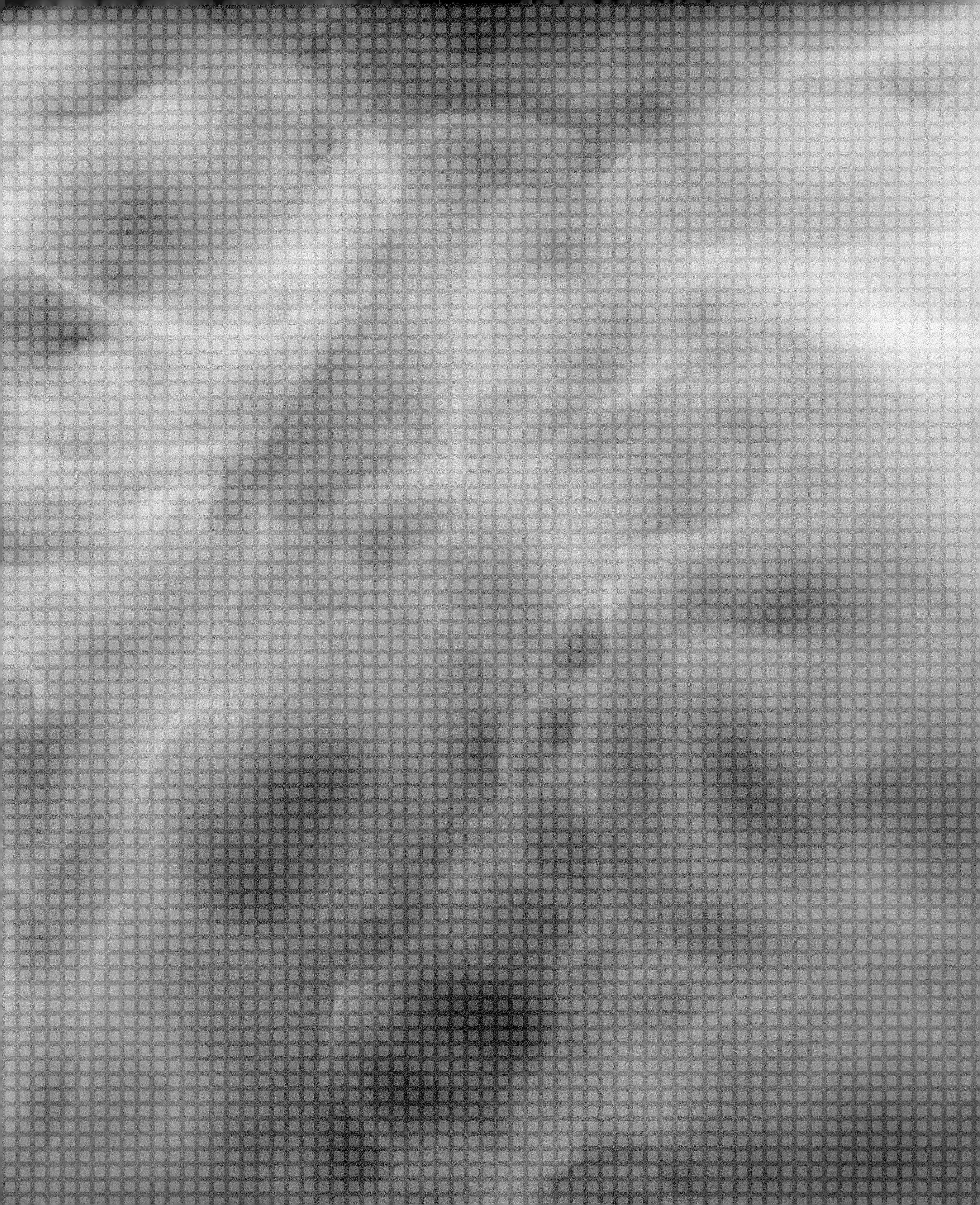

RAFAEL LOZANO-HEMMER

EDITED BY RUDOLF FRIELING AND FRANÇOIS LETOURNEUX

Published to accompany the exhibition co-organized by the
Musée d'art contemporain de Montréal and the San Francisco Museum of Modern Art

SAN FRANCISCO MUSEUM OF MODERN ART IN ASSOCIATION WITH
DELMONICO BOOKS · PRESTEL, MUNICH, LONDON, NEW YORK

NOTE TO THE READER

The cover of this book is printed with ink that appears only in sunlight. To activate distinct effects, expose the book to sunlight both with and without the jacket in place. The stability of the effects will wane over time.

CONTENTS

FOREWORD

NEAL BENEZRA

Helen and Charles Schwab Director
San Francisco Museum of Modern Art

JOHN ZEPPETELLI

Director and Chief Curator
Musée d'art contemporain de Montréal

In a 2014 interview, Rafael Lozano-Hemmer said, "A good artwork is like a good nightclub—you create the music, the ambience . . . but it's only when the public comes in that you know if it's going to be a good party or not. The public brings the energy and the content, and the artist just creates the conditions for an experiment to take place over time."

Rafael Lozano-Hemmer: Unstable Presence, the first major survey of the artist's work organized in the United States and Canada, includes a wide range of installations that deeply engage—and indeed depend on—the viewer. And while Lozano-Hemmer's works often deploy sophisticated technologies, they are also profoundly human, summoning our sense of play as much as our anxieties. They are immersed, and in turn immerse us, in the complex realities of our broader social and political context. Lozano-Hemmer's installations make tangible our impact on one another and our environment. Within each work, a kind of community building takes place: we are made aware of the implications of our presence within a larger group or are united, either knowingly or unwittingly, with a broader community.

Lozano-Hemmer, who was born in Mexico City in 1967 and lives in Montreal, is a key figure in the intersecting fields of contemporary art and new media. Over the past few decades, he has become well known for large-scale, participatory installations involving ambitious light projections and the architecture of public sites. The Musée d'art contemporain de Montréal (MAC) and the San Francisco Museum of Modern Art (SFMOMA) are honored to have co-organized and co-curated *Rafael Lozano-Hemmer: Unstable Presence*, which focuses primarily on works produced by the artist over the past decade. More than a midcareer survey, this exhibition offers a new conceptual viewpoint on the artist's output, exploring its poetic and political dimensions through the underlying notion of co-presence. It explores dialogue among singular voices, experiences, and perspectives in Lozano-Hemmer's work. Conversely, it also makes visible more asymmetrical types of relationships and uneasy cohabitations in the age of technological surveillance.

Both of our organizations have longstanding relationships with the artist. *Rafael Lozano-Hemmer: Unstable Presence* debuted at MAC, which has collected the artist's work since 2011 and included it in exhibitions such as *La beauté du geste*, in 2006, and *Articulated Intersect*, during the 2011 Quebec Triennial. At SFMOMA, where the exhibition closes, Lozano-Hemmer was previously featured in *The Art of Participation: 1950 to Now* (2008), *Field Conditions* (2010), *Rafael Lozano-Hemmer: Frequency and Volume* (2011), and *Soundtracks* (2017), which included a work by the artist from SFMOMA's collection, *Last Breath* (2012).

Between its presentations in Montreal and San Francisco, the show traveled to the Museo de Arte Contemporáneo de Monterrey, Mexico (MARCO). We are grateful to our colleagues at MARCO, including board director Alfonso González Migoya, administrative director Jaime Rosales, and exhibitions and collection manager Elisa Téllez, for their partnership. Our gratitude also goes to the Canada Council for the Arts for supporting the presentation of the exhibition at MARCO and to Debbie and Andy Rachleff and Carlie Wilmans for their support of the exhibition at SFMOMA.

We extend our heartfelt thanks to Rudolf Frieling, SFMOMA curator of media arts, and Lesley Johnstone, curator and head of exhibitions and education at MAC, as well as to MAC associate curator François LeTourneux, who served, with Frieling, as coeditor of this publication. Their deep commitment to and passion for this project and this artist have yielded an astonishing exhibition. It is a thrill to share *Rafael Lozano-Hemmer: Unstable Presence* in our galleries, and to see our visitors take part in the extraordinary experiments the works on view present.

Our ultimate thanks go to the artist and his entire team at Antimodular Research for their groundbreaking work and tireless collaboration on all aspects of this complex exhibition.

NOTE

Opening quote: Caroline Menezes, "Rafael Lozano-Hemmer Interview," *Studio International*, September 16, 2014, http://www.studiointernational.com/index.php/rafael-lozano-hemmer-new-media-art-digital-technology-sphere-packing.

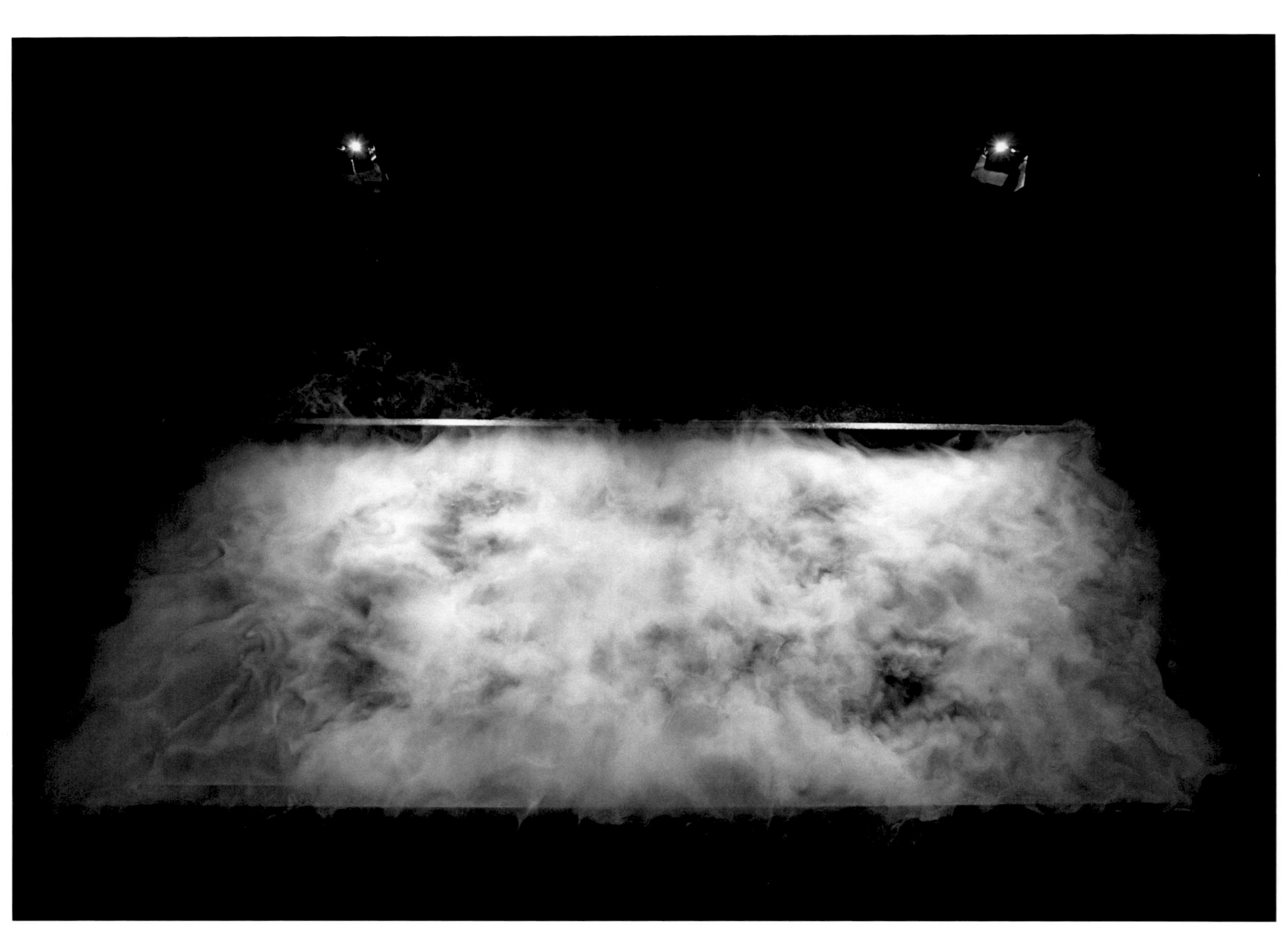

ACKNOWLEDGMENTS

RUDOLF FRIELING
Curator of Media Arts
San Francisco Museum of Modern Art

LESLEY JOHNSTONE
Curator and Head of Exhibitions
and Education
Musée d'art contemporain de Montréal

The development and presentation of this long-overdue survey exhibition was only possible with the enthusiastic support of many colleagues. We wish to expressly acknowledge the trust and support extended by our two directors, John Zeppetelli, director and chief curator at the Musée d'art contemporain de Montréal (MAC), and Neal Benezra, Helen and Charles Schwab Director of the San Francisco Museum of Modern Art (SFMOMA), both of whom embraced our proposal for this exhibition from the outset.

At MAC, the curatorial team included Lesley Johnstone, who collaborated closely with François LeTourneux on the Montreal presentation of the exhibition, assisted by Marjolaine Labelle. They received support from Chantal Charbonneau in publications and the administration team of Nathalie Dupuis, Maryse Elias, and Yves Théoret. The complexities of a large survey were masterfully handled by the registration team of Béatriz Leyva-Calderon, Eve Katinoglou, Gabriel Lalonde-Savage, Manon Pouliot, and Anne-Marie Zeppetelli, working closely with conservator Marie-Chantale Poisson and the installation crew of Denis Labelle, Alexandre Perreault, Carl Solari, and Josée St-Louis. Additional appreciation goes to Anne-Marie Barnard, Roxane Dumas-Noël, Carol Jungpeter, Valérie Sirard in communications, Pascale Tremblay in rights and reproductions, Laureen Bardou in development, Chantal St-Cyr in visitor services, and educators Luc Guillemette and Sylvie Pelletier.

At SFMOMA, the curatorial team included Rudolf Frieling with Andrea Nitsche-Krupp, assisted by Karen Cheung. Exhibitions staff, under the supervision of Jessica Woznak, skillfully and professionally supported the project. We are exceptionally grateful to Jillian Aubrey, Alexander Cheves, Sarah Choi, Steve Dye, David Funk, Sean Horchy, and Brandon Larson, in close collaboration with Eliza Chiasson in registration. Our cordial thanks go to the conservation team led by Michelle Barger, and to Meghan Berckes, Summer Li, and Michelle Thomas under the supervision of Bosco Hernández in our design studio. We appreciate the substantial support of our marketing and communications department, headed by Ann von Germeten, with Clara Hatcher Baruth, Taylor Brandon, Cristina Chan, Emma LeHocky, and Jill Lynch. Further thanks go to Jennifer Snyder and Vincent Sulit in digital experience; Alison Bowman,

Samantha Leo, and Caroline Stevens in development; and the education and community engagement team led by Chad Coerver. We also wish to thank Emily Quist in visitor experience for her thoughtful oversight. Anna Tang in finance and Mike Chominski, Courtney Costello, Walter Logue, Christo Oropeza, and Tim Tengonciang, in operations, provided additional support.

SFMOMA's excellent publications team guided us expertly through developing an enduring yet dynamic catalogue in response to this exhibition. We thank Kari Dahlgren and Brianna Nelson, along with Lucy Medrich. Our thanks also go to the catalogue's designer, James Brendan Williams, who responded so beautifully to our desire for an "unstable presence" in this publication. Kristin Swan ably served as copy editor, while staff members at Lucia | Marquand, including Melissa Duffes, Tom Eykemans, Leah Finger, Adrian Lucia, Meghann Ney, and Kestrel Rundle oversaw the book's production. We are also grateful to Mary DelMonico and Amelia Rina of our copublishing partner DelMonico Books / Prestel. Our contributing authors—Olivier Asselin, Merete Carlson, Sean Cubitt, Tatiana Flores, Robin Adèle Greeley, François LeTourneux, Ulrik Schmidt, and Gloria Sutton—wrote profoundly about the artist's complex work, providing the multiplicity of voices, perspectives, and histories we had hoped to include.

Rafael Lozano-Hemmer has offered trust and friendship every step of the way, making the experience of working on this exhibition particularly special. Our tremendous gratitude goes to the artist and his entire team of collaborators at his studio, Antimodular Research, who in many different ways have been instrumental in realizing this project. We are particularly grateful to Karine Charbonneau for her deft handling of all manner of logistics and coordination, and to Stephan Schulz and Guillaume Tremblay for their technical expertise and meticulous execution. Our appreciation extends to invaluable members of the studio team Sarah Amarica, Kitae Kim, Jesse Morrison, Rebecca Murdock, Carolina Murillo-Morales, Matthew Palmer, Jean Philippe Pierre-Louis, Caroline Record, and Tegan Scott for their enthusiasm, resilience, and groundbreaking work. The studio further wishes to thank Generique Design and Conroy Badger, Jessica Blanchet, Nikolaos Chandolias, Sergio Clavijo, Sébastien Dallaire, Pierre Fournier,

Call on Water, 2016. Installation view, Museo de Arte Contemporáneo de Monterrey, Mexico, 2019

Miguel Legault, Jakob Lorenz, Leo Maraviglia, Frederic
Monast, and Orion Szydel. Special gratitude goes to Susie
Ramsay, Antimodular Research cofounder and Rafael's
partner in life.

An exhibition of this size and technological complexity
does not tour easily. We were thus excited to be able to
work with our colleagues at Museo de Arte Contemporáneo
de Monterrey, Mexico (MARCO), whose board director,
Alfonso González Migoya, and administrative director,
Jaime Rosales, supported exhibitions and collection
manager Elisa Téllez in seamlessly and impeccably
mounting this first survey exhibition of Lozano-Hemmer's
work in northern Mexico. We were thrilled to witness this
homecoming to an institution and community where the
artist had exhibited at the beginning of his career.

A large-scale survey cannot be executed without the
generosity of private and institutional lenders. We are
especially grateful to Ahmet Kocabiyik, Yağız Zaimoğlu,
and former artistic director Kathleen Forde of Borusan
Contemporary, Istanbul, for their extraordinary support
in commissioning both *Vicious Circular Breathing* and
Sphere Packing: Bach. We also thank Sergio Fontanella of
Cisneros Fontanals Art Foundation (CIFO), Rosa María
Rodríguez Garza of FEMSA Collection, François Rochon of
Giverny Capital, and SFMOMA trustee Pat Wilson, as well as
Frances Morris and conservator Patricia Falcão, Tate,
London, who facilitated the presentation of *Subtitled Public*
for display at MAC.

Early on, the Canada Council for the Arts provided support
for the presentation of the exhibition at MARCO; the
SFMOMA presentation was generously supported by
Debbie and Andy Rachleff and Carlie Wilmans. To them,
and to all supporters not mentioned here, we express
our sincere gratitude and our hope that the exhibition
resonated with each one of them in very personal ways.
For us, it was a pleasure all the way through.

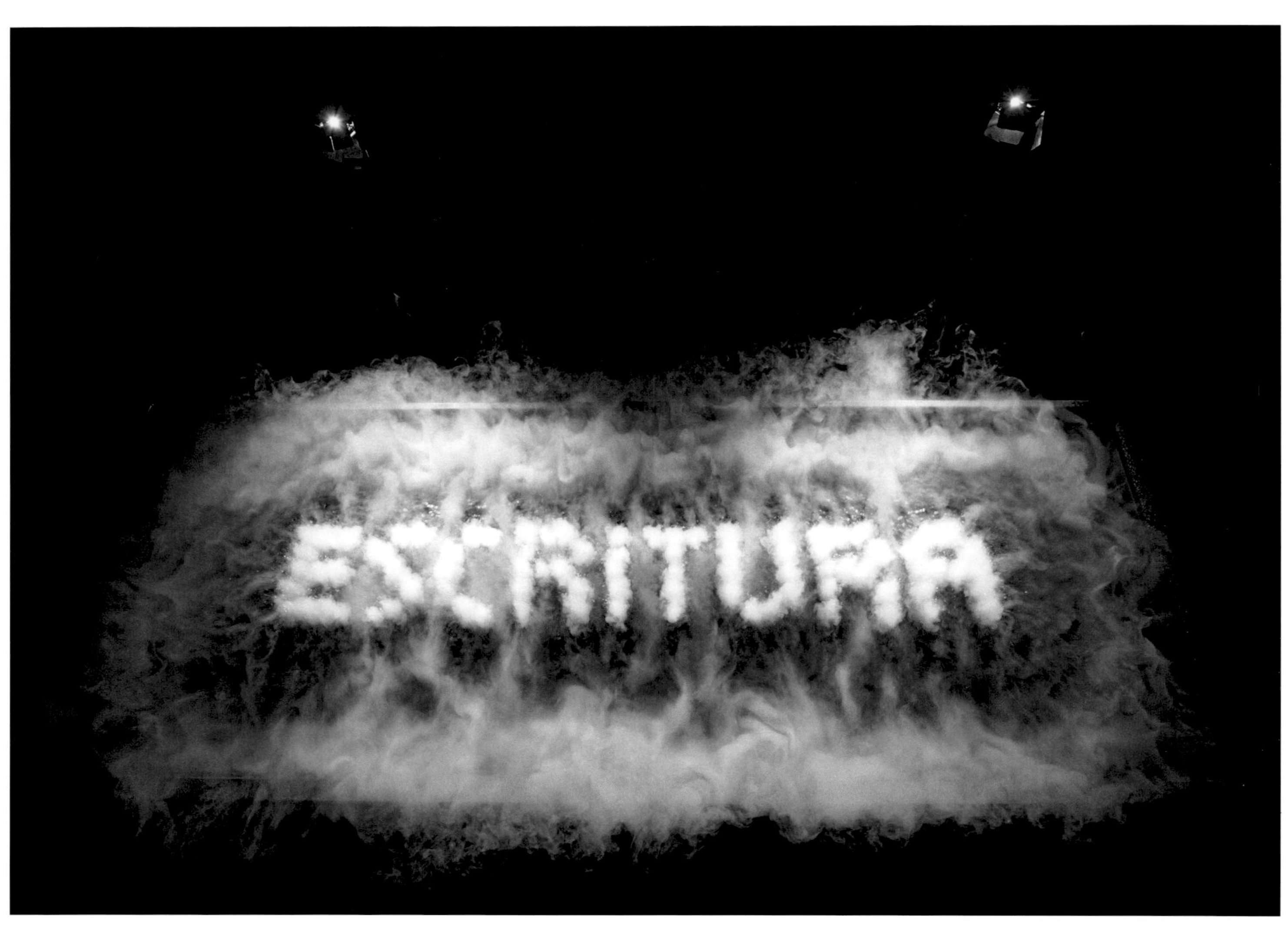
ESCRITURA

INTRODUCTION

RUDOLF FRIELING AND
LESLEY JOHNSTONE

Los cuatro puntos cardinales son tres: el Sur y el Norte.
("The four cardinal directions are three: North and South.")
—Vicente Huidobro, *Altazor*

This absurdist epigram, taken from the preface to a poem by Chilean writer Vicente Huidobro, is the only content displayed on the monitor of the responsive sculpture *Cardinal Directions* (2010; see page 150) by Rafael Lozano-Hemmer. The text slowly unfolds as the viewer walks alongside the rotating monitor, following it in its circular movement, enacting the profound instability central to the artist's work. When presented as the opening of the exhibition *Rafael Lozano-Hemmer: Unstable Presence* for its last iteration, in San Francisco, Huidobro's line, originally meant to describe the geography of Chile, becomes an emblematic instance of the artist's appropriation of poetry in his work. Taking the visitor on a short walk that leads nowhere—or back to the beginning—it opens the door to an understanding of a complex body of responsive, participatory, and performative work that the artist has developed over almost three decades. Once the visitor enters the artist's literal and symbolic space, any simplistic notion of playful performance is subverted. Lozano-Hemmer's artworks offer experiences that are ambiguous and yet precise, poetic and political, material and ephemeral. They present an instant of palpable recognition, even joy, but tentatively and fleetingly. Like the voice of a nearby stranger heard once and then never again, these works offer, for the briefest of moments, an invitation to connect.

Lozano-Hemmer began developing theatrical performances incorporating sound, projections, and tracking systems in the late 1980s. During the 1990s, he explored the performative potential of interaction and, in particular, the integration of different artistic disciplines through technology. Over the last twenty-five years, he has become known for large-scale, computerized installations that employ both light projections and the architecture of public spaces to address the political and cultural history of these sites. The largest of these "anti-monuments" are displayed in spectacular outdoor spaces to optimize their impact and accessibility. While these works of *Relational Architecture*—a series he started in 1997—were designed to be sited in public space and address the agency of the public, a survey exhibition inside a museum necessarily operates on a different scale.

The works selected for *Rafael Lozano-Hemmer: Unstable Presence* offer more intimate experiences in a setting that, at times, recalls a studio, as in *Sphere Packing: Bach* (2018; see page 110), or an immersive social tableau, as in *Zoom Pavilion* (with Krzysztof Wodiczko, 2015; see page 98). The "set" might even be the entire exhibition space, envisioned as the environment into which nanoparticles of a text are dispersed into the air and inhaled by visitors, as in *Babbage Nanopamphlets* (2015; see page 84). A similar instance of porous proximity between bodies and the work occurs in *Pulse Spiral* (2008; see page 132), where one's heartbeat is amplified visually and sonically, exhibiting publicly a most personal signature. To experience the cadence of our own heartbeat in relation to those of visitors who came before or after us is decidedly destabilizing. To become aware of the wide range of rates of heartbeats is to fathom the diversity of the human species, but also to acknowledge our own vulnerability. To see this intimate information projected onto such a large scale is both intimidating and empowering. However, whereas many of the works from the *Pulse* series are exhibited outdoors (often at spectacular scale[1]), the museum presentation of *Pulse Spiral* in an enclosed space introduces yet another dimension to the experience of intimacy and intersubjectivity the series explores.

Commissioned for the opening of Moscow's Garage Center for Contemporary Culture in 2008, *Pulse Spiral* takes its structural inspiration from engineer Vladimir Shukov's collaboration with architect Konstantin Melnikov. The latter's role in the history of constructivism gives the piece an added layer of meaning, echoing modernism's distant models of social fabric and collective agency. As a somber counterpoint to this particular history of co-presence (and like many of the artist's other works), *Pulse Spiral*'s abstraction and technical concentration of bodily traces point to the artist's interest in the broader spaces of political history, and in totalitarianism's historical manipulation of the masses and aestheticization of politics.

Participation in the creation of a condensed, collective "space" also factors in *Vicious Circular Breathing* (2013;

see page 78), albeit on a barely perceptible level, as we breathe the air that others have breathed before us within the confines of a hermetically sealed glass pavilion. Like *Pulse Spiral*, *Vicious Circular Breathing* is a literal embodiment that affects us somatically, but also resonates with every visitor differently in its political invocation of the current global context. All—or most of us, at least—will agree, however, that we have entered an unstable macro-reality in a much more profound and disturbing way at a time of economic and ecological crisis, when the boundaries between public and private space are more and more permeable, and when our own agency is more and more restricted. What is in the air and what dissipates before our eyes into the atmosphere is demonstrably theatrical, all the while operating underneath the visible and legible surface of this exhibition, very much in the manner of the numerous invisible and complex forces that shape our networked daily reality. What is "present" is more than meets the eye.

The exhibition's title refers explicitly to the turbulence that characterizes such social and technical interrelations, and their materialization on various scales, from the personal to the geopolitical. We think of these interrelated layers of presence as a "co-presence" whose instability is powerfully echoed in the sheer physical impact of the various major installations on display, and in their intensive material and sculptural quality. Exploring the works' poetic and political dimensions via the notion of co-presence led us to focus on the coexistence of viewpoints, active voices, and singular experiences, the relationships formed between spectators, and the situations elicited by the works' dialogic devices. Co-presence also alludes to various types of asymmetrical relationships, forced cohabitations, and issues of power, evoking the question of observation, the interplay of gazes, and bodies subjected to today's many techniques of surveillance and control.

The playful, collective dimensions of Lozano-Hemmer's work are locked in a fraught relationship with more disturbing aspects. *Rafael Lozano-Hemmer: Unstable Presence* offers an experience that is seemingly playful and yet never without a sentiment of anxiousness. *Voz Alta* (Out Loud, 2008; see page 40), for example, is a powerful reminder of this interrelationship. Commissioned to commemorate the fortieth anniversary of the massacre of hundreds of students in Mexico City in 1968, this "anti-monument" offered participants the opportunity to speak freely about the tragedy while their amplified voices were transmitted to powerful searchlights, making the project visible to millions throughout the city. We can and must speak up against unjust regimes or the corrupt politics of a place. Nonetheless, eschewing any sort of "techno-optimism," the artist suggests that the aesthetics of participation and new technologies are double edged, and cannot be understood solely as a liberating experience. The participants' role in constructing the experience of Lozano-Hemmer's works is not without spectacular aspects, but the artist reminds us that the devices these works employ also belong to a broader social system. We must confront the ways that economics, politics, and our behaviors are interwoven in a complex and often problematic fashion through technologies of identification and control.

Likewise, the surveillance cameras, facial recognition software, and algorithms of *Zoom Pavilion* (2015, with Krzysztof Wodiczko; see page 98) are subverted to signal how technologies determine and control the circulation of information, images, and data. The piece explicitly articulates the interrelationships between visitors, but also implicitly feeds into the ubiquitous desire to take selfies, even in a space that is constructed to capture comparable images of participants. There is an undeniable, immediate seduction in the works at hand, as visitors see and hear their own heartbeats or their faces or bodies projected on the walls, or relish the power to activate light on a large scale. Entering the sealed air chamber in *Vicious Circular Breathing* engenders a kind of morbid fascination. A visitor may interact joyfully with their shadow on the pages of projected texts in the *Airborne* series (2013; see page 90), even as this destructive presence renders any content illegible. Traces of presence are not just traces; they are embedded in a temporality of obsolescence or loss. This is a quality in Lozano-Hemmer's work that we sought to exhibit in its fullest potential. Language is on display as a forceful but endangered species. It survives in the artist's world through his insistence on the poetic dimension, which often oscillates between emergence, disappearance, and reemergence.

The automated questions of *33 Questions per Minute* (2000; see page 18), presented at the title's speed, mark the threshold of legibility—an experience that is all the more frustrating as viewers have very little time to consider/register the questions' often absurdist meanings. The confusion of who speaks, the mystery of the interrogative form, and the possible references to the context or surroundings (the exhibition site, the artist, the spectators, the present moment) help create a synergy, where the signs of the work and those of the world intermingle as if in an oracular enigma. Presenting questions in multiple languages further enhances the illegibility of the work. Questions generated by the work appear throughout this book; their placement in a consistent position on the page yields varying degrees of legibility.

Underscoring the physical dimension of language, the beautiful fountain of poetry *Call on Water* (2016; see page 86) suggests that words temporarily and shakily materialize in the air, carried by minuscule particles—and on a more metaphorical level, by the breath of those who read and speak them. The fragments of texts by poet Octavio Paz evoke language—the way we see the world through words, and the way words conversely reflect our own image back to us. These metaphors weave through the exhibition a thread of ambiguous legibility best expressed by a turbulent speech act captured on camera and transformed into a sturdy physical thing in *Volute 1: Au clair de la lune* (2016; see page 46). Inspired by Charles Babbage's 1837 statement that the atmosphere is a vast library that contains all the words that have been spoken, the work renders the French phrase in three dimensions as turbulent clouds, containing layers of complex folds and vortices.

Matter still matters. Not everything can or will be unstable. The act of finding physical support structures for ephemeral events encapsulates the artist's—and also our own— imagination, as in the beautiful design of the final iteration of his *Sphere Packing* series, *Sphere Packing: Bach*. To enter the space in which the entire musical production of this most prolific composer may be experienced on a bodily scale is to fathom how data may be translated into physical form, how sound can be made visibly perceptible, and how immateriality may be transformed back into immersive, physical space. Ultimately, it manifests an act of optimism by constructing a new reality, despite the darker implica-

tions and deconstructed realities of many of the assembled works in this exhibition. Participating in these temporal and fluid situations and events is an act of faith in art and the artist.

NOTES

Lesley Johnstone co-curated the Montreal presentation of this exhibition in close collaboration with François LeTourneux, coeditor of this publication.

Epigraph: From the preface to Vicente Huidobro, *Altazor o el viaje en paracaídas, poema de VII cantos* (Madrid: Compañía Iberoamericana de Publicaciones, 1931).

1. See, for example, *Articulated Intersect*, presented by the Musée d'art contemporain de Montréal, in collaboration with the Quartier des Spectacles, on Place des Festivals during the 2011 Quebec Triennial.

33 QUESTIONS PER MINUTE ²⁰⁰⁰

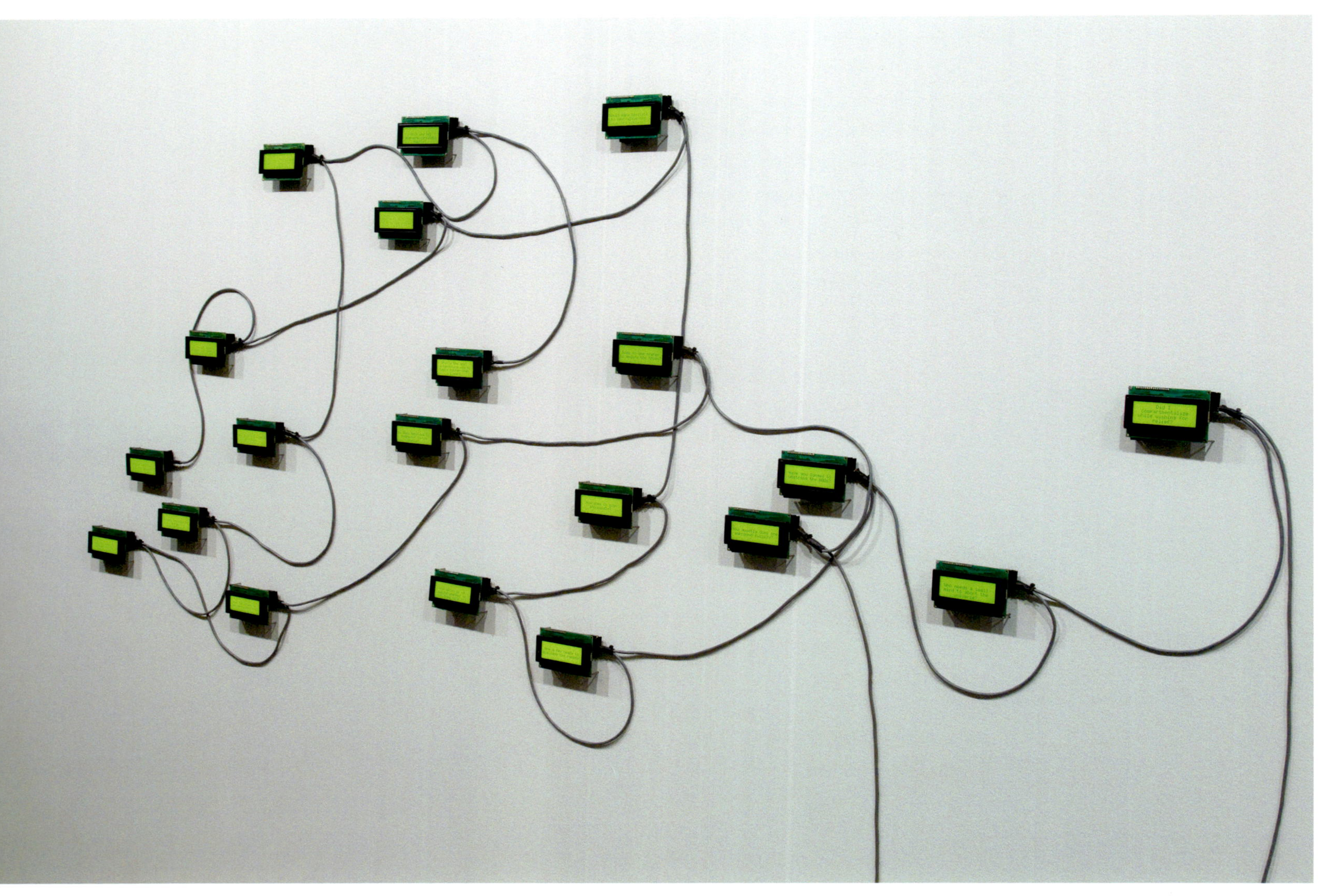

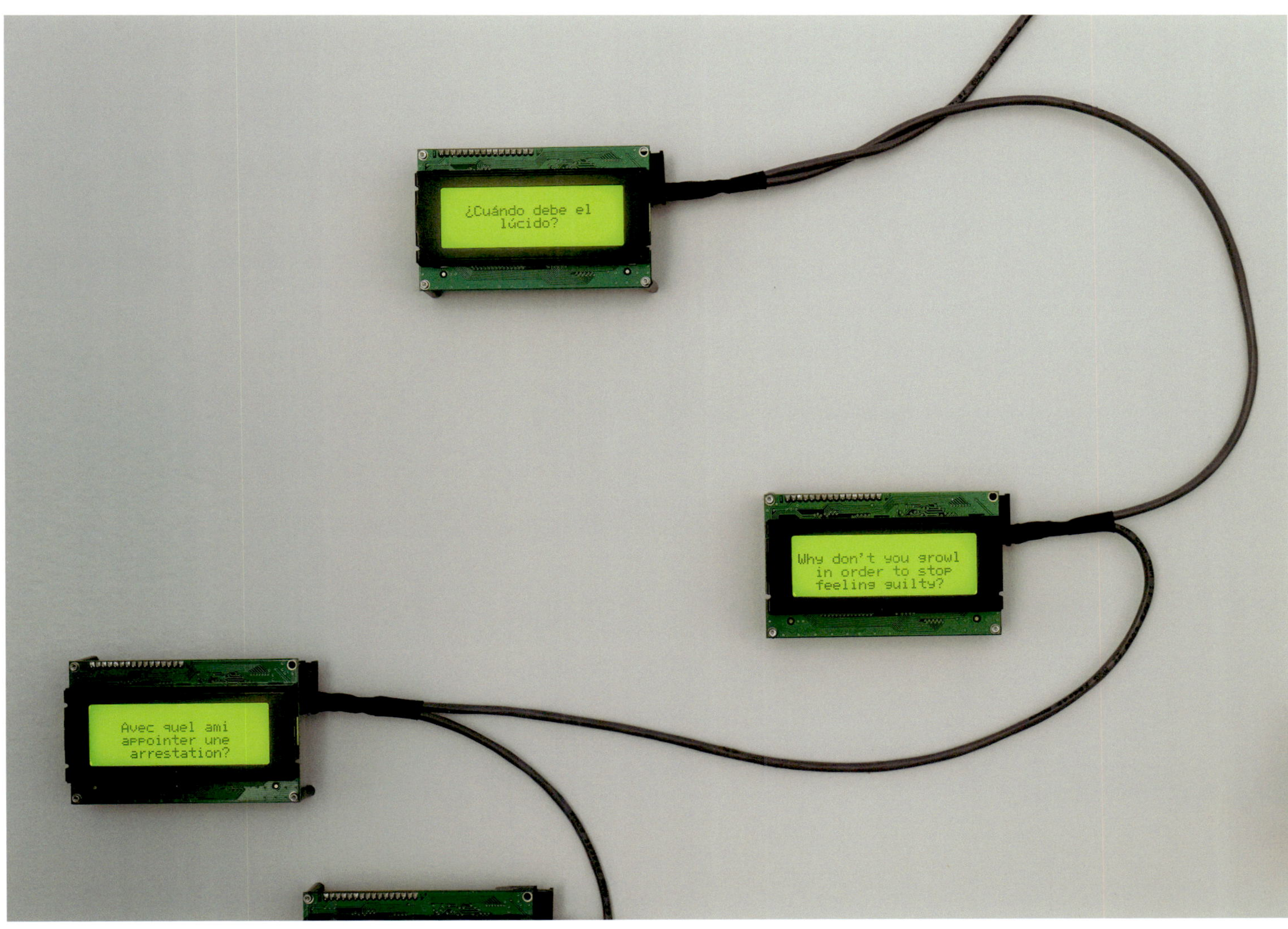

Installation views, Museum of Contemporary Art, Sydney, 2011 (left), and Musée d'art contemporain de Montréal, 2018 (right)

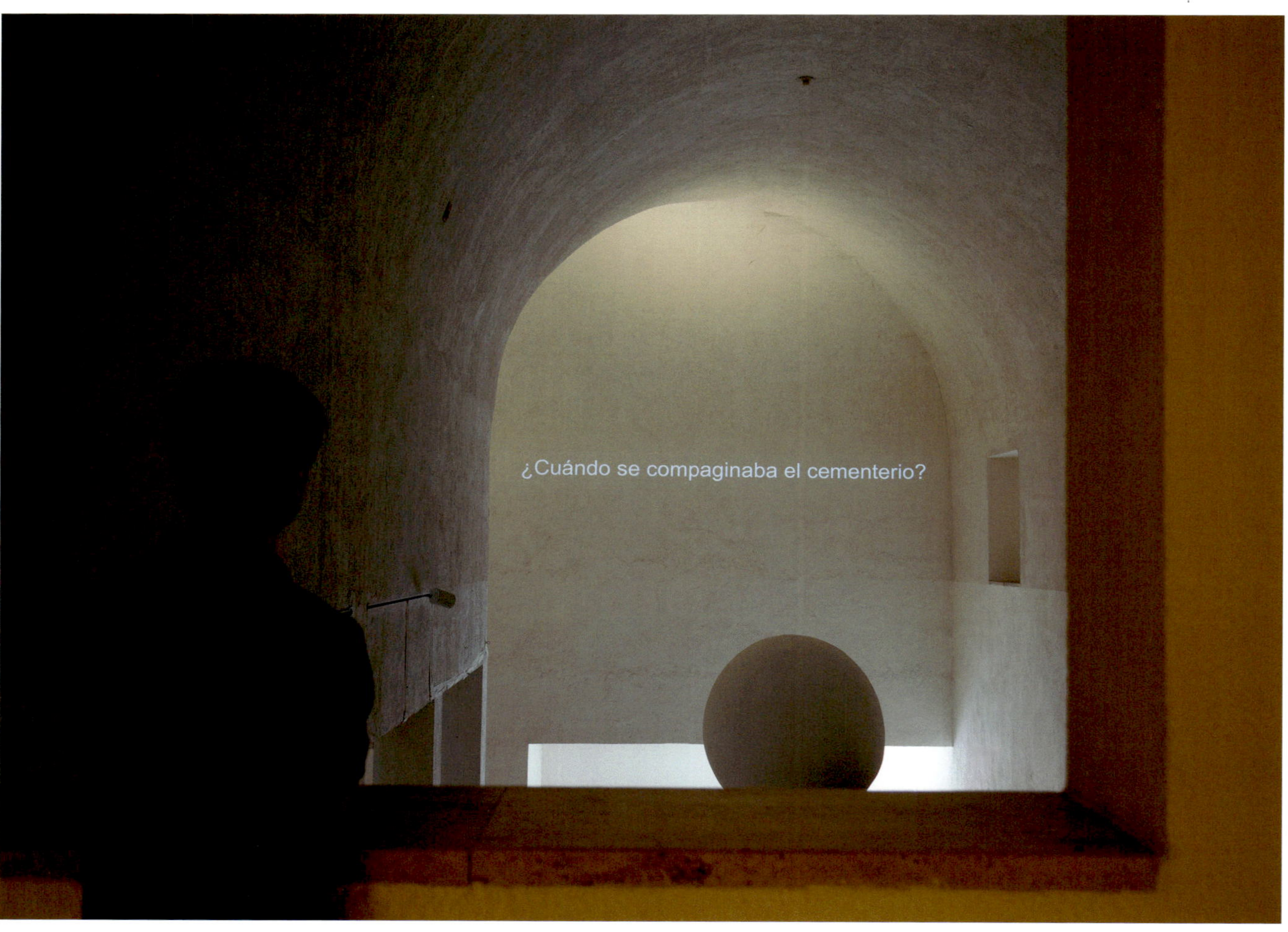
¿Cuándo se compaginaba el cementerio?

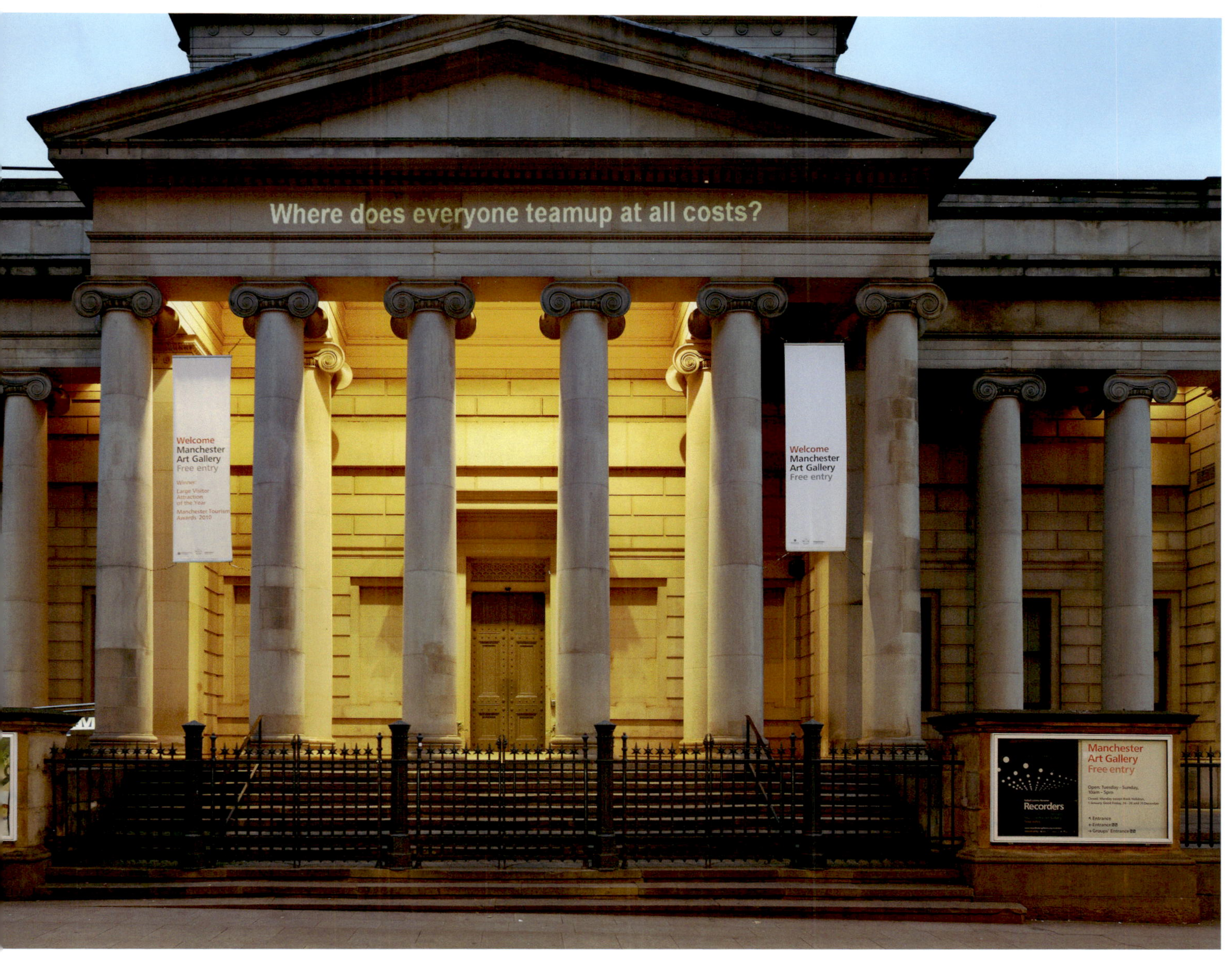

Installation views, Museo de Arte Contemporáneo de Monterrey, Mexico, 2019 (left), and Manchester Art Gallery, England, 2010 (right)

ACTUAL - Nº1
Hoja de Vanguardia
Comprimido Estridentista
de Manuel Maples Arce

Iluminaciones Subversivas de Renée Dunan, F. T. Marinetti, Guillermo de Torre, Lasso de la Vega, Salvat-Papasseit, etc., y Algunas Cristalizaciones Marginales.

E MUERA EL CURA HIDALGO
X ABAJO SAN-RAFAEL-SAN
I LÁZARO ————————————
T ESQUINA ————————————
O SE PROHIBE FIJAR ANUNCIOS

N nombre de la vanguardia actualista de México, sinceramente horrorizada de todas las placas notariales y rótulos consagrados de sistema cartulario, con veinte siglos de éxito efusivo en farmacias y droguerías subvencionadas por la ley, me pongo en el vértice eclatante de mi insustituible categoría presentista, equilibrada y eminentemente revolucionaria, mientras que todo el mundo fuera del eje, se contempla esféricamente atónito con las manos torcidas, imperativa y categóricamente afirmo, sin más excepciones a los "players" diametralmente explosivos en incendios fonográficos y gritos acorralados, que mi estridentismo deshiciente y acendrado para defenderme de las pedradas literales de los últimos plebiscitos intelectivos: Muera el Cura Hidalgo, Abajo San Rafael, San Lázaro, Esquina, Se prohibe fijar anuncios.

I.- Mi locura no está en los presupuestos. La verdad, no acontece ni sucede nunca fuera de nosotros. La vida es sólo un método sin puertas que se llueve a intervalos. De aquí que insista en la literatura insuperable en que se prestigian los teléfonos y diálogos perfumados que se hilvanan al desgaire por hilos conductores. La verdad estética, es tan sólo un estado de emoción incohercible desenrrollado en un plano extrabasal de equivalencia integralista. Las cosas no tienen valor intrínseco posible, y su equivalencia poética, florece en sus relaciones y cordinaciones, las que sólo se manifiestan en un sector interno, más emocionante y más definitivo que una realidad desmantelada, como puede verse en fragmentos de una de mis anticipaciones poemáticas novilatitudinales: "Esas Rosas Eléctricas..." (Cosmópolis.—No. 34). Para hacer una obra de arte, como dice Pierre Albert-Birot, es preciso crear, y no copiar. "Nosotros buscamos la verdad en la realidad pensada, y no en la realidad aparente". En este instante asistimos al espectáculo de nosotros mismos. Todo debe ser superación y equivalencia en nuestros iluminados panoramas a que nos circunscriben los esféricos cielos actualistas, pues pienso con Epstein, que no debemos imitar a la Naturaleza, sino estudiar sus leyes, y comportarnos en el fondo como ella.

II.- Toda técnica de arte, está destinada a llenar una función espiritual en un momento determinado. Cuando los medios expresionistas son inhábiles o insuficientes para traducir nuestras emociones personales,—única y elemental finalidad estética,—es necesario, y esto contra toda la fuerza estacionaria y afirmaciones rastacueras de la crítica oficial, cortar la corriente y desnucar los "swichs". Una pechera reumática se ha carbonizado, pero no por esto he de abandonar el juego. ¿Quién sigue? Ahora el cubilete está en Cipriano Max-Jacob, y es sensacionalísimo por lo que respecta a aquel periodista circunspecto, mientras Blaise Cendrars, que siempre está en el plano de superación, sin perder el equilibrio, intencionalmente equivocado, ignora, si aquello que tiene sobre los ojos es un cielo estrellado o una gota de agua al microscopio.

III.- "Un automóvil en movimiento, es más bello que la Victoria de Samocracia". A esta eclatante afirmación del vanguardista italiano Marinetti, exaltada por Lucini, Buzzi, Cavacchioli, etc., yuxtapongo mi apasionamiento desisivo por las máquinas de escribir, y mi amor efusivísimo por la literatura de los avisos económicos. Cuanta mayor, y más honda emoción he logrado vivir en un recorte de periódico arbitrario y sugerente, que en todos esos organillerismos pseudo-líricos y bombones melódicos, para recitales de changarro gratis a las señoritas, declamatoriamente inferidos ante el auditorio disyuntivo de niñas fox-troteantes y espasmódicas y burgueses temerosos por sus concubinas y sus cajas de caudales, como valientemente afirma mi hermano espiritual Guillermo de Torre, en su manifiesto yoista leído en la primera explosión ultráica de Parisiana, y ésto, sin perforar todas esas poematizaciones (sic) entusiastamente aplaudidas en charlotadas literarias, en que sólo se justifica el reflejo cartonario de algunos literaturípedos "specimen".

IV.- Es necesario exaltar en todos los tonos estridentes de nuestro diapasón propagandista, la belleza actualista de las máquinas, de los puentes gímnicos reciamente extendidos sobre las vertientes por músculos de acero, el humo de las fábricas, las emociones cubistas de los grandes trasatlánticos con humeantes chimeneas de rojo y negro, anclados horoscópicamente —Ruiz Hidobro— junto a los muelles efervescentes y congestionados, el régimen industrialista de las grandes ciudades palpitantes, las bluzas azules de los obreros explosivos en esta hora emocionante y conmovida; toda esta belleza del siglo, tan fuertemente intuida por Emilio Verhaeren, tan sinceramente amada por Nicolás Beauduin, y tan ampliamente dignificada y comprendida por todos los artistas de vanguardia. Al fin, los tranvías, han sido redimidos del dicterio de prosaicos, en que prestigiosamente los había valorizado la burguesía ventruda con hijas casaderas por tantos años de retardarismo sucesivo e intransigencia melancólica de archivos cronológicos.

V.- Chopín a la silla eléctrica! He aquí una afirmación higienista y detersoria. Ya los futuristas anti-selenegráficos, pidieron en letras de molde el asesinato del claro de luna, y los ultraistas españoles, transcriben, por voz de Rafael Cansinos Assens, la liquidación de las hojas secas, reciamente agitada en periódicos y hojas subversivas. Como ellos, es de urgencia telegráfica emplear un metodo radicalista y eficiente. Chopín a la silla elétrica! (M. M. A. trade mark) es una preparación maravillosa; en veinte y cuatro horas extermina todos los gérmenes de la literatura putrefacta y su uso es agradabilísimo y benéfico. Agítese bien antes de usarse. Insisto. Perptuemos nuestro crímen en el melancolismo trasnochado de los "Nocturnos", y proclamemos, sincrónicamente, la aristocracia de la gasolina. El humo azul de los tubos de escape, que huele a modernidad y a dinamismo, tiene, equivalentemente, el mismo valor emocional que las venas adorables de nuestras correlativas y exquisitas actualistas.

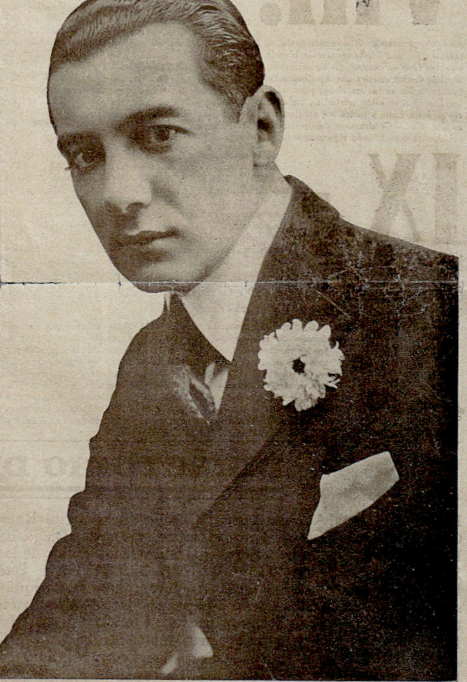

TATIANA FLORES

RAFAEL LOZANO-HEMMER AND THE DREAM OF ESTRIDENTISMO

In December 1921, the Mexican poet Manuel Maples Arce distributed an audacious and irreverent avant-garde manifesto—*Actual No. 1* (1921; opposite and fig. 1)—that sought to renovate Mexican aesthetics by embracing technological modernity.[1] Modeled after futurist prototypes, *Actual No. 1* called for an art grounded in the experience of the modern city whose form and content would defy the lyrical poetry then in vogue. "Chopin to the electric chair!" its author scandalously proclaimed.[2] He instead directed artists to "exalt in all the strident tones . . . the currentist [*actualista*] beauty of machines, of gymnastic bridges freshly extended over the slopes by muscles of steel, the smoke of factories, the cubist emotions of the great transatlantic ships with smoking chimneys of red and black."[3] Predicting that technology would shrink the world, making possible the "psychological unity of the century," Maples Arce advocated for globalization avant la lettre.[4] One of his most-cited lines foregrounds that the tension between the global and the local that is characteristic in contemporary art discourse was already pertinent: "Let us become cosmopolitan. It is no longer possible to be contained in conventional chapters of national art."[5] This manifesto, drafted in the period immediately following the Mexican Revolution (1910–20), would launch the avant-garde movement Estridentismo ("stridentism").[6] Maples Arce's demands for art, however, were too disconnected from the local context to take root.[7] After an explosion of activity during the 1920s, Estridentismo fell into oblivion for nearly half a century.[8]

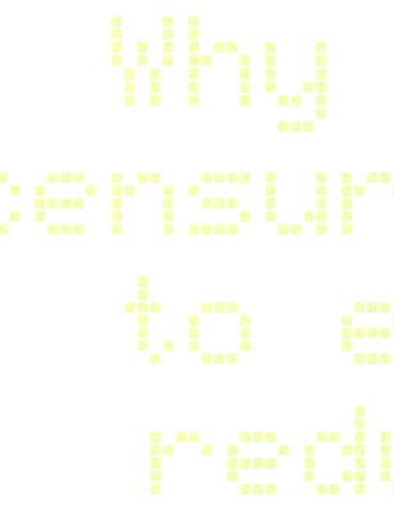

Manuel Maples Arce, *Actual No. 1* (recto), December 1921
Broadsheet
23 7/16 × 15 3/4 in. (59.5 × 40 cm)
Museo Nacional de Arte / INBA, Mexico City

The art of Rafael Lozano-Hemmer shows us how Estridentismo's technological dreams have now been fully realized.[9] Nothing would have pleased Manuel Maples Arce

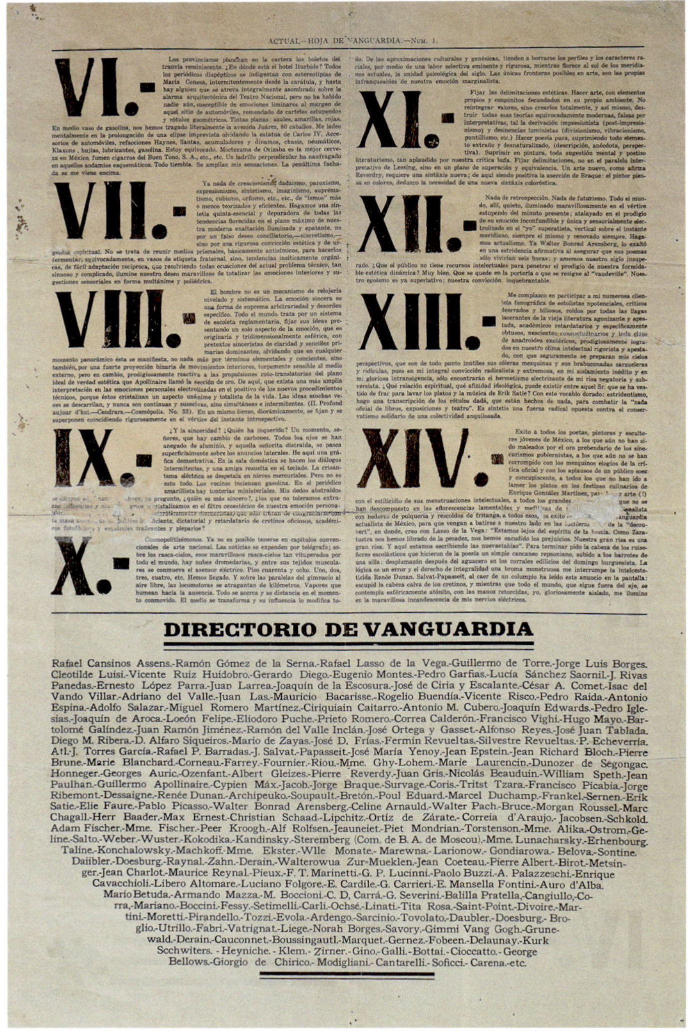

more than to witness the celebration of the turn of the millennium in Mexico City, validating, as it did, his foresight in *Actual No. 1*. For this symbolic date, Mexico's most emblematic public space, the Zócalo, played host to a light show quite unlike the spectacular fireworks on view in every other major city at the stroke of midnight. Lozano-Hemmer presented the interactive installation *Vectorial Elevation* (1999; figs. 2 and 3), featuring eighteen searchlights placed around the perimeter of the plaza that projected beams from 7,000-watt xenon lamps into the night sky.[10] The lights could be seen from a radius of fifteen kilometers, but they could be configured from anywhere in the world. Participants employed an online interface to create and view designs through three-dimensional simulation. Once these had been programmed, they were placed in a queue, waiting their turn to be projected. The user was given an estimate of when his or her pattern would appear. A new configuration became visible every six seconds, held long enough to be photographed. The photographs were then posted online, alongside the original prototypes and an email sent to the author of the particular design.[11]

Through its sophisticated technology, Lozano-Hemmer's project provided a spectatorial experience that could be both real and virtual. Passersby witnessed, most of them unexpectedly, a unique light show, and Internet users could try their hand at programming

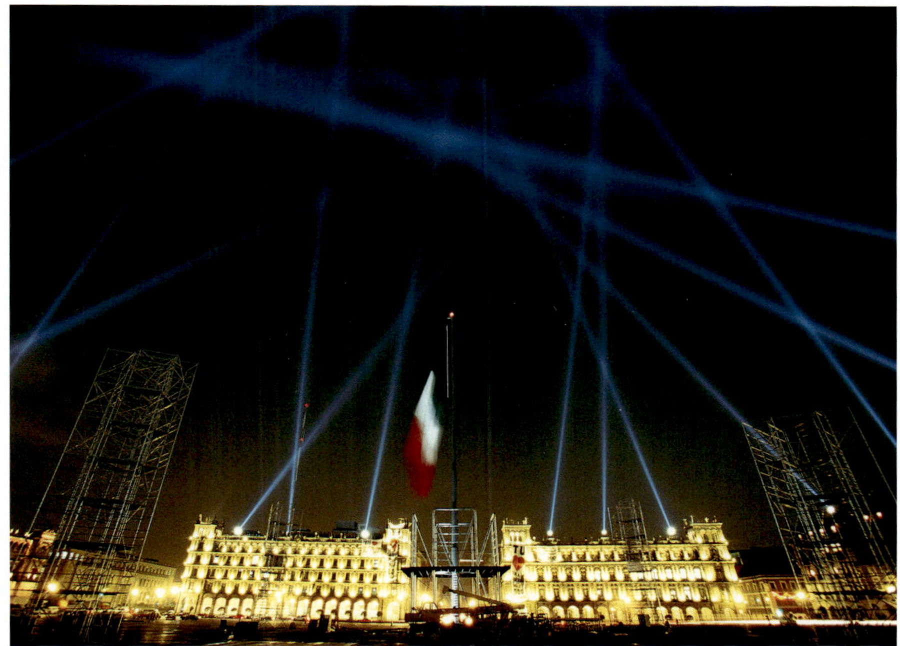

and later examine the results. By the end of its two-week run, more than 700,000 people from eighty-nine countries had designed light patterns for the installation, and countless others had viewed it from the ground. In his engagement both of masses of locals and a global audience, Lozano-Hemmer achieved a milestone in Mexican art. Not only did he demonstrate the relationship that Maples Arce had established between technology and globalization, he was also able to address and connect to a mass audience in a manner that had eluded the Mexican muralists.

With his use of cutting-edge technology, technical prowess, and ability to conceive of and execute projects on a global scale, Lozano-Hemmer has expanded the boundaries of the visual arts in unexpected and unprecedented ways. Though certainly breaking new ground, his projects also engage—consciously or not—with significant historical models. These connections add depth and nuance to his work while transforming our understanding of the past. Lozano-Hemmer recalls that when he received the commission for *Vectorial Elevation,* he was asked to "refer to a chapter of Mexican history."[12] Well aware of the weight of muralism in Mexican art history and national self-fashioning, he mused, "Perhaps what could have been expected is to have a new kind of virtual muralism, consisting of projections of parading national heroes."[13] Instead he turned to geometric abstraction as one means of making his art as democratic as possible.

The rejection of the dogmatism that came to be associated with Social Realism in favor of a socially conscious abstract visual language has been a familiar tactic in Latin American art, beginning with the work of Joaquín Torres-García in the 1930s. Geometric abstraction claimed to be a universal aesthetic that could be experienced collectively—especially in public space—while also engaging with the individual on an experiential level. Lozano-Hemmer repeatedly invokes this legacy, particularly in his *Relational Architecture* series. In a more recent public light installation, *Pulse Corniche*

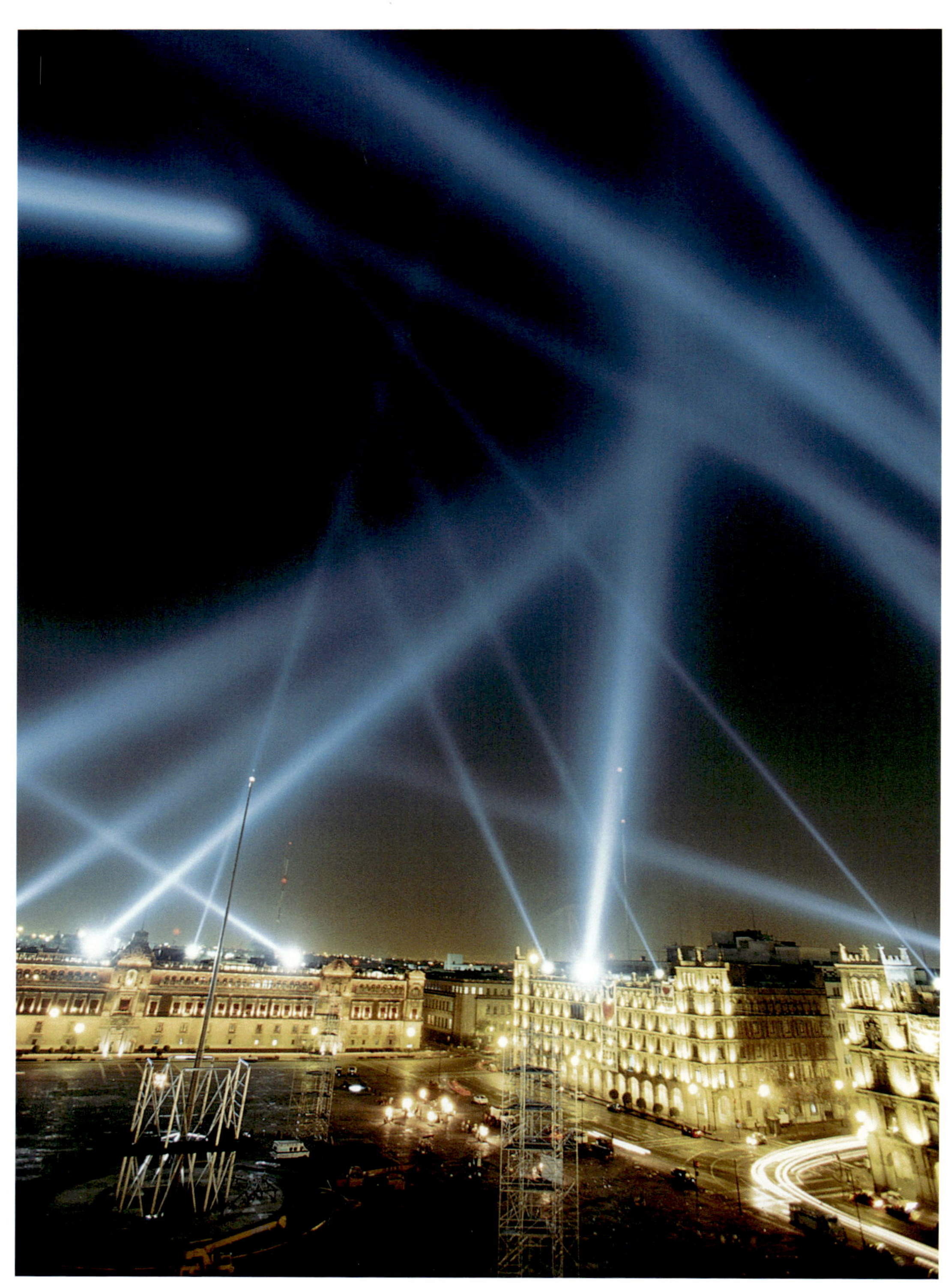

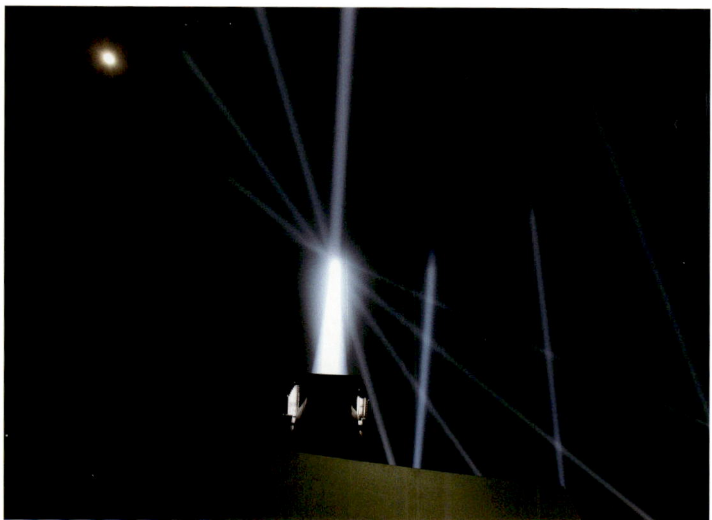

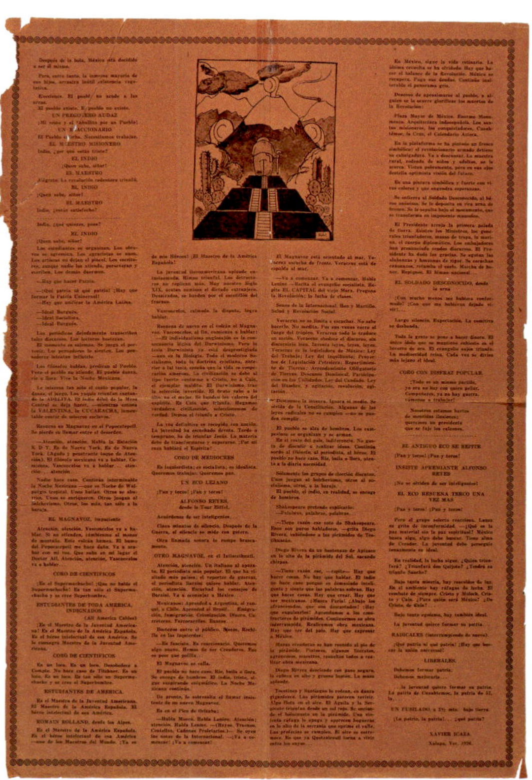

(2015; fig. 4), he relied on searchlights drawing vectors in the sky to fuse the individual and the collective.[14] Spectators placed their hands on a sensor that measured their heartbeats, which, in turn, were converted into light pulsations echoing their unique biorhythms, allowing, in the words of the artist, "public space [to] be personalized by individual participants."[15] The use of searchlights and biometrics also suggests the ominous overtones of surveillance, challenging the utopic connotations of geometric abstraction as well as Maples Arce's untrammeled optimism about technology.

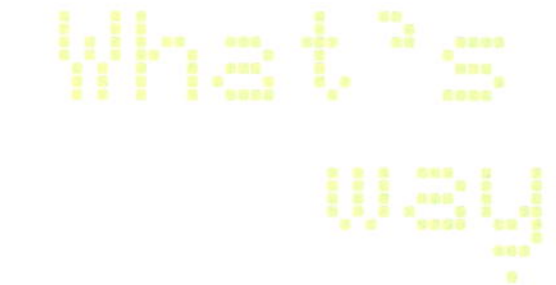

Maples Arce's aesthetic presciently imagined what geometric abstraction would later hope to achieve and also anticipated Lozano-Hemmer's and others' interest in the relational.[16] "Things don't have an intrinsic possible value," Maples Arce wrote in *Actual No. 1*, "and their poetic equivalence flourishes in their relations and coordinations, which are only manifested in an internal zone, more exciting and more definitive than a dismantled reality."[17] He distrusted both realism and lyricism, but he could not fully articulate what he wanted for visual art except that it should capture the tumult of modern experience through an aesthetic of simultaneity. What most interested him was how the changes brought about by new technologies affected the contemporary individual, but the artistic models in existence at the moment he was writing were insufficient to give form to his vision. Almost eight decades later, Lozano-Hemmer began fulfilling the promises of Maples Arce's 1921 manifesto.

Lozano-Hemmer's *Voz Alta* (Out Loud, 2008; see page 40) recalled another estridentista text—Xavier Icaza's broadsheet *Magnavoz* (1926; fig. 5)—in a way that was nothing short of uncanny.[18] *Voz Alta* was commissioned as a memorial for the 1968 student massacre at Tlatelolco, where government security forces shot and killed dozens of

Figure 3
Vectorial Elevation, 1999
Robotic searchlights, webcams, Linux servers, GPS, and Java 3-D DMX interface
Dimensions variable
Installation view, Zócalo Square, Mexico City, 1999

Figure 4
Pulse Corniche, 2015
Robotic searchlights, heart rate sensor, computer, DMX controller, speakers, subwoofers, custom software, and generators
393 ¾ ft. (120 m) semicircle diameter
Commissioned by Guggenheim Abu Dhabi
Installation view, Abu Dhabi, United Arab Emirates, 2015

Figure 5
Xavier Icaza, *Magnavoz*, with image by Ramón Alva de la Canal, 1926, published 1928
Broadsheet
18 7/16 × 12 3/16 in. (46.8 × 31 cm)
Private collection

students who had gathered at the Plaza de las Tres Culturas to protest violations of university autonomy.[19] On the plaza, Lozano-Hemmer placed a megaphone into which visitors could say anything they wanted. Their words were broadcast over the radio station of the Universidad Nacional Autónoma de México (UNAM), and they were also transformed into beams of light that flashed according to their enunciations. The light would hit a nearby building, the former Ministry of Foreign Affairs, and was then relayed by three powerful searchlights to significant points—the Zócalo (Mexico City's central plaza), the Monument to the Revolution, and northward—where they could be seen over a nine-mile radius. *Voz Alta* was an extraordinary anti-monument that empowered Mexicans to speak for themselves. Some of the participants movingly remembered the massacre, while others made no reference to it in their speeches. The artist employed elements associated with surveillance (the searchlights) and demagoguery (the radio discourse) and inverted their associations by placing them in the hands of his audience.[20]

When *Voz Alta* is exhibited, a prototype version is shown: the megaphone originally placed at Tlatelolco has been adapted with a searchlight inside that beams in relation to what is spoken. The megaphone also connects to a radio transmitter so that participants' words may be heard through FM signals on transistor radios. Lacking the site specificity of the Mexico City version, the prototype foregrounds the associations between broadcast speech and the potential for incendiary, bombastic, or demagogic rhetoric.

Eight decades earlier, Icaza's avant-garde text also used the trope of the megaphone combined with the radio. Part manifesto, part theatrical script, *Magnavoz* (Megaphone) presents competing proposals for the direction of Mexico in the postrevolutionary period through three megaphones projecting radio transmissions. Like the megaphone in *Voz Alta*, these are placed at strategic points—the two volcanoes of the Valley of Mexico (Popocatépetl and Iztaccihuatl) and the country's three tallest peaks (the Pico de Orizaba). The speeches that emanate from them offer the masses different perspectives on their priorities as citizens. The public remains an abstraction, restless and bored. It isn't until the painter Diego Rivera makes an appearance and, speaking with his own booming voice from the top of the Pyramid of the Sun, urges creation instead of speechmaking that the crowd gets excited.

Typically, Lozano-Hemmer's uses of technology stray far from the idealism and optimism that Icaza's contemporary Maples Arce projected onto it. Yet new technologies in Lozano-Hemmer's work do invoke wonder and make his art accessible to a great number of people. They often create an open text to be infused with meaning by viewer-participants and that exists only in relation to them, addressing Maples Arce's question of how art's engagement with new technologies might affect a spectator's subjectivity. But once the participants animate a work, they often lack control over it, and interacting with it is not necessarily an uplifting experience. Themes of surveillance, uneven power relations, and loss of privacy recur in Lozano-Hemmer's work. Rather than being a vehicle toward utopia, technology is simply a medium through which to express the contemporary condition of a globalized world. Forcing the questions of whether technology equals progress and challenging the utopic ideals of collectivism, Lozano-Hemmer considers the failure of such historical avant-gardes from a twenty-first-century perspective. Nevertheless, as a public, site-specific artwork, *Voz Alta* empowered the audience in a way that many of the artist's other works do not. The guarantee that people were free to speak their minds offered the possibility of catharsis in the declarations made through the megaphone. Broadcasting their speech symbolically through the lights and literally through the radio lent the "masses" a presence that was both visible and audible.

With Icaza, the inverse holds true. Whereas *estridentista* texts conventionally celebrate technology and project faith in its utopic potential, *Magnavoz* shows us that this was not always the case. The author calls attention to the radio as a tool for demagoguery and the manipulation of collective mentality. The masses are always just that, never individuals with hopes, dreams, or opinions. They are skeptical of the radio, however, refusing to listen to the disembodied voices; only Diego Rivera's presence is able to animate them. Icaza's text poses the question of how to create avant-garde art that is socially conscious, relevant, and engages *el pueblo* ("the masses"). Lozano-Hemmer demonstrates that these concerns continue to be central in the twenty-first century.

In the last decade, Lozano-Hemmer's production has continued to resonate with the aesthetics of Estridentismo. Whereas Maples Arce, following the Futurists, sought the "assassination of the *clair de lune*," referring to Claude Debussy's famous piano suite, Lozano-Hemmer does him one better, materializing the phrase *au clair de la lune* as a 3-D-printed speech bubble in *Volute 1: Au clair de la lune* (2016; see page 46).[21] The sculpture and accompanying video documentation refer to the earliest extant audio recording of human speech, made by Édouard-Léon Scott de Martinville, who captured that very phrase in 1860. Lozano-Hemmer's sculpture is an amorphous mass of polished aluminum with a complex grooved surface. It reproduces an evanescent cloud of speech uttered in an instant and translated, through laser tomography, from the audible to the visible. For Maples Arce, the complexity of the instant was precisely what he sought to represent. The silencing of the lyrical in the hands of the early twentieth-century poet and the contemporary artist is a byproduct of the search by both men for an art that is utterly current.

Lozano-Hemmer and Maples Arce also share an interest in technology's impact on traditional aesthetic experience. In their exploration of new media's effects on the spectator, neither is afraid to court dissonance. For Maples Arce, stridency becomes his calling card. His manifesto is characterized by language that assaults the reader, not only with actual insults but also through form and syntax—the poet favors long words and neologisms in run-on, overly complex sentences, making them confusing and hard to follow, but also giving the impression of being uttered quickly. This overall aesthetic is a sensorial onslaught that mimics the experience of simultaneity. The reader is presumed to be a pedestrian in a modern city who is overwhelmed by sights,

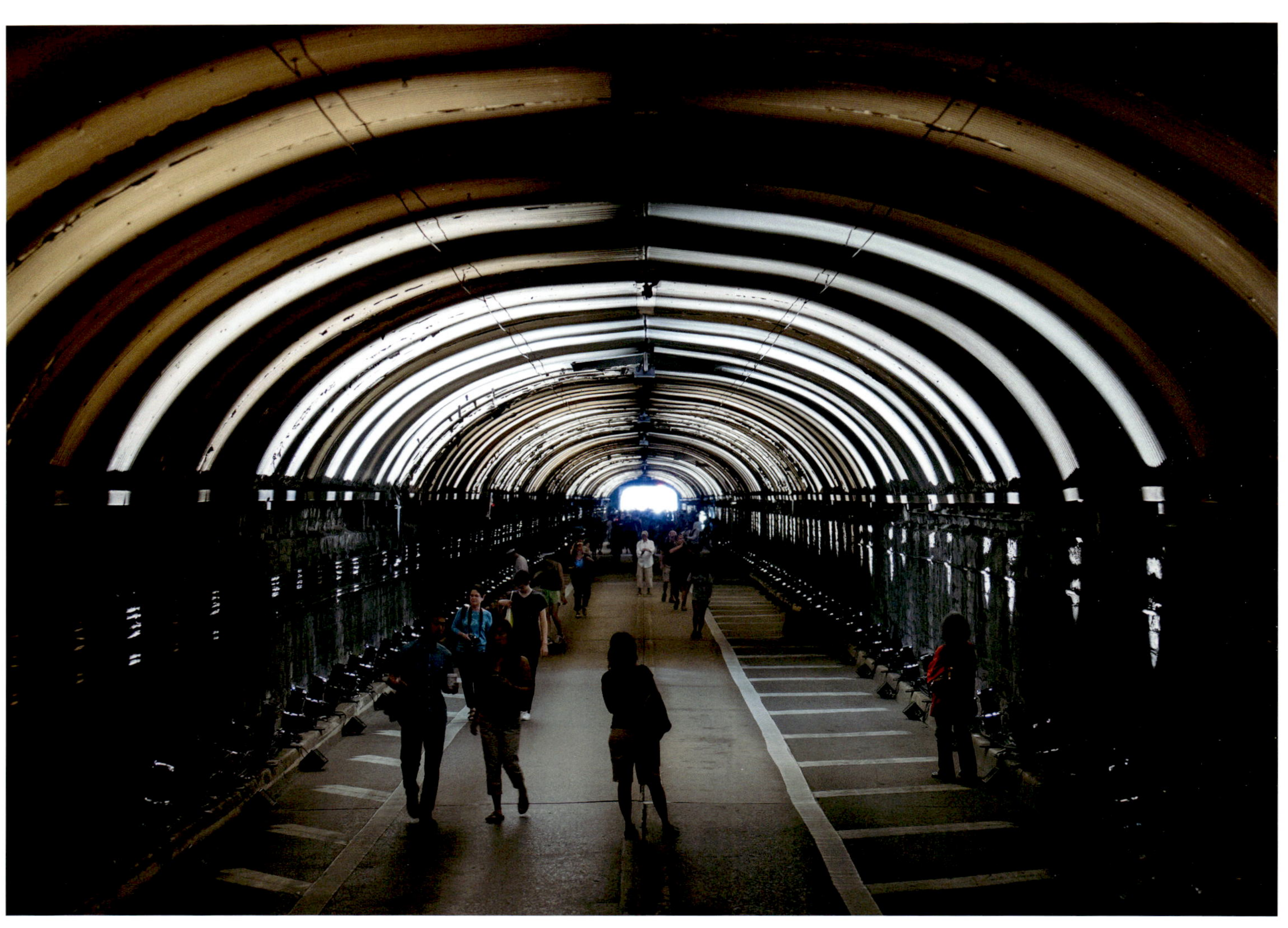

sounds, and sensations. Maples Arce aims to incite "the positively electrolyzed personal emotions of the new technical procedures because these crystallize a unanimous and totalizing aspect of life. Ideas often get derailed, and are never continuous or successive, but simultaneous and intermittent."[22]

Lozano-Hemmer has produced numerous projects with multiple, overlapping voices and sounds, including *Pan-Anthem* (2014; see page 106), the *Sphere Packing* series (2013–18; see page 110), *Voice Array* (2011; see page 126), and *Voice Tunnel* (2013; fig. 6). *Pan-Anthem* is an interactive installation consisting of speakers that play various national anthems and may be arranged according to various metrics, including population or gross domestic product.[23] As spectators approach the work, their proximity triggers the nearest speakers to play; multiple visitors may prompt various tunes to play simultaneously, creating an overpowering cacophony of sounds. The piece speaks to the individual's lack of agency in the face of power and authority and shares the skepticism expressed in Icaza's *Magnavoz*. The *Sphere Packing* series also groups together musical compositions by various composers. The series consists of 3-D-printed spheres with embedded speakers, one speaker for each piece in a composer's oeuvre. They hang from the ceiling at ear level, with each sphere playing the complete works of its respective composer simultaneously—among them Mozart, Beethoven, and Mahler.[24] *Sphere Packing: Bach* (2018; see page 110) gathers the entire musical output of Johann Sebastian Bach, which is so vast as to require a room-sized installation: a sphere made of wood and aluminum with 1,128 speakers.[25] The *Sphere Packing* works probe the nature of contemporary spectatorship by exploring how masterpieces of Western music become transformed through reproduction and simultaneity, recalling Maples Arce's notion that the experience of art after the technological revolution can never again purport to be a unique or transcendent experience. This idea, in turn, anticipated Walter Benjamin's argument that new technologies of reproduction bring about the loss of art's aura: "They neutralize a number of traditional concepts—such as creativity and genius, eternal value and mystery."[26]

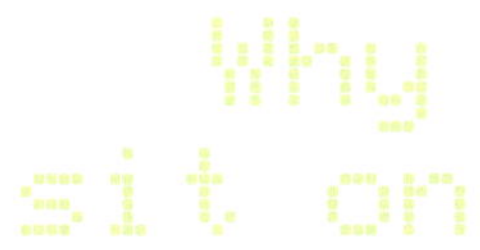

Whereas these audio pieces presume a silent spectator, *Voice Array* and *Voice Tunnel*, like *Voz Alta*, allow for audience interaction. *Voice Array* consists of a thin horizontal metal band along with a device through which each spectator records a message.[27] The audio is replayed and converted into a flashing light that syncs with the sound. These components are then merged with the recordings of previous participants in a sweeping accumulation that "travels down" the strip. After the collective voices play and the corresponding lights are activated, the voice of the individual who is being "pushed out" of the work by the incoming one emerges a final time. *Voice Tunnel* was a temporary public art installation in the Park Avenue Tunnel in New York City in summer 2013. Spanning from Thirty-Third to Fortieth Streets, the space had never been open to pedestrians since its inauguration in 1834. Within the tunnel, Lozano-Hemmer placed 300 spotlights, divided along each side and spaced seven feet apart, creating arches of light along the ceiling. They were interspersed with 150 loudspeakers that communicated the voices of participants who spoke into a microphone in the middle of the tunnel. People lined up to make short statements of their choosing, which were

Figure 6
Voice Tunnel, 2013
Spotlights, dimmer racks, speakers, computers, generators, microphone, and custom software and hardware
Tunnel: 1,400 ft. (427 m) long
Commissioned by the Public Art Program of the Department of Transportation, New York
Installation view, Summer Streets, Park Avenue Tunnel, New York Department of Transportation, 2013

projected into the loudspeakers sequentially, beginning at the center of the tunnel. As new participants added their voices, the preceding remarks shifted outward by one speaker, along either side of the tunnel, until they disappeared after 75 new recordings. Each speaker was synchronized to the lights, which blinked according to the sound modulation, creating a correlation between vision and hearing. Because each speaker conveyed a single voice at any given time, the resulting sounds were intriguing snippets rather than a jumble of dissonant noises. The work created a communal experience among strangers, allowed the public to roam within an otherwise inaccessible space, and permitted the audience to talk back rather than remain passive spectators. Both *Voice Tunnel* and *Voice Array* also revisited the legacy of geometric abstraction as a means of creating a shared aesthetic experience.

In 1921, Maples Arce proposed an avant-garde model for Mexico that was far ahead of his time. It took almost eighty years for a Mexican artist to come along who could bring to life his vision of the marriage of art and technology while also calling attention to consequences that the poet did not consider. In the intervening years, Latin American art has championed and then rejected social realism, embraced abstraction, and today grapples with issues of representation, accessibility, and social justice, all of which similarly concern Lozano-Hemmer. For all his innovations in new media, many recurring themes in the artist's work are grounded in history. He has addressed the interplay between figurative and abstract languages, the individual and the collective, and the global and the local in ways that underscore the intensely interconnected nature of our contemporary condition, bringing to life John Tomlinson's notion of "complex connectivity" as "the ever-densening network of interconnections and interdependences that characterize modern social life."[28] In so doing, Lozano-Hemmer challenges geopolitical hierarchies and Eurocentrism, arguing for a shift in planetary consciousness—much like his predecessor Maples Arce did almost a century earlier when he stated, "The medium transforms itself, and its influence changes everything."[29]

The first part of this essay is drawn from the introduction to my book *Mexico's Revolutionary Avant-Gardes: From Estridentismo to ¡30–30!* (New Haven, CT: Yale University Press, 2013), 7–12.

1. Manuel Maples Arce, *Actual No. 1* (broadsheet, Mexico City, 1921). *Actual No. 1* is reprinted in Luis Mario Schneider, *El estridentismo: México, 1921–1927* (Mexico City: Universidad Nacional Autónoma de México, 1985), 41–48. For an English translation, see the appendix in Dawn Ades with Guy Brett, Stanton Loomis Catlin, and Rosemary O'Neill, *Art in Latin America* (New Haven, CT: Yale University Press, 1989), 306–9.

2. "Chopin a la silla eléctrica," Maples Arce, *Actual No. 1*, point V in Schneider, *El estridentismo: México*, 43. This and all ensuing translations from Spanish are my own unless otherwise noted.

3. "Es necesario exaltar en todos los tonos estridentes . . . la belleza actualista de las máquinas, de los puentes gímnicos reciamente extendidos sobre las vertientes por músculos de acero, el humo de las fábricas, las emociones cubistas de los grandes transatlánticos con humeantes chimeneas de rojo y negro." Maples Arce, point IV, in Schneider, *El estridentismo: México*, 43. In Spanish, *actualista* is a made-up word, which was characteristic of Maples Arce throughout this text.

4. "La unidad psicológica del siglo," Maples Arce, point X, in Schneider, *El estridentismo: México*, 45.

5. "Cosmopoliticémonos. Ya no es posible tenerse en capítulos convencionales de arte nacional," Maples Arce, point X, in Schneider, *El estridentismo: México*, 45.

6. See Tatiana Flores, *Mexico's Revolutionary Avant-Gardes: From Estridentismo to ¡30–30!* (New Haven, CT: Yale University Press, 2013).

7. See Tatiana Flores, "*Murales Estridentes*: Tensions and Affinities between Estridentismo and Early Muralism," in *Mexican Muralism: A Critical History*, ed. Alejandro Anreus, Leonard Folgarait, and Robin A. Greeley (Berkeley: University of California Press, 2012), 108–24.

8. For the first scholarly study of Estridentismo, see Luis Mario Schneider, *El estridentismo, o una literatura de la estrategia* (Mexico City: Instituto Nacional de Bellas Artes, Departamento de Literatura, 1970).

9. I first made the connection between Lozano-Hemmer and Estridentismo in an article written in 2008. See Tatiana Flores, "The Historical (Self) Consciousness of Rafael Lozano-Hemmer," *Art Nexus* 7, no. 71 (December 2008–February 2009): 66–71.

10. The light installation was on view from December 26, 1999, to January 7, 2000. For a comprehensive analysis, see Rafael Lozano-Hemmer, ed., *Alzado Vectorial / Vectorial Elevation* (Mexico City: Consejo Nacional para la Cultura y las Artes, 2000).

11. The website is www.alzado.net. Currently it features the most recent incarnation of the project, Vancouver, February 4–28, 2010. Accessed April 13, 2019.

12. Lozano-Hemmer, *Alzado Vectorial / Vectorial Elevation*, 29.

13. Lozano-Hemmer, 57. This was precisely the case for a November 2010 light show on the Zócalo that commemorated the centennial of the revolution. See BicentenarioMexico, "Yo México. Ciudad de México. Del 11 al 23 de noviembre de 2010," *YouTube*, November 21, 2010, https://www.youtube.com /watch?v=GJMqroBQ3CE.

14. See Rafael Lozano-Hemmer, "Pulse Corniche," http://www.lozano-hemmer .com/pulse_corniche.php, accessed June 3, 2019.

15. Anna Seaman, "Artist Rafael Lozano-Hemmer Talks about Interactive Exhibition on Display at East Plaza on the Corniche," *The National*, January 6, 2015, http://www.thenational.ae/arts-culture/artist-rafael-lozano-hemmer -talks-about-interactive-exhibit-on-display-at-east-plaza-on-the-corniche -1.113547#full.

16. For Lozano-Hemmer's remarks on the concept of "relational architecture," see Daniele Mancini, "Relational Architecture: Interview with Rafael Lozano-Hemmer," *Unpacked*, November 30, 2006, http://unpacked .wordpress.com/2006/11/30/relational-architecture-interview-with -rafael-lozano-hemmer/.

17. "Las cosas no tienen valor intrínseco posible, y su equivalencia poética, florece en relaciones y coordinaciones, las que sólo se manifiestan en un sector interno, más emocionante y más definitivo que una realidad desmantelada," Maples Arce, *Actual No. 1*, point I, in Schneider, *El estridentismo: México*, 42.

18. Xavier Icaza, *Magnavoz* (Xalapa, Mexico: Talleres Gráficos del Estado de Veracruz, 1926). In 2008, when I first learned about the plans for *Voz Alta*, I shared a facsimile of this text, which has never been in wide circulation, with the artist. It is reproduced on his website: http://www.lozano-hemmer.com /showimage.php?img=mexico%20-%202008&proj=38&type=artwork&id=36, accessed June 3, 2019.

19. The number of casualties is still disputed, and estimates vary widely, from 30 to 1,000.

20. See Rafael Lozano-Hemmer, "Voz Alta," http://www.lozano-hemmer.com /voz_alta.php, accessed May 10, 2019.

21. See Rafael Lozano-Hemmer, "Volute 1: Au clair de la lune," http://www .lozano-hemmer.com/volute_1_au_clair_de_la_lune.php, accessed May 10, 2019.

22. "Las emociones personales electrolizadas en el positivo de los nuevos procedimientos técnicos, porque éstos cristalizan un aspecto unánime y totalista de la vida. Las ideas muchas veces se descarrilan, y nunca son continúas y sucesivas, sino simultáneas e intermitentes," Maples Arce, *Actual No. 1*, point VIII, in Schneider, *El estridentismo: México*, 44.

23. See Rafael Lozano-Hemmer, "Pan-Anthem," http://www.lozano-hemmer .com/pan-anthem.php, accessed May 10, 2019.

24. See Rafael Lozano-Hemmer, "Sphere Packing," http://www.lozano -hemmer.com/sphere_packing.php, accessed May 10, 2019.

25. See Rafael Lozano-Hemmer, "Sphere Packing: Bach," http://www .lozano-hemmer.com/sphere_packing_bach.php, accessed May 10, 2019.

26. Walter Benjamin, "The Work of Art in the Age of Its Technological Reproducibility: Second Version," in *The Work of Art in the Age of Its Technological Reproducibility, and Other Writings on Media* (Cambridge, MA: Harvard University Press, 2008), 20. I further discuss Maples Arce in relation to Benjamin in Tatiana Flores, "Beyond Centre–Periphery: Modernism in Latin American Art," in *The Modernist World*, ed. Allana Lindgren and Stephen Ross (London: Routledge, 2015), 426–35.

27. See Rafael Lozano-Hemmer, "Voice Array," http://www.lozano-hemmer .com/voice_array.php, accessed May 10, 2019.

28. John Tomlinson, *Globalization and Culture* (Chicago: University of Chicago Press, 1999), 2.

29. "El medio se transforma y su influencia lo modifica todo," Maples Arce, *Actual No. 1*, point X, in Schneider, *El estridentismo: México*, 45.

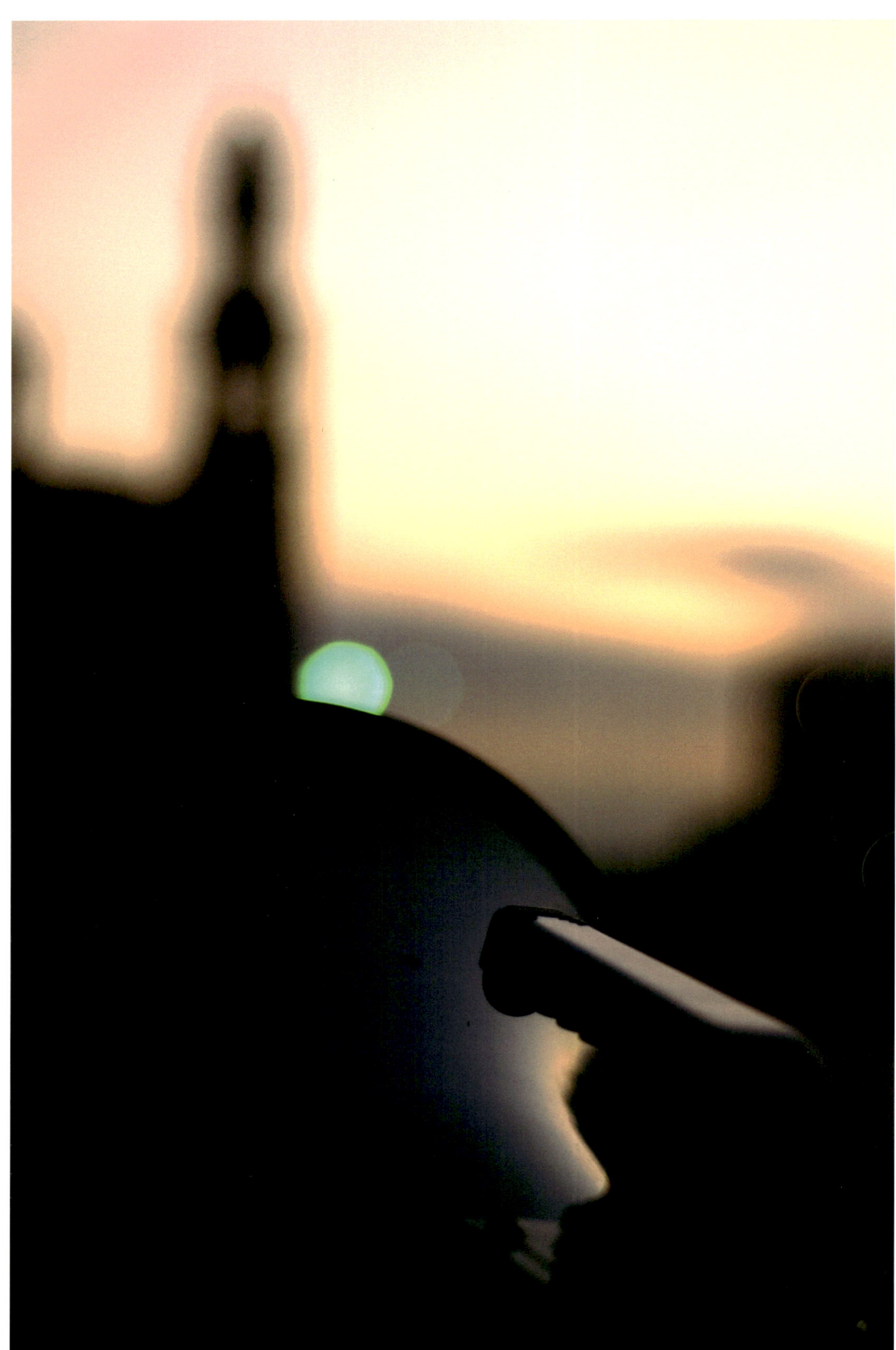

ROBIN ADÈLE GREELEY

PERFORMATIVITY, PUBLIC SPACE, AND AESTHETICS IN THE POLITICIZATION OF MEXICO'S PUBLIC SPHERE

On October 2, just ten days before the opening of the 1968 Olympic Games in Mexico, a large student demonstration had gathered in the Plaza de las Tres Culturas, in Mexico City's Tlatelolco housing complex, to demand a democratization of Mexico's political system that would match the country's rapid industrialization under the so-called "Mexican Miracle."[1] On orders from Interior Minister Luis Echeverría and President Gustavo Díaz Ordaz, government troops opened fire on the rally, killing several hundred people and wounding many more.[2] The government instituted an immediate information blackout and mobilized its corporatized support networks to reassert very effective control over the public sphere, characterizing the student movement as a treasonous act of sabotage against the nation. This act of state terrorism, known as the Tlatelolco massacre, marked an abrupt end to the 1968 movement's powerful challenge to the political order imposed by the Mexican state, and it initiated a level of political polarization not seen since the Mexican Revolution of 1910–20. Under the subsequent *guerra sucia* ("dirty war") imposed by the state, hundreds "disappeared" or were forced into hiding and exile. In the aftermath of 1968, the combined use of repressive and ideological state apparatuses proved remarkably effective in the state's reassertion of control over the public sphere. Despite state pledges to prosecute those responsible for the massacre, no convictions have ever been handed down.[3] But the state's open use of brute force in 1968 plunged what has famously been called "the perfect dictatorship" into a crisis of legitimacy that even the election, in the year 2000, of the first non-PRI (Institutional Revolutionary Party) president in more than seven decades could not overcome.[4] More than any other event in the twentieth century, the Tlatelolco massacre ruptured the state's claim to be the self-declared

Voz Alta, 2008. Memorial for the Tlatelolco student massacre, Mexico City, 2008

heir to the Mexican Revolution's promise of social justice and political inclusion—to represent the nation's citizenry. Since 1968, the Tlatelolco killings have festered as an unhealed trauma in Mexico's public psyche.[5] But they have also prompted numerous responses from civil society, including massive popular demonstrations against the 2014 disappearance and probable murder of forty-three students from the rural town of Ayotzinapa.[6] Rafael Lozano-Hemmer's *Voz Alta* (Out Loud, 2008; see page 40) sought to bring together a plurality of voices into a concentrated articulation to further democratic expansion of Mexico's public sphere.

A simple proposal: for several hours over the course of ten nights in 2008, to transform the uncensored voice of the public into powerful light beams that would shine across the vast metropolis of Mexico City. Installed in the site of the Tlatelolco massacre—the Plaza de las Tres Culturas, a monumental open space surrounded by the modernist Tlatelolco housing complexes erected in the 1960s—Lozano-Hemmer's interactive light-sound project invited anyone to speak into a megaphone on any topic, completely free of monitoring or censorship. The voices of participants stimulated a searchlight, which flashed in response to their frequency and volume, beaming those illuminated voice patterns to the top of the former Ministry of Foreign Affairs building (now Centro Cultural Tlatelolco). Vastly increasing the project's visibility to the scale of the entire city, further antiaircraft searchlights relayed the flashing beams to three other signifi-cant public locations: the Zócalo, the traditional political and social heart of the city and nation; the Basilica of the Guadalupe Virgin, patron saint of Mexico; and the Monument to the Revolution, commemorating the violent upheaval that launched the nation into twentieth-century modernity. The light flashes were then retransformed into sound, transmitted by radio waves to a listening public via the National University's radio station. In the pauses between live presentations, *Voz Alta* transmitted archival recordings of 1968 music, as well as archival testimonials from 1968 survivors, intellec-tuals, and public figures. Thousands from all ranks of society participated, comment-ing on everything from their memories of the massacre, to calls for political action in the name of freedom and democracy, to poetry and sound art, to marriage proposals. Many called for the prosecution of those responsible for the massacre; many also spoke on the relationship between everyday life and politics. Others pointed to the long-term and consistent state censorship and repression in Mexico, and to the collusion between the news media and the government in controlling access to information.[7]

Voz Alta sought to reappropriate Tlatelolco, turning it from a site whose history had been carefully managed by a single voice of authoritative power—the Mexican state—into a public space whose history was the result of a multitude of citizen voices.[8] Against the state's production of Tlatelolco as a space of spectacle and truncated remembrance aimed at bolstering its own power, Lozano-Hemmer's sound-light piece provided an expanding sensorial forum specifically aimed at bridging, temporally and spatially, disparate private thoughts and a collective public discourse that would activate historical memory in the present in all its complexity. As person after person spoke into the megaphone, individual soliloquies interwove to produce an ever-thickening web of collective testimonial, a corporate witnessing in the public

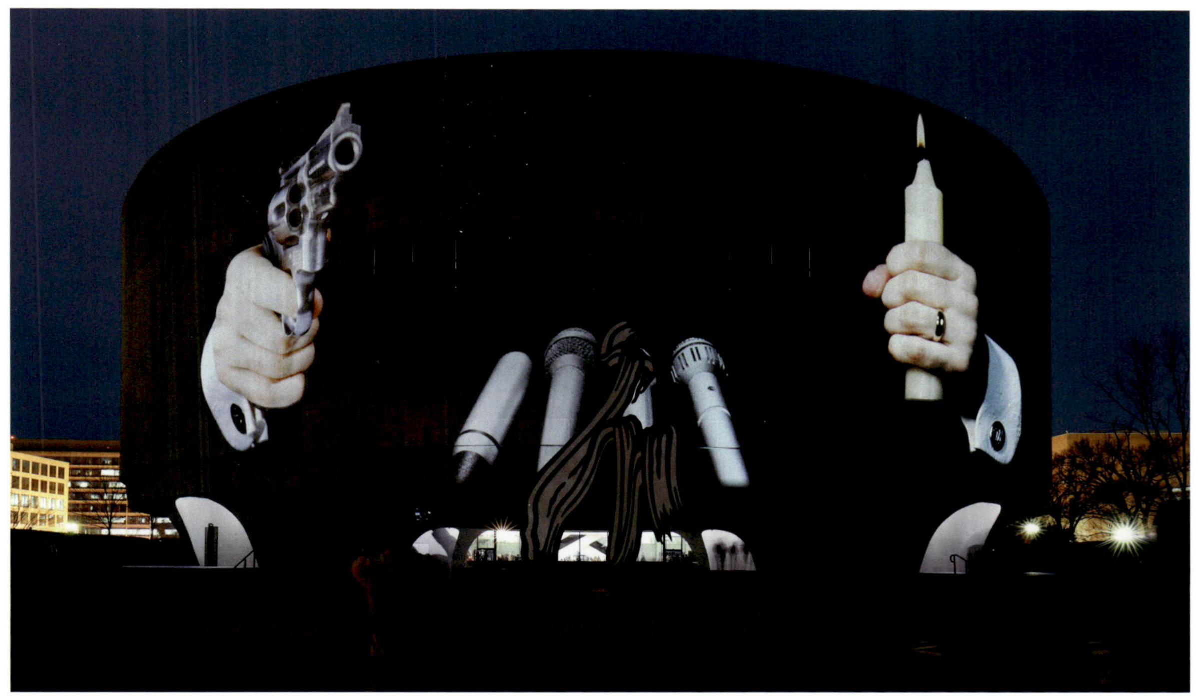

sphere that shattered hegemonic state narratives blaming others—the students, "communists," foreign terrorists, rogue political elements—for the Tlatelolco massacre. Individual memories lost their isolated, idiosyncratic character and became nodal points for drawing the past into the present and for marking experiential connections across previously segregated arenas of civil society. Historical memory became a communal affair, such that even children could testify as community witnesses to events long past.

Voz Alta offered an egalitarian model of civic association structured through unscripted collective action in public space, articulating the conditions of contemporary civic engagement without monumentalizing them. Light and sound formed a principle measure and structure of that engagement, with a spatial demarcation that turned spectacle into deliberately ephemeral yet powerful critique. Luminosity, translated from sound and beamed across the city's sky, became the means through which citizens activated their participation in social space. Lozano-Hemmer, in speaking about his consistent use of light, has invoked scientific models—particularly contemporary quantum physics—that have a "flexible understanding of the phenomenon of light" in which "observation is complicit with what is observed." He correlates this with Duchamp's maxim *c'est le regardeur qui fait le tableau* ("the beholder makes the painting") to posit an explicitly interactive art that foregrounds the "performative role of the observer."[9] This sets his work in sharp contrast to that of predecessors such as Krzysztof Wodiczko, who focuses on deconstructing the authoritative power narratives of specific monuments and buildings (fig. 7). At the other end of the political scale, Lozano-Hemmer's light-based works are antithetical to the "cathartic intimidation" of coercive political spectacle embodied in Nazi architect Albert Speer's Nuremberg Cathedral of Light, even as he uses similar technologies, such as powerful antiaircraft searchlights. Rather, Lozano-Hemmer argues, "personal interactivity [transforms] intimidation into 'intimacy': the possibility for people to constitute new relationships with the urban landscape and therefore to reestablish a context for a building's social performance."[10] Spaces of social control historically engineered through the aestheticization of scientific technological regimes are inverted in *Voz Alta*: opened outward versus closed-in; fragile, ephemeral pulses of light and sound versus monumental concrete, glass, and steel; performative versus static; anti-hierarchical, inclusive, and collective versus coercive models of mass society.

All the performative interventions in Tlatelolco's plaza, from the 1968 student demonstrations to *Voz Alta* and the contemporary Ayotzinapa 43 protest movement, tapped into the energies of popular unrest in the face of government manipulation, providing those energies with a conduit to a generative presence in the public sphere. And as much as this process is about popular voices struggling against the state to enact a public political identity, so too is it about the changes the state must undergo. Like civil society, the state is neither monolithic nor conflict-free, despite all its efforts to present itself as such. Nor is its hegemony ever fully or irrevocably consolidated. *Voz Alta* took place on the fortieth anniversary of the Tlatelolco massacre, as Mexico was falling into an extended period of violence sparked by rampant government corruption and impunity, unchecked drug-war carnage, and skyrocketing levels of social inequality under presidents Felipe Calderón and Enrique Peña Nieto. In these circumstances, movements like the Ayotzinapa 43 protests have opened new—if fragile—parameters for civic engagement in public space. *Voz Alta*, in plumbing such ongoing dilemmas around social justice and political democratization, reveals the dialectical conditions of performative social engagement as an imperative for mounting a non-spectacularized citizen reclamation of public space.

A longer version of this text was published in Sophie Halart and Mara Pologovsky Ezcurra, eds., *Sabotage Art: Politics and Iconoclasm in Contemporary Latin American Art* (London and New York: I. B. Tauris, 2016).

1. On the Mexican Miracle, see Sarah L. Babb, "The Mexican Miracle," in *Managing Mexico: Economists from Nationalism to Neoliberalism* (Princeton: Princeton University Press, 2001), 75–105.

2. It is now widely recognized that Echeverría was principally responsible for orchestrating the massacre. Casualty figures vary enormously and have never been fully confirmed. John Rodda concluded that more than three hundred had been killed, a number that has since been frequently cited. See John Rodda, "The Killer Olympics," *The Guardian*, August 18, 1972; and Julio Scherer García and Carlos Monsiváis, *Parte de Guerra, Tomo I: Tlatelolco 1968: Documentos del general Marcelino García Barragán. Los hechos y la historia* (Mexico City: Nuevo Siglo and Aguilar, 1999).

3. President Vicente Fox (PAN, or National Action Party) was elected against the PRI (Institutional Revolutionary Party) in 2000, in part, on his pledge to prosecute the Tlatelolco criminals—a promise that remained unfulfilled. See "Las promesas incumplidas del presidente Fox," *El Mundo*, December 9, 2001; Carlos Monsiváis, *El 68. La tradición de la Resistencia* (Mexico City: Editorial Era, 2008); Alfredo Méndez, "Echeverría ni siquiera ha sido llevado ante un juez federal de primera instancia," *La Jornada* (Mexico City), October 2, 2008.

4. See Matthew Gutmann, *The Romance of Democracy: Compliant Defiance in Contemporary Mexico* (Berkeley: University of California Press, 2002).

5. In 2012, Elena Poniatowska contrasted the impact of the Tlatelolco massacre to that of Mexico's current drug war: "1968 cannot be compared with the more than 60,000 dead and disappeared of today, but one can compare the treatment accorded to the victims who have concerned [Movement for Justice with Peace and Dignity leader] Javier Sicilia since the day his son was murdered in Cuernavaca, Morelos. Still, the 1968 student movement and the October 2 massacre in Tlatelolco was the kick-off to the violence that Mexico has suffered during the past fifty years. . . . Until Cuauhtémoc Cárdenas decided to lower the flag to half-mast on 2 October, when he was mayor of Mexico City in 1997, the student movement and its mortal turn was taboo in Mexican newspapers. Why is it just and necessary to remember it now? Because it forms part of our history." Poniatowska, quoted in Kent Paterson, "Mexico Remembers the Massacre of Tlatelolco," *The Cutting Edge*, October 4, 2012, http://www.thecuttingedgenews.com/index.php?article=76359.

6. On September 26, 2014, a group of students from a rural teacher-training school in Ayotzinapa, in the Mexican state of Guerrero, was attacked by local and federal police while en route to the neighboring town of Iguala to protest state discrimination in educational resources. Several students were killed outright, and the police rounded up forty-three others at gunpoint, handing them over to a local drug cartel, which purportedly assassinated them and burned their bodies. Although just one incident among many in the rampant violence unleashed in recent years by Mexico's drug wars, for vast swaths of the Mexican citizenry, the Ayotzinapa disappearances proved to be the straw that broke the camel's back. The refusal of President Peña Nieto's government to accept responsibility regarding the Ayotzinapa tragedy, along with government failure to implement effective rule of law, sparked massive popular demonstrations, and eventually led to the 2018 landslide election of President Andrés Manuel Lopez Obrador on the promise of cleaning up state corruption, halting Mexico's violence, and establishing a truth commission.

7. Lozano-Hemmer recounts, for example, the son of a soldier involved in the massacre, who spoke in *Voz Alta* of having lived with that guilt his whole life, and quotes a firefighter who participated in *Voz Alta* in order to denounce the government's requirement that he put coloring in the water used to spray protestors so that they could be easily identified: "I became a fireman to protect people, not to be part of the apparatus of repression." Rafael Lozano-Hemmer with Marie-Pier Boucher and Patrick Harrop, "Alien Media," *Inflexions* 5 (2012): 148–59.

8. Even as I recognize that the Mexican state has never truly had a "single voice" but was rather always itself riven with tensions and contradictions, what I point to here is the will of the state to present the image of a unified authoritative voice—something at which the Mexican government has long excelled and used to great effect, particularly in terms of presenting itself as the benevolent arbiter of Mexico's modernizing progress. On this issue, specifically in relation to Tlatelolco and its surrounding housing development, see George Flaherty, "Uncanny Tlatelolco, Uncomfortable Juxtapositions," in *Desafío a la estabilidad: Procesos artísticos en México / Defying Stability: Artistic Processes in Mexico, 1952–1967*, ed. Rita Eder (Mexico City: UNAM and Turner, 2014), 401–17.

9. Rafael Lozano-Hemmer, quoted in Geert Lovink, "Real and Virtual Light of Relational Architecture: An Interview with Rafael Lozano-Hemmer," in *Uncanny Networks: Dialogues with the Virtual Intelligentsia* (Cambridge, MA: MIT Press, 2002), 305. *Voz Alta* also capitalizes on the history of popular performativity generated in response to the government censorship that erased almost all traces of the massacre from the official news media. To counter the state's disinformation campaign and to disseminate their own concerns and views, students formed ad hoc news brigades (*las brigadas*), staging street theater plays and producing posters and flyers. Participants in *las brigadas* noted the connection between performativity, public space, and information circulation: "We were like mobile newspapers." Ana Ignacia Rodríguez, quoted in Celeste González de Bustamante, "1968 Olympic Dreams and Tlatelolco Nightmares: Imagining and Imaging Modernity on Television," *Mexican Studies / Estudios Mexicanos* 26, no. 1 (2010): 23. Of course, the interesting parallel of *las brigadas* with the Ayotzinapa movement's savvy use of social media should also be underscored.

10. Lozano-Hemmer, quoted in Lovink, "Real and Virtual Light," 306.

VOZ ALTA ²⁰⁰⁸

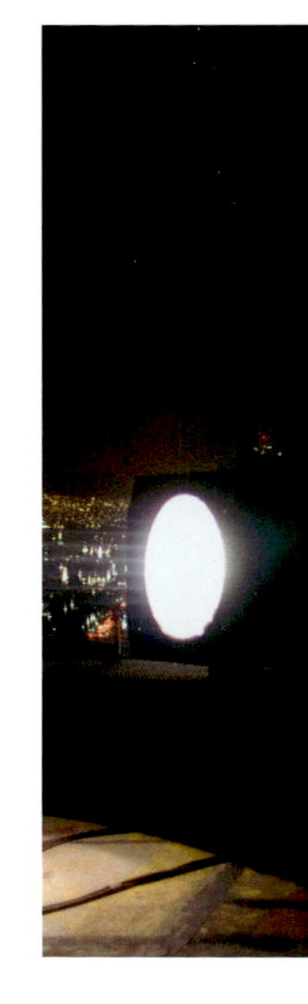

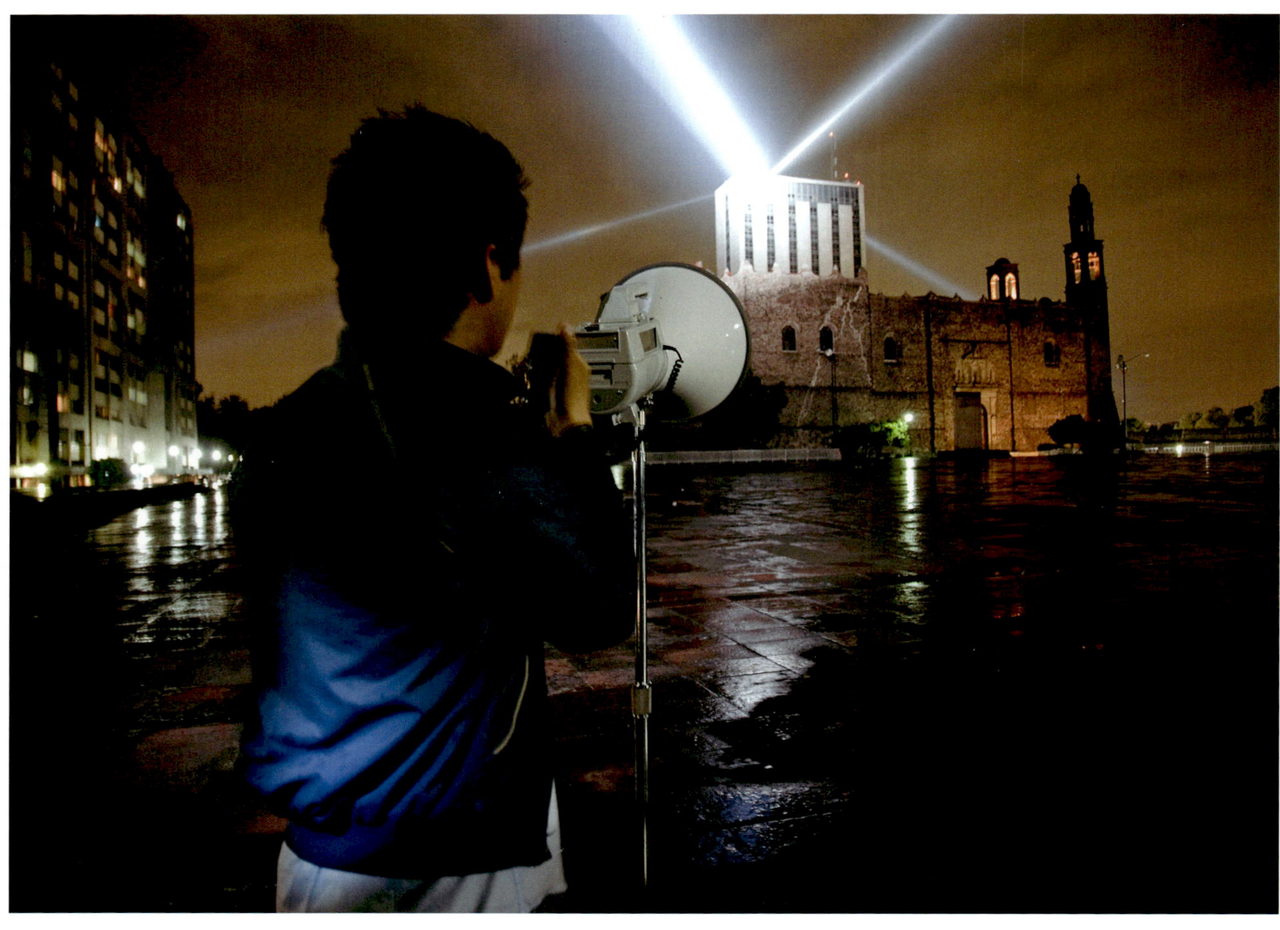

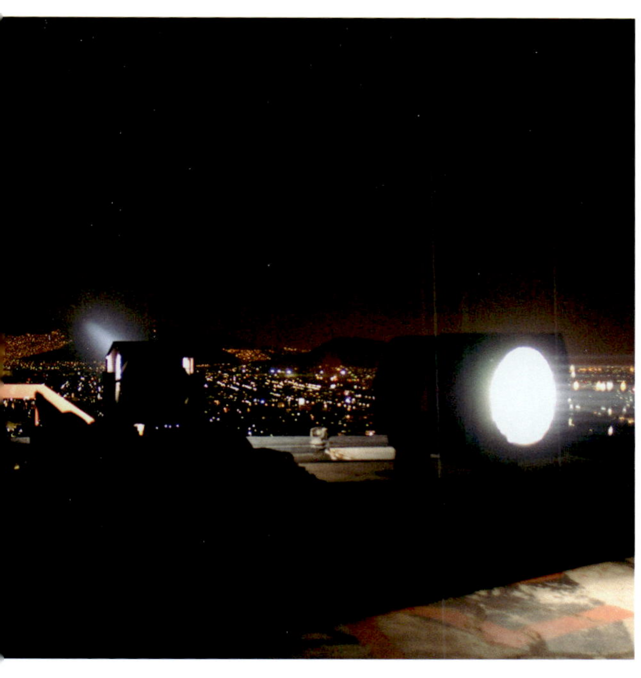

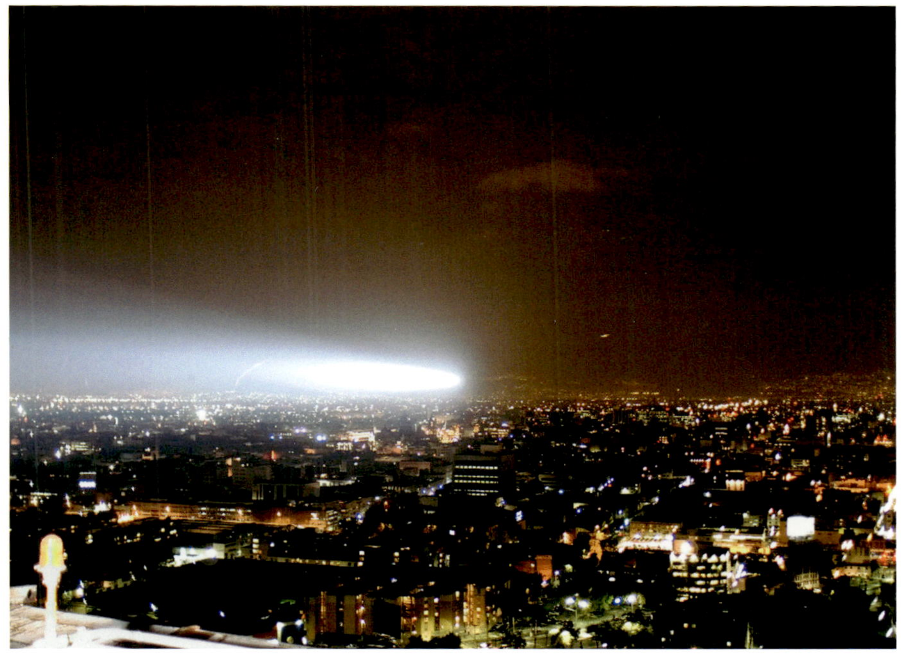

Memorial for the Tlatelolco student massacre, Mexico City, 2008

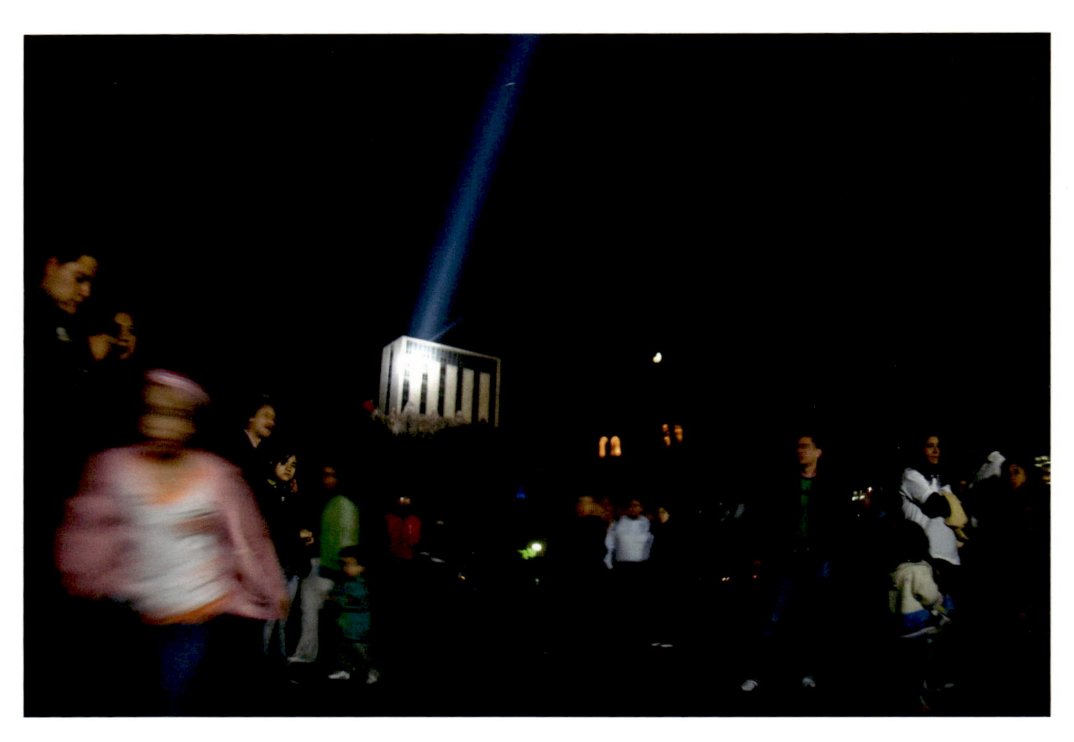

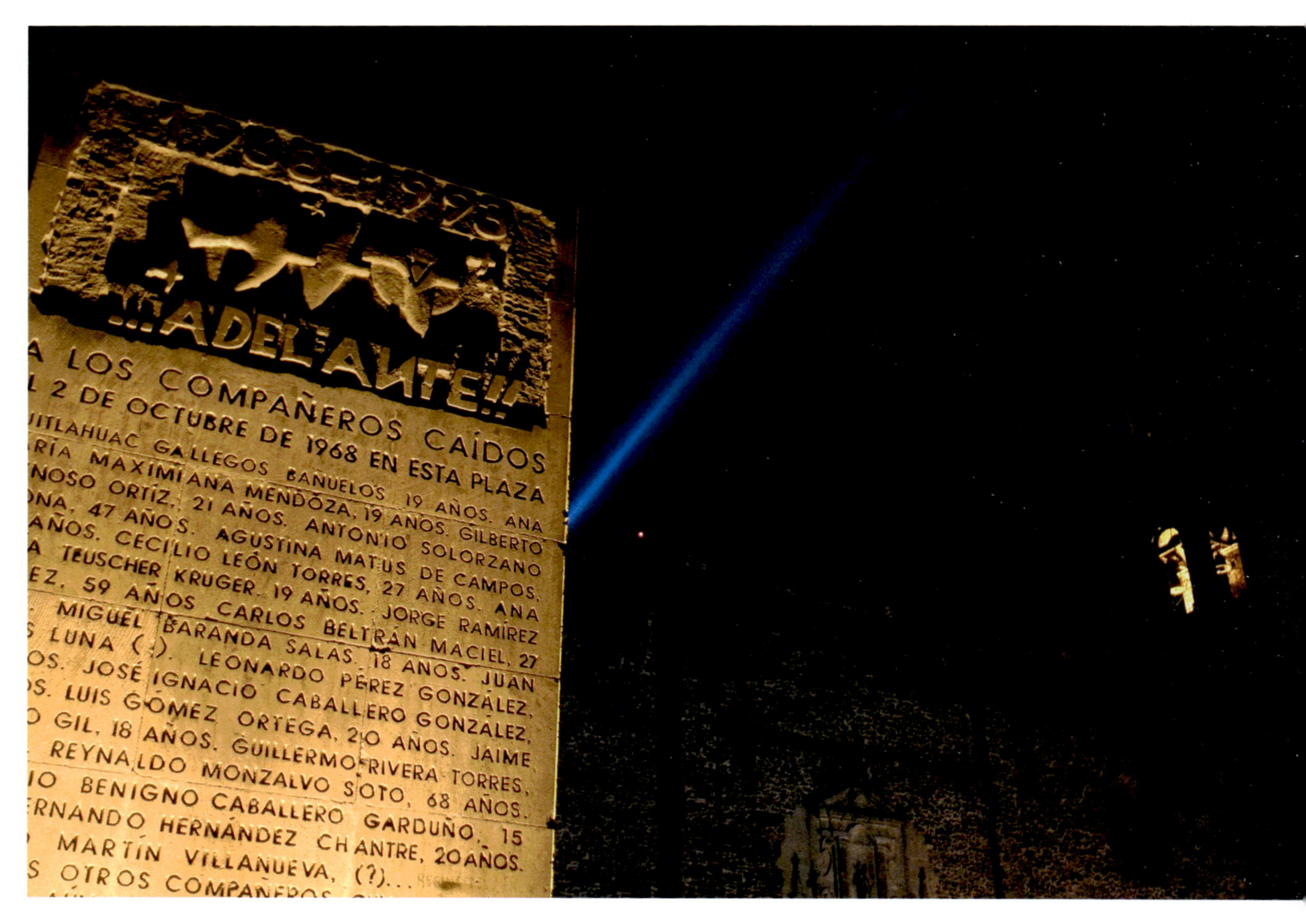
1968 - 1993
¡¡¡ADELANTE!!!
A LOS COMPAÑEROS CAÍDOS
L 2 DE OCTUBRE DE 1968 EN ESTA PLAZA
UITLAHUAC GALLEGOS BAÑUELOS 19 AÑOS. ANA
RÍA MAXIMIANA MENDOZA, 19 AÑOS. GILBERTO
NOSO ORTÍZ, 21 AÑOS. ANTONIO SOLORZANO
NA, 47 AÑOS. AGUSTINA MATUS DE CAMPOS,
AÑOS. CECILIO LEÓN TORRES, 27 AÑOS. ANA
A TEUSCHER KRUGER, 19 AÑOS. JORGE RAMÍREZ
EZ, 59 AÑOS. CARLOS BELTRÁN MACIEL, 27
MIGUEL BARANDA SALAS, 18 AÑOS. JUAN
S LUNA ( ). LEONARDO PÉREZ GONZÁLEZ,
OS. JOSÉ IGNACIO CABALLERO GONZÁLEZ,
S. LUIS GÓMEZ ORTEGA, 20 AÑOS. JAIME
O GIL, 18 AÑOS. GUILLERMO RIVERA TORRES,
REYNALDO MONZALVO SOTO, 68 AÑOS.
IO BENIGNO CABALLERO GARDUÑO, 15
ERNANDO HERNÁNDEZ CHANTRE, 20 AÑOS.
MARTÍN VILLANUEVA, (?)...
S OTROS COMPAÑEROS

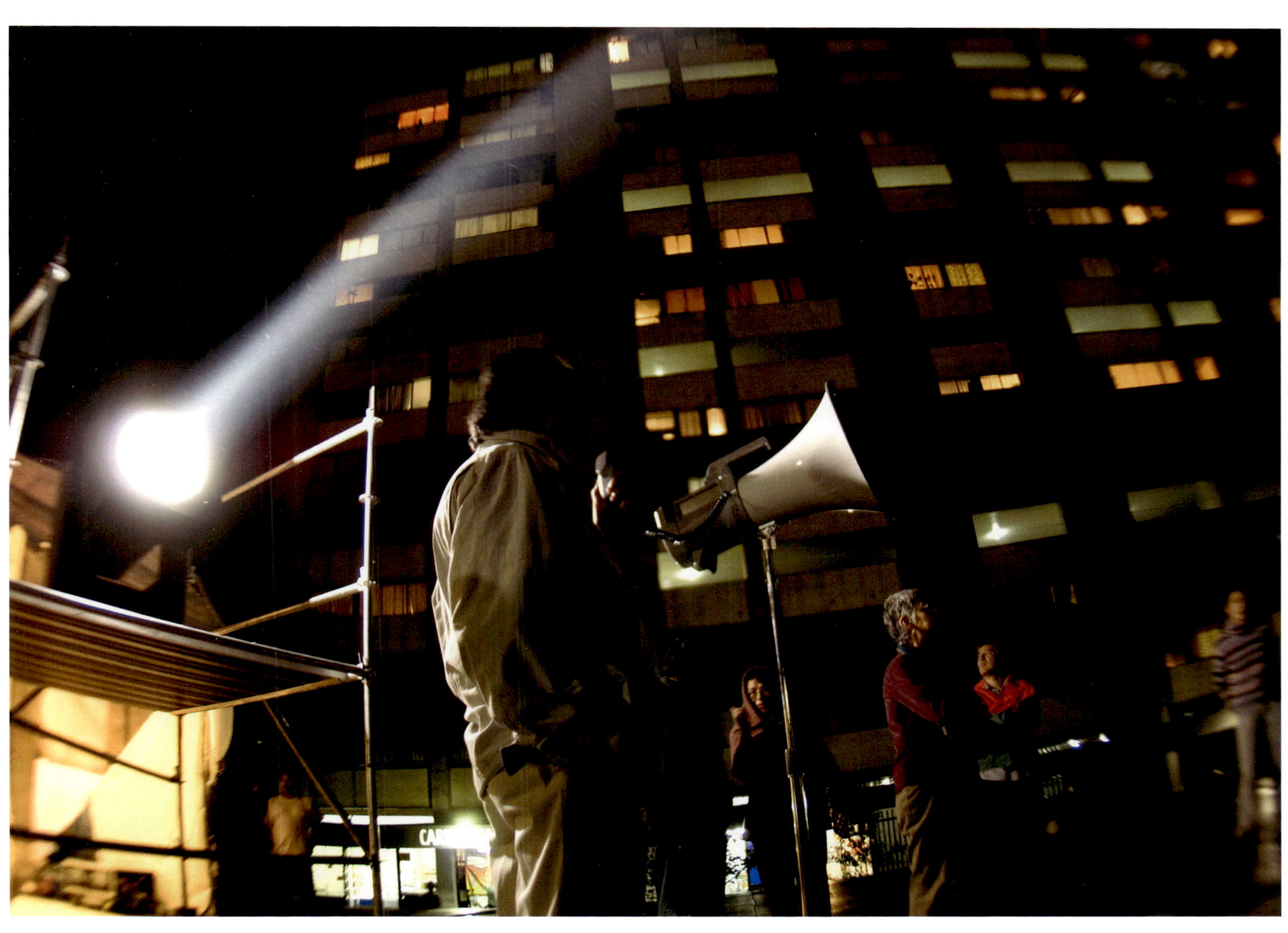

Memorial for the Tlatelolco student massacre, Mexico City, 2008

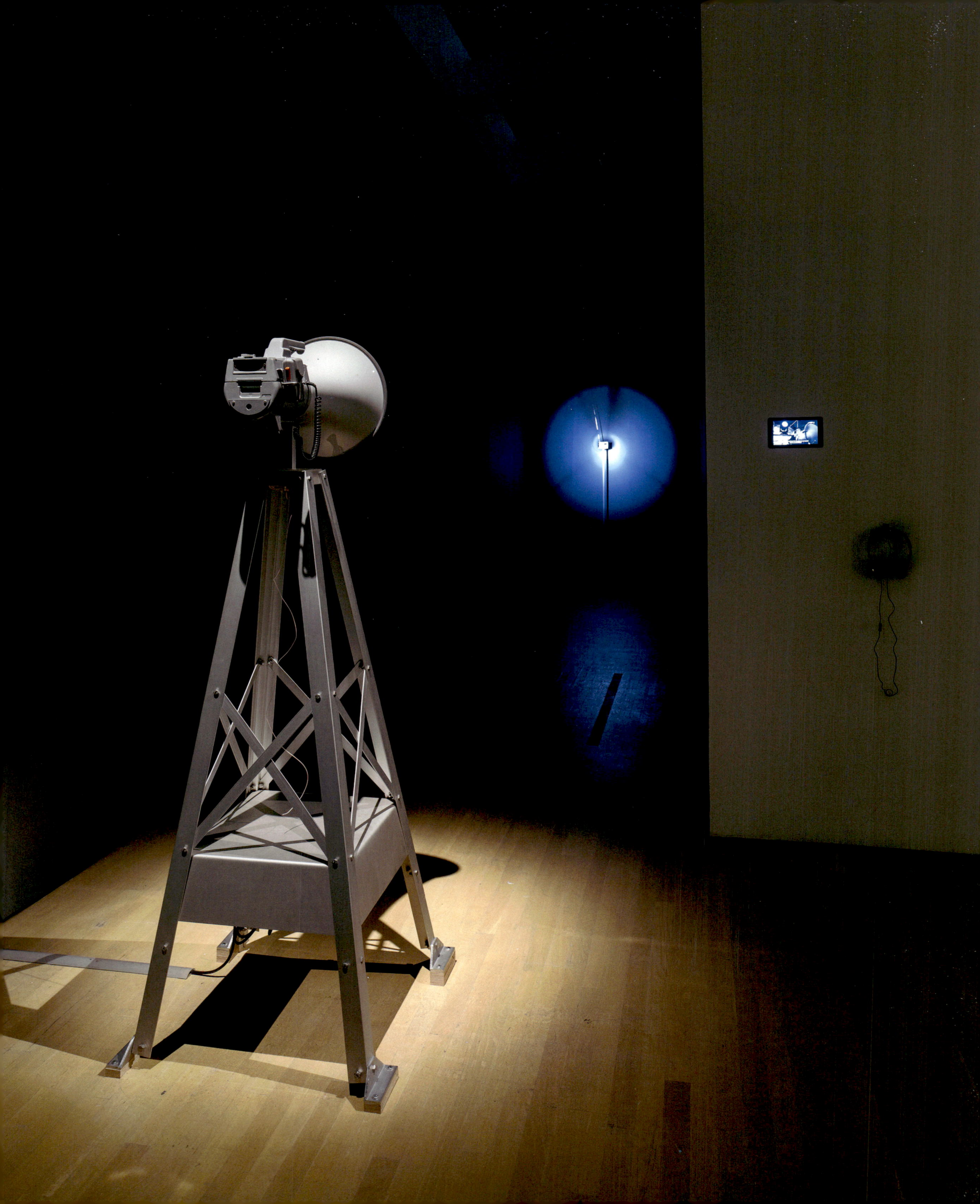

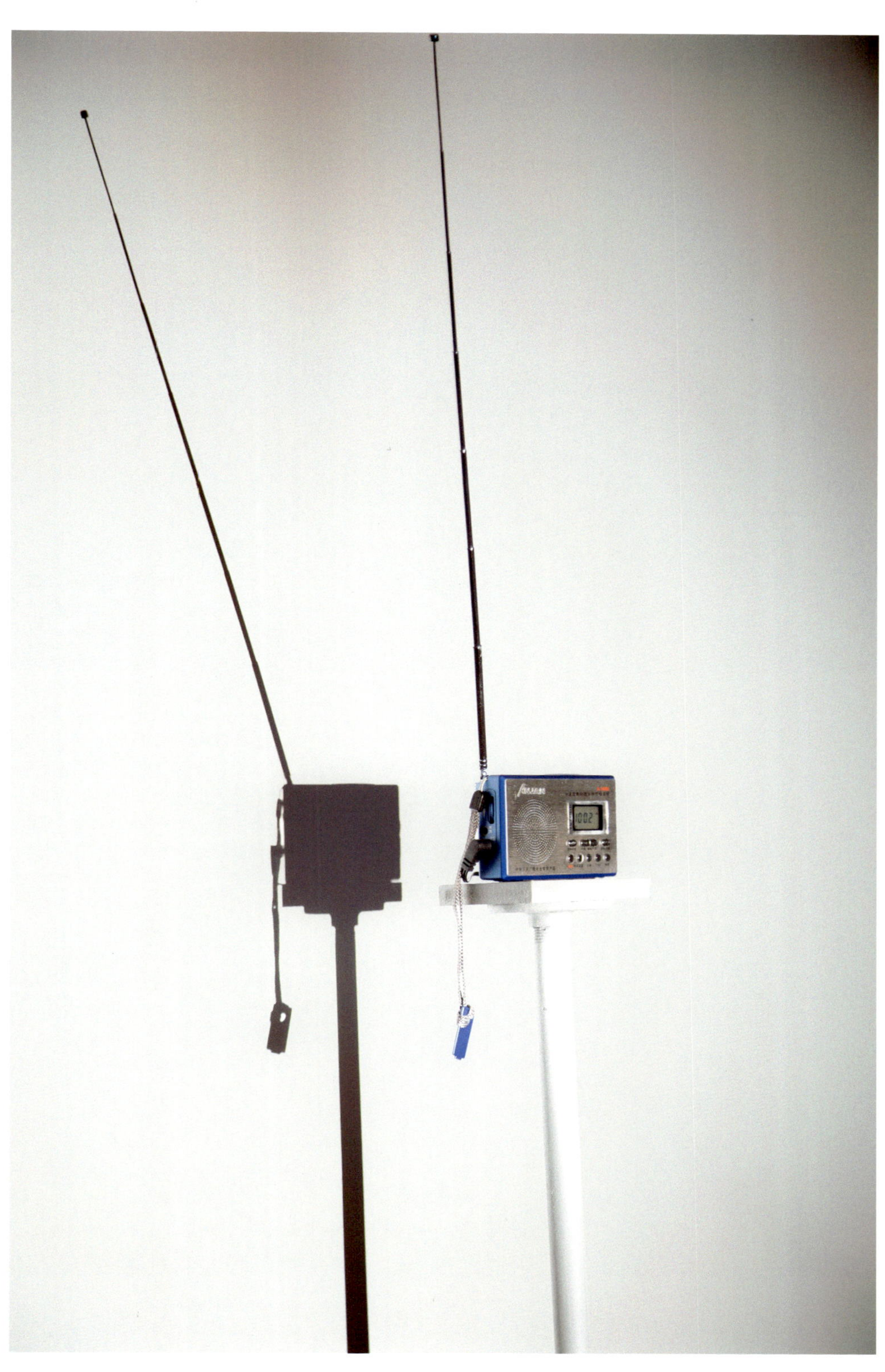

Voz Alta and Prototype, 2008. Installation views, Musée d'art contemporain de Montréal, 2018 (left), and Museo de Arte Contemporáneo de Monterrey, Mexico, 2019 (right)

VOLUTE 1: AU CLAIR DE LA LUNE 2016

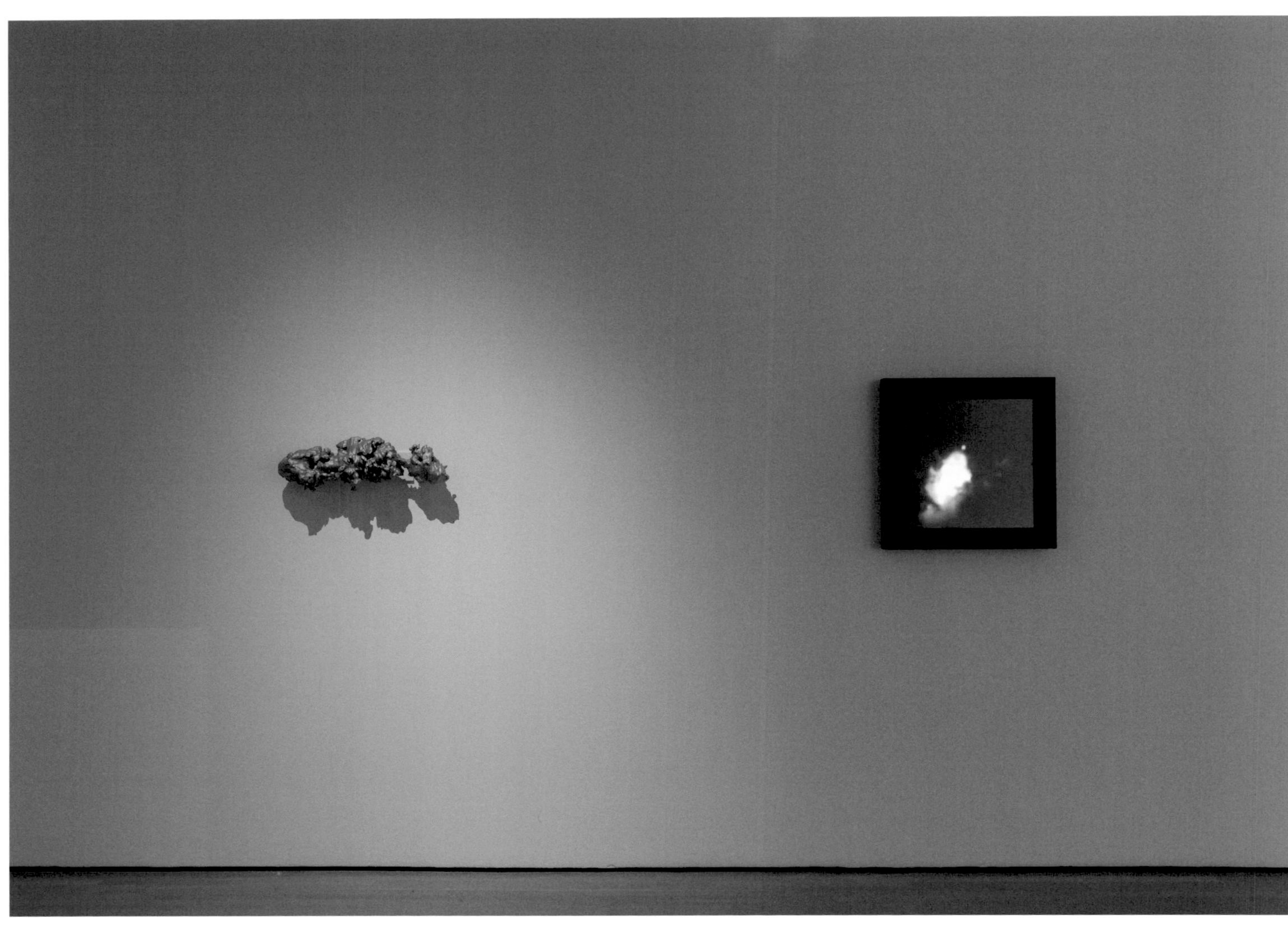

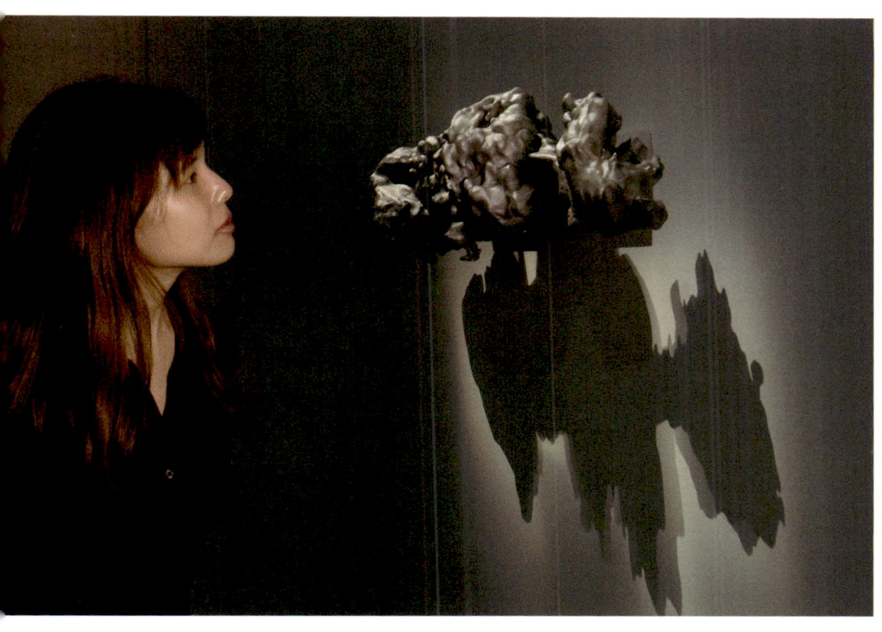

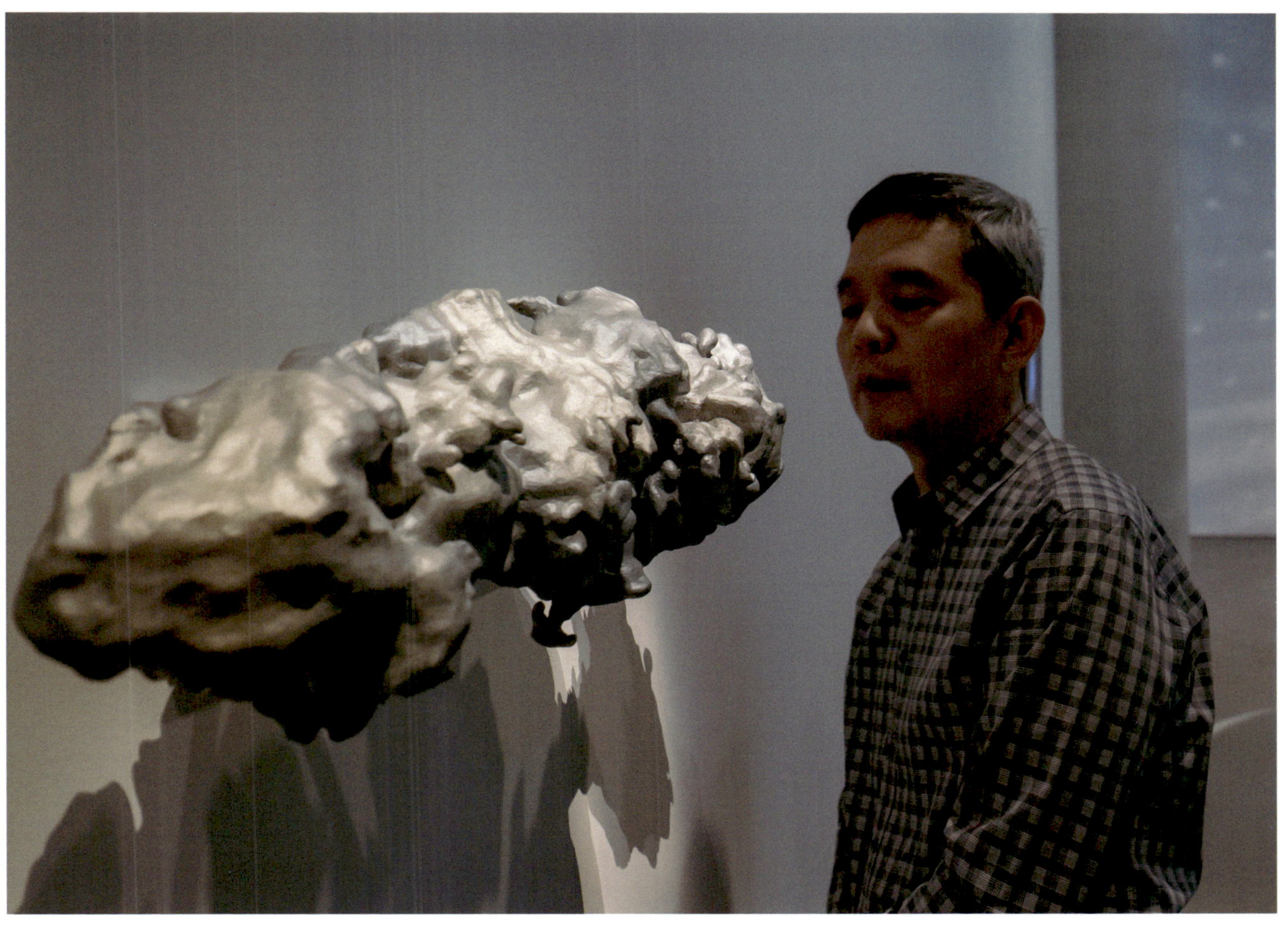

Installation views, Musée d'art contemporain de Montréal, 2018 (left), and Amorepacific Museum of Art, Seoul, 2018 (top and right)

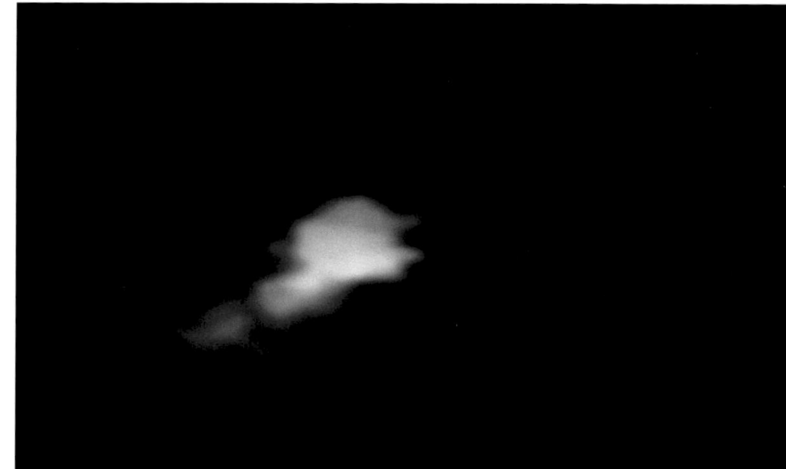

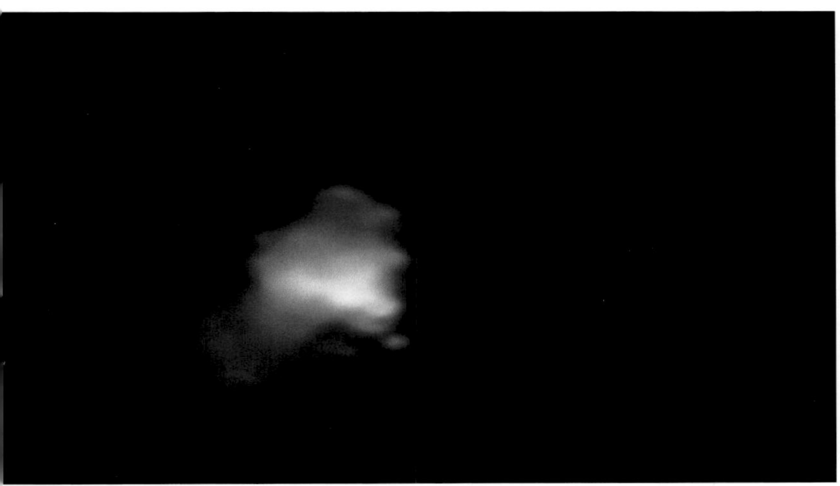 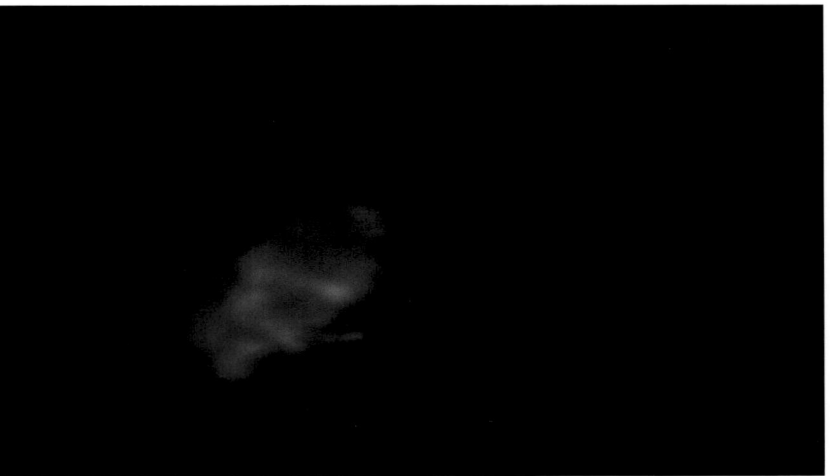

Laser tomograph cross sections of the density of breath exhaled with the spoken phrase *au clair de la lune*, used to generate the sculpture *Volute 1: Au clair de la lune*

BIFURCATION 2012

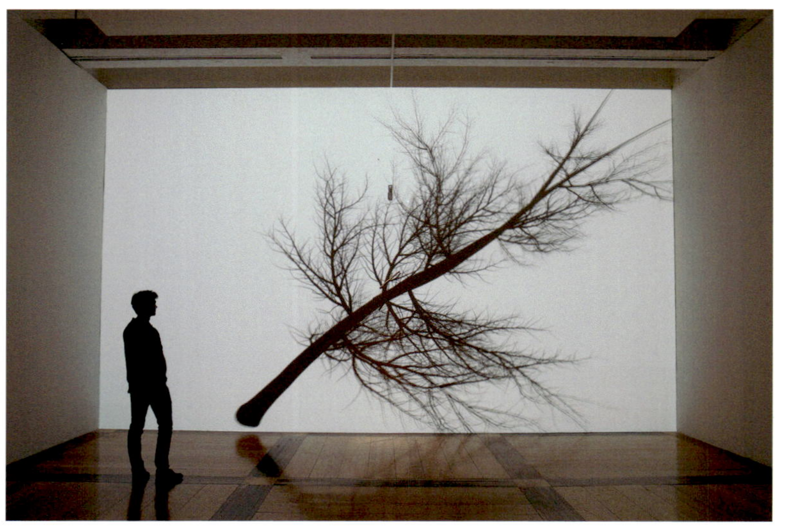

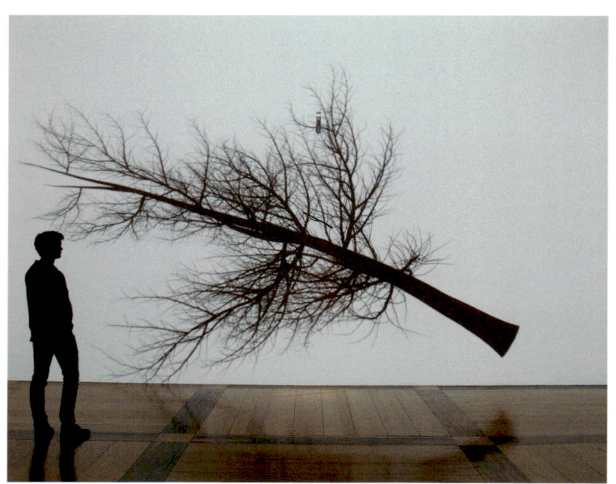

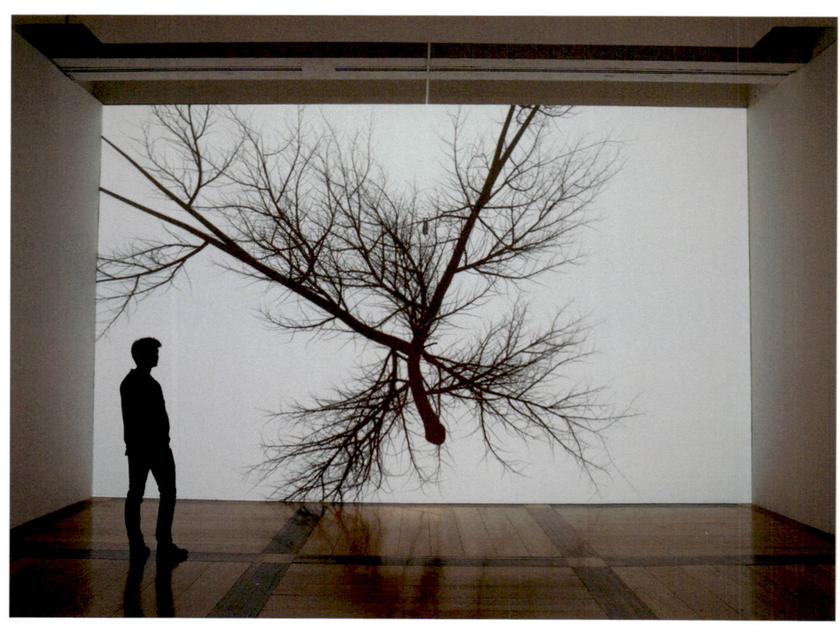

Installation views, Museo de Arte Contemporáneo de Monterrey, Mexico, 2019

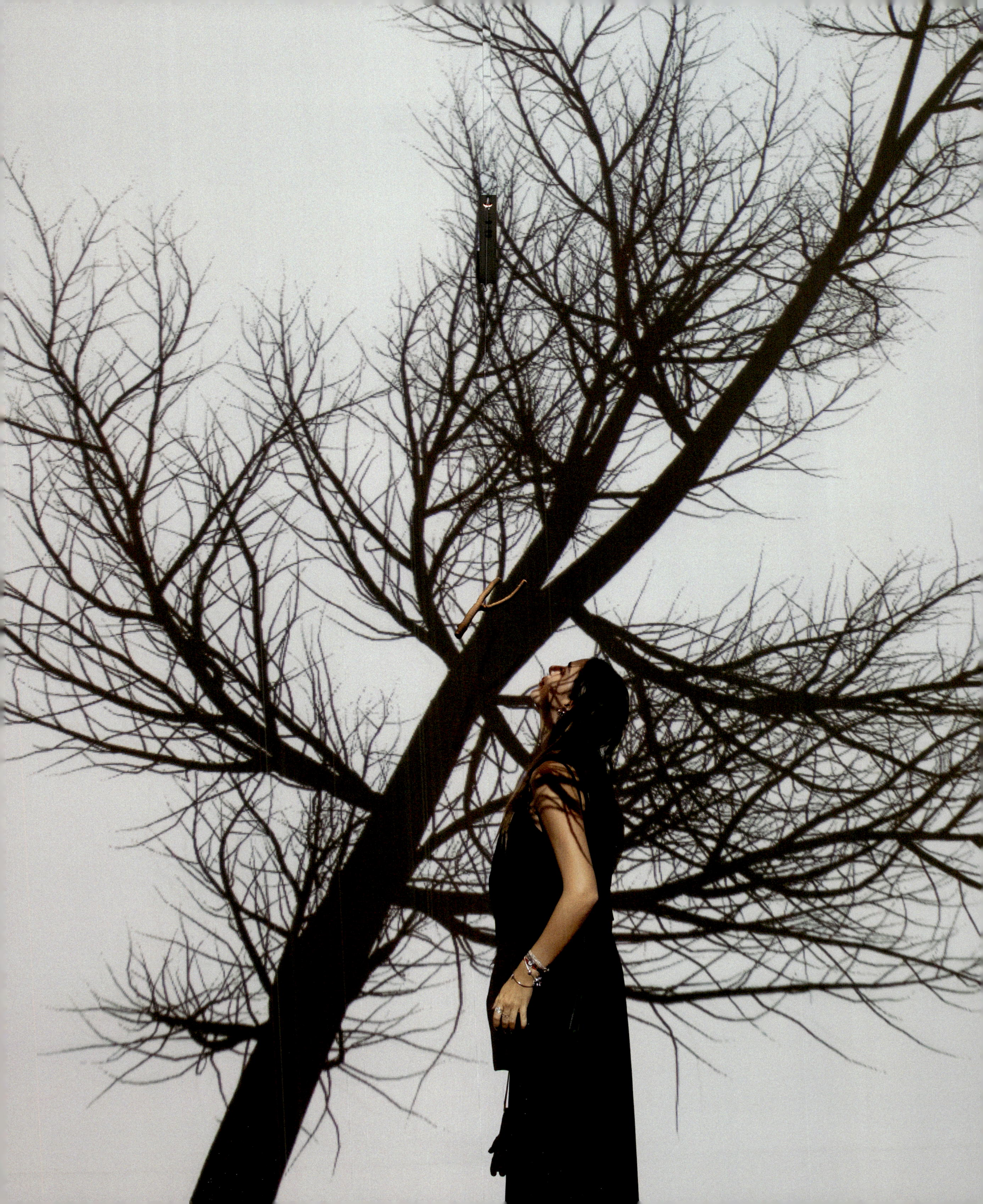

SEISMOSCOPES 2009

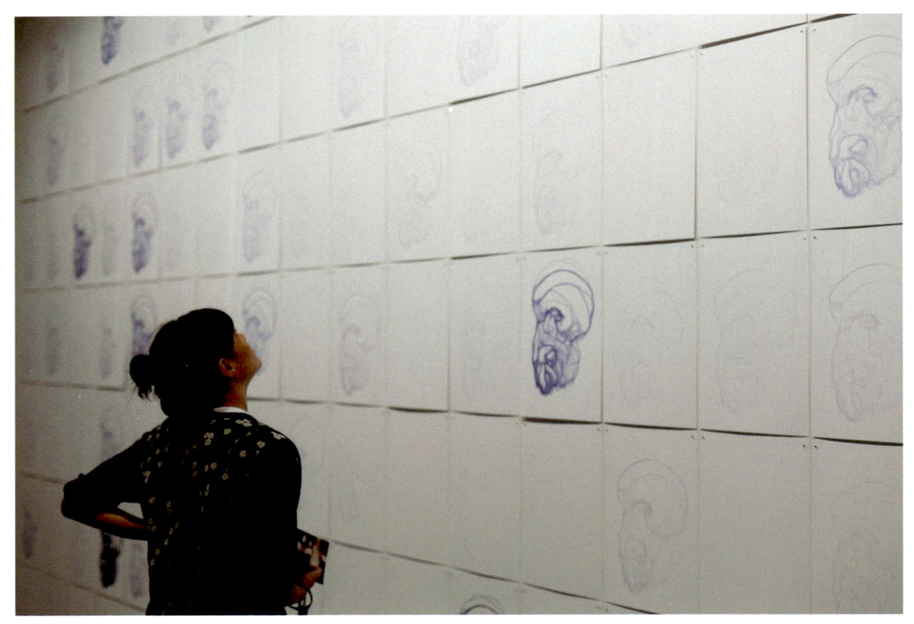

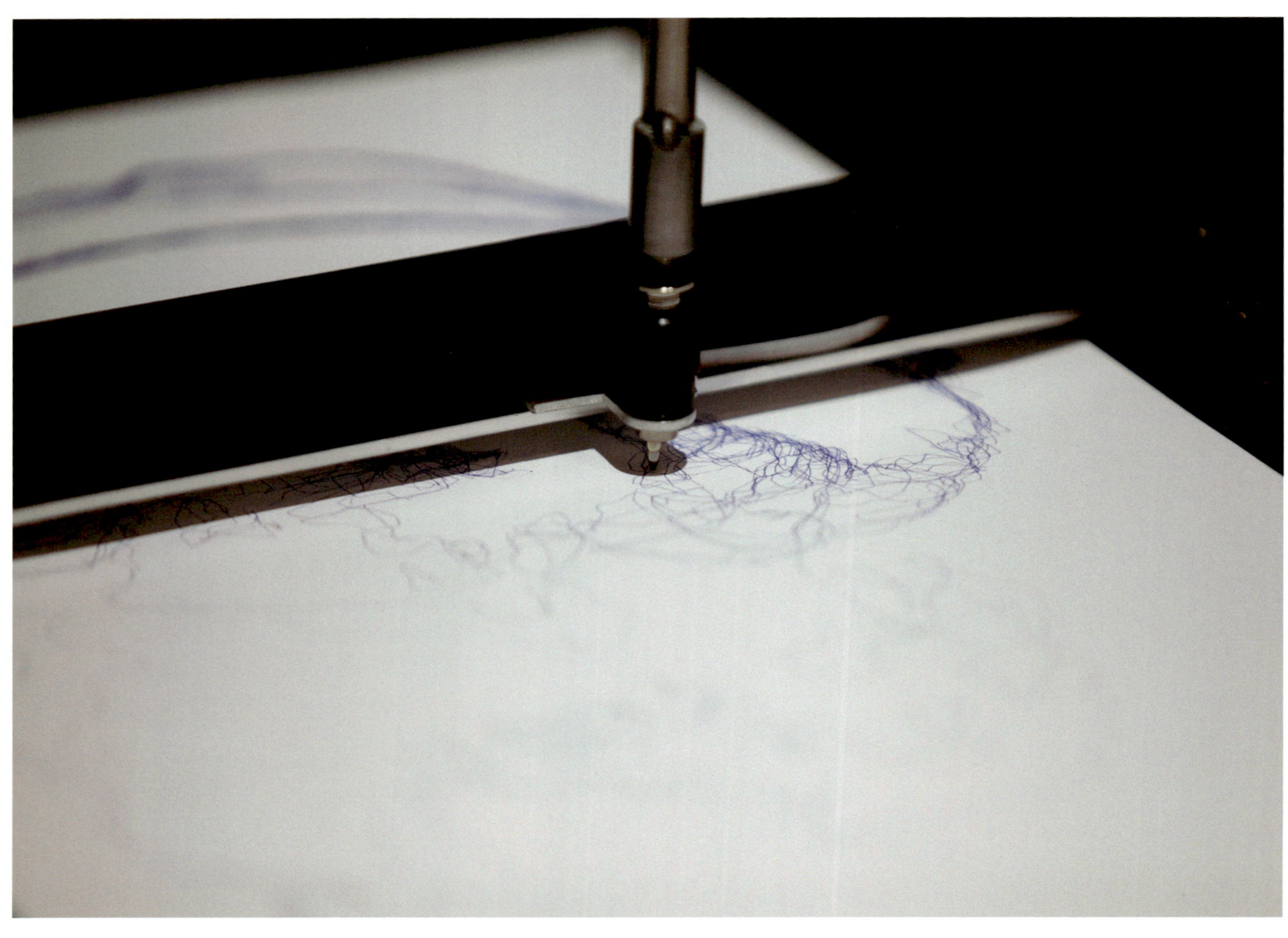

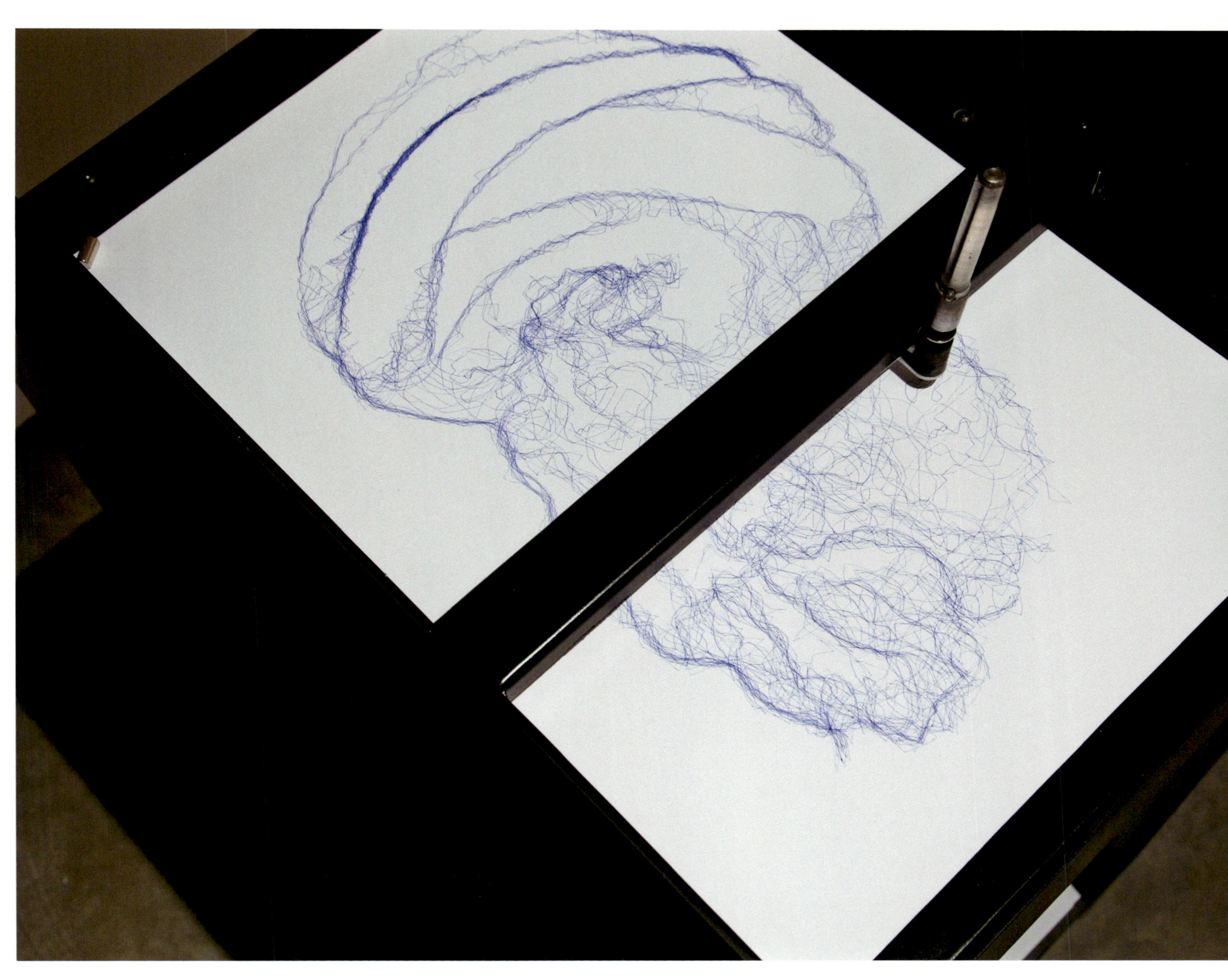

Installation views, Museum of Contemporary Art, Sydney, 2011

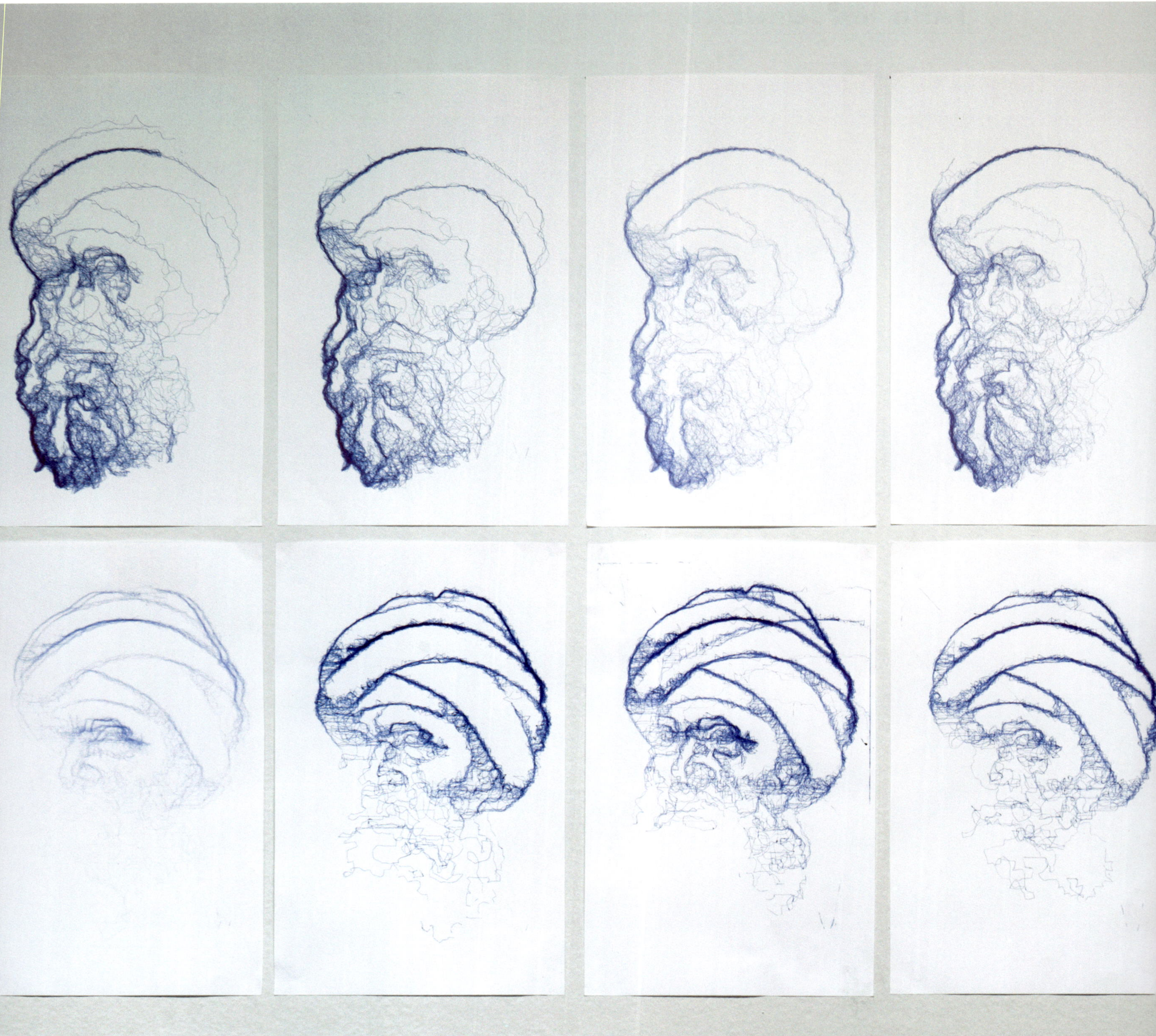

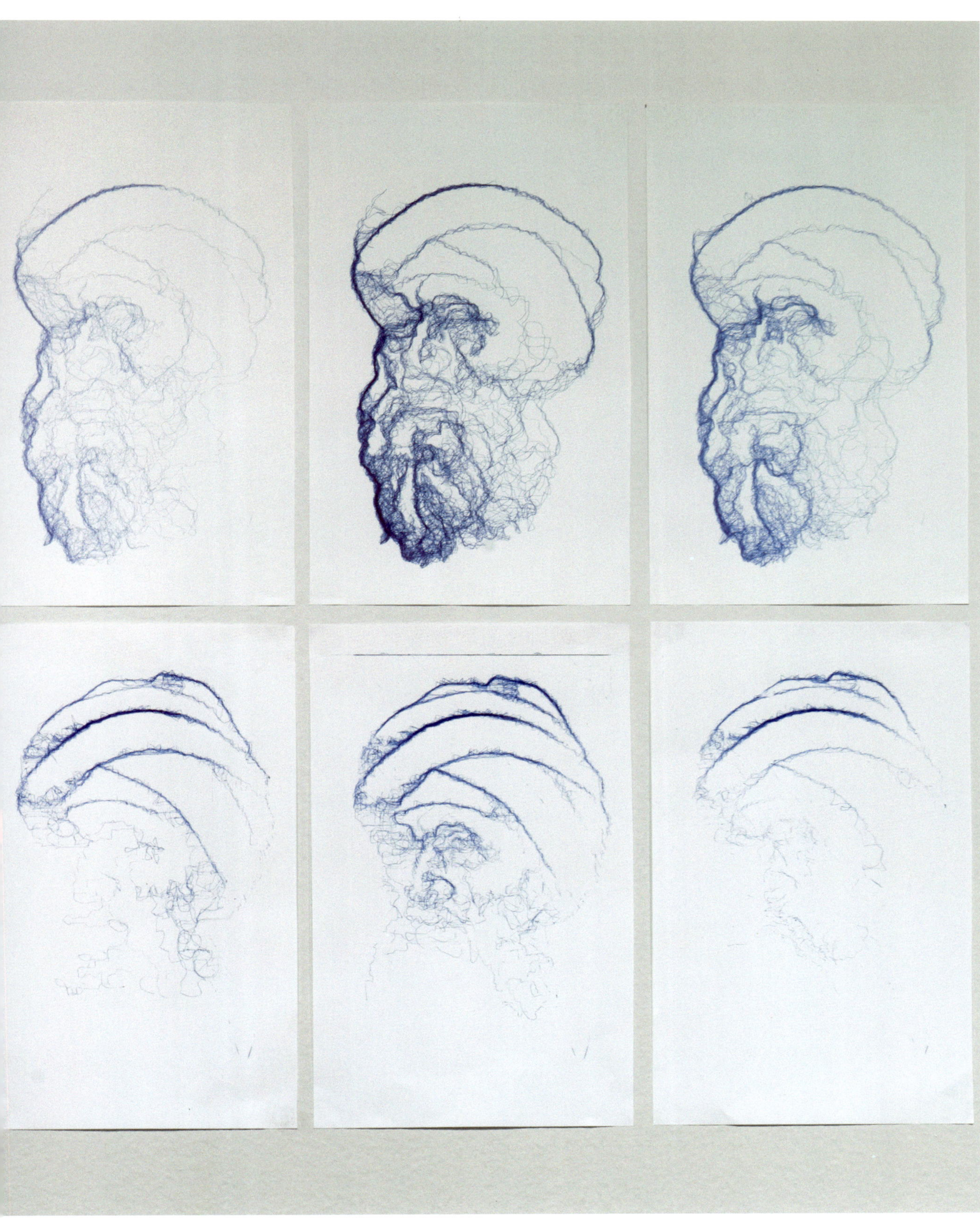

Installation view, Museo de Arte Contemporáneo de Monterrey, Mexico, 2019

TAPE RECORDERS 2011

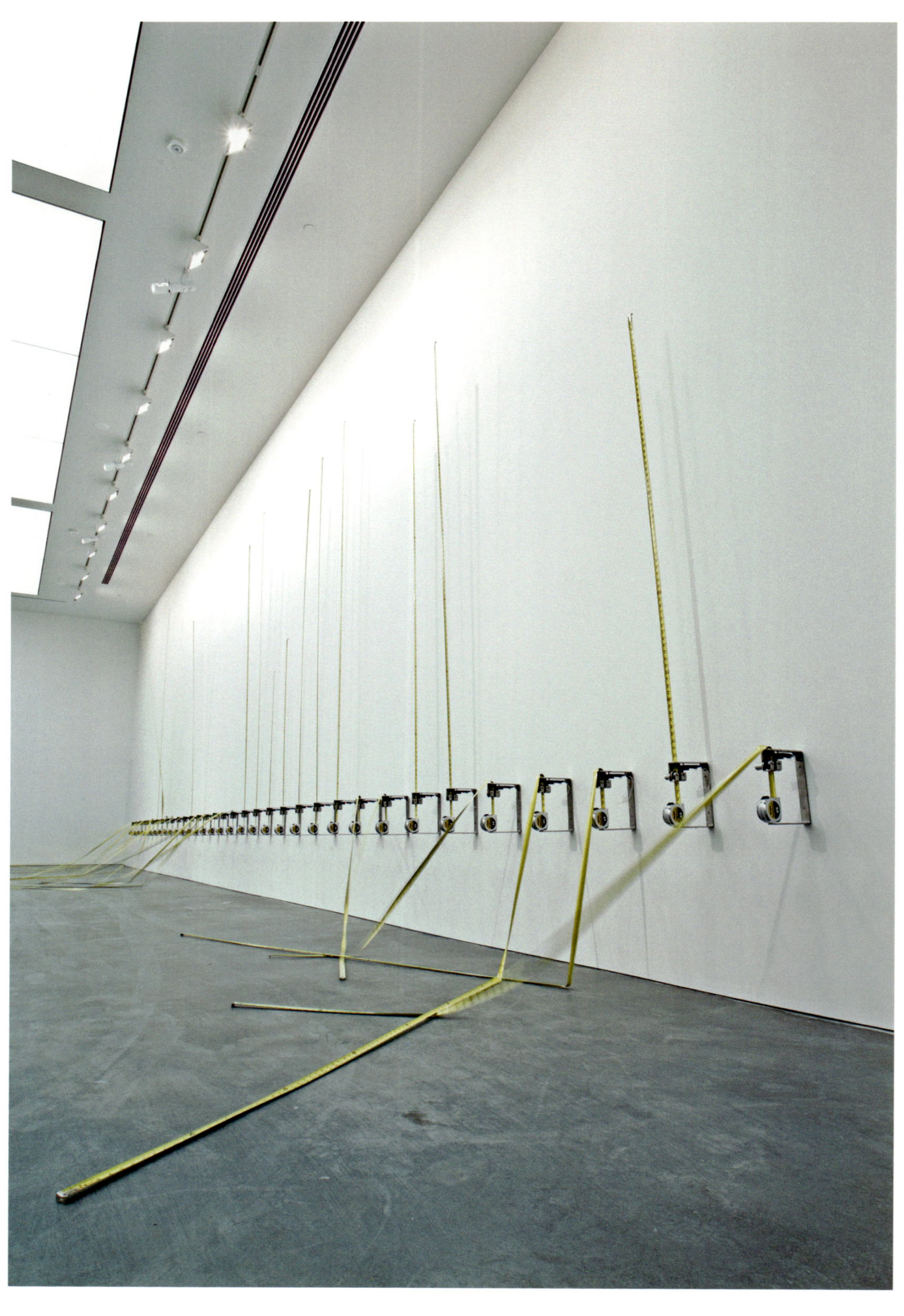

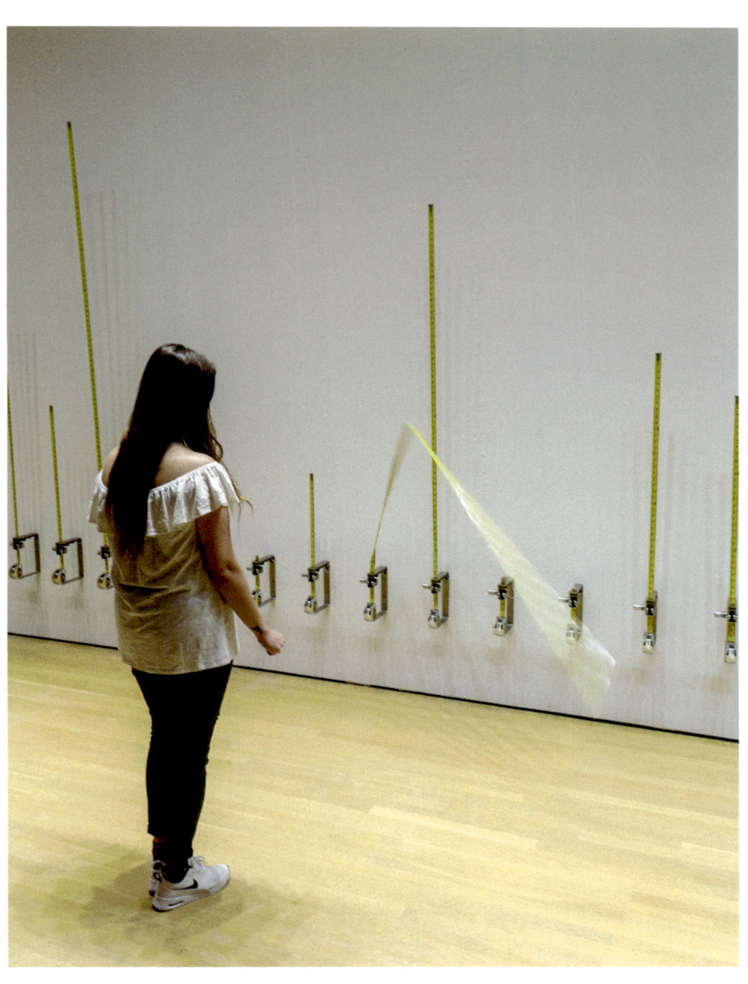

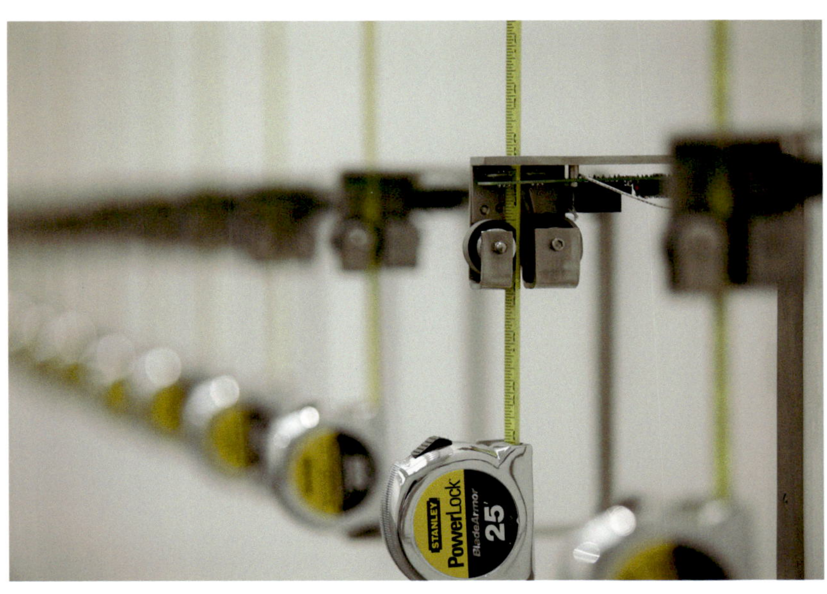

Installation views, Museum of Contemporary Art, Sydney, 2011 (left and right), and Musée d'art contemporain de Montréal, 2018 (top)

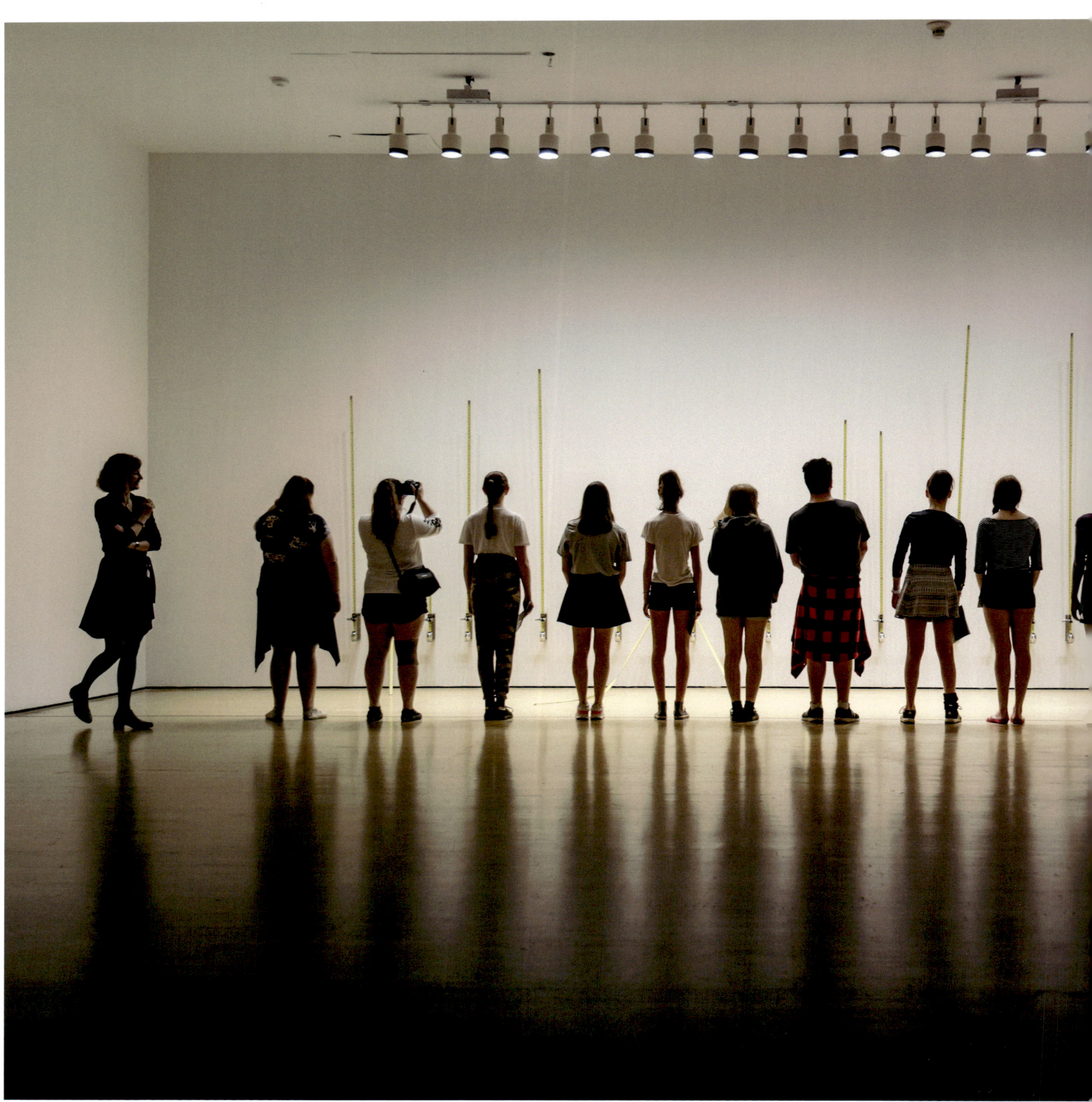

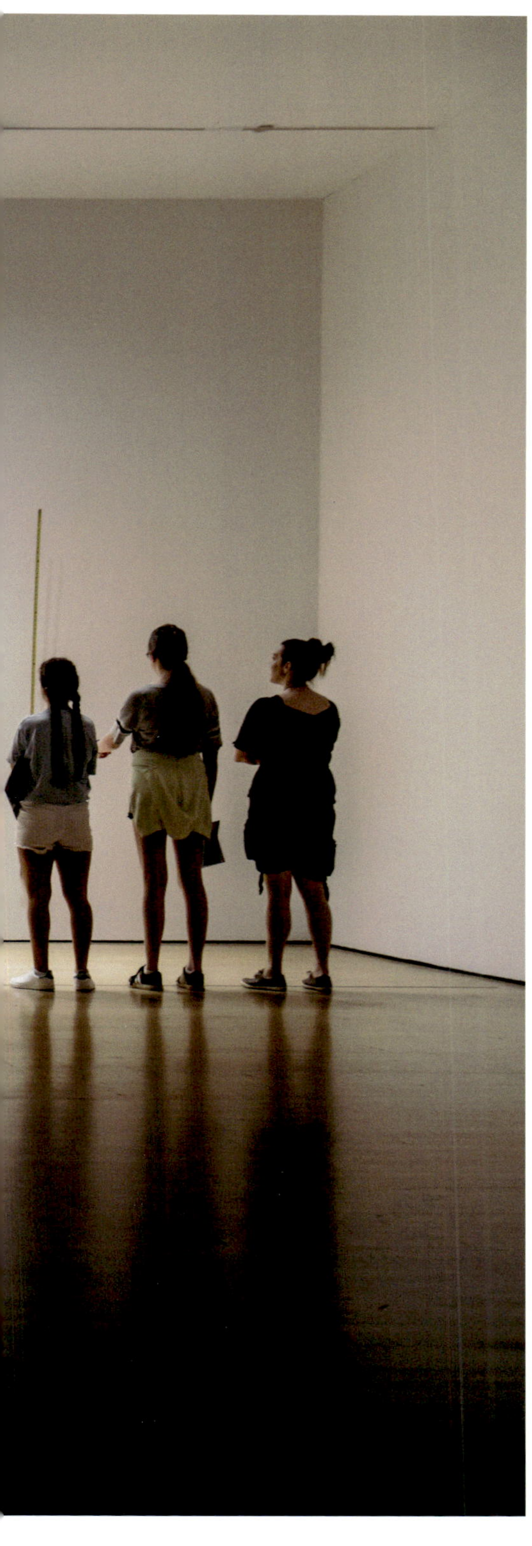

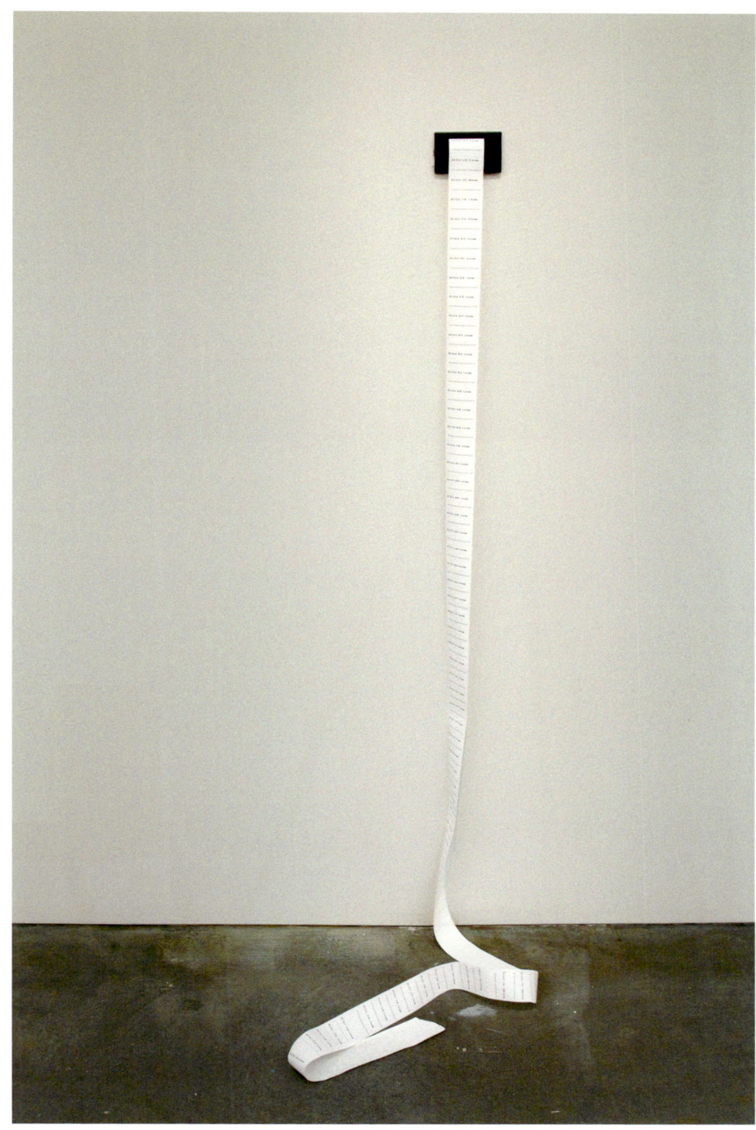

Installation views, Musée d'art contemporain de Montréal, 2018 (left), and Museum of Contemporary Art, Sydney, 2011 (right)

SYNAPTIC CAGUAMAS 2004

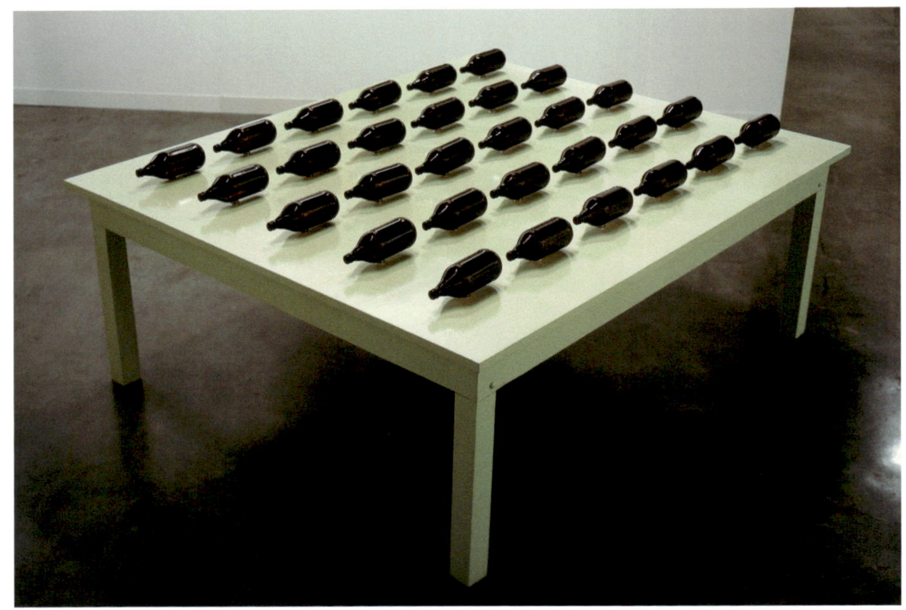

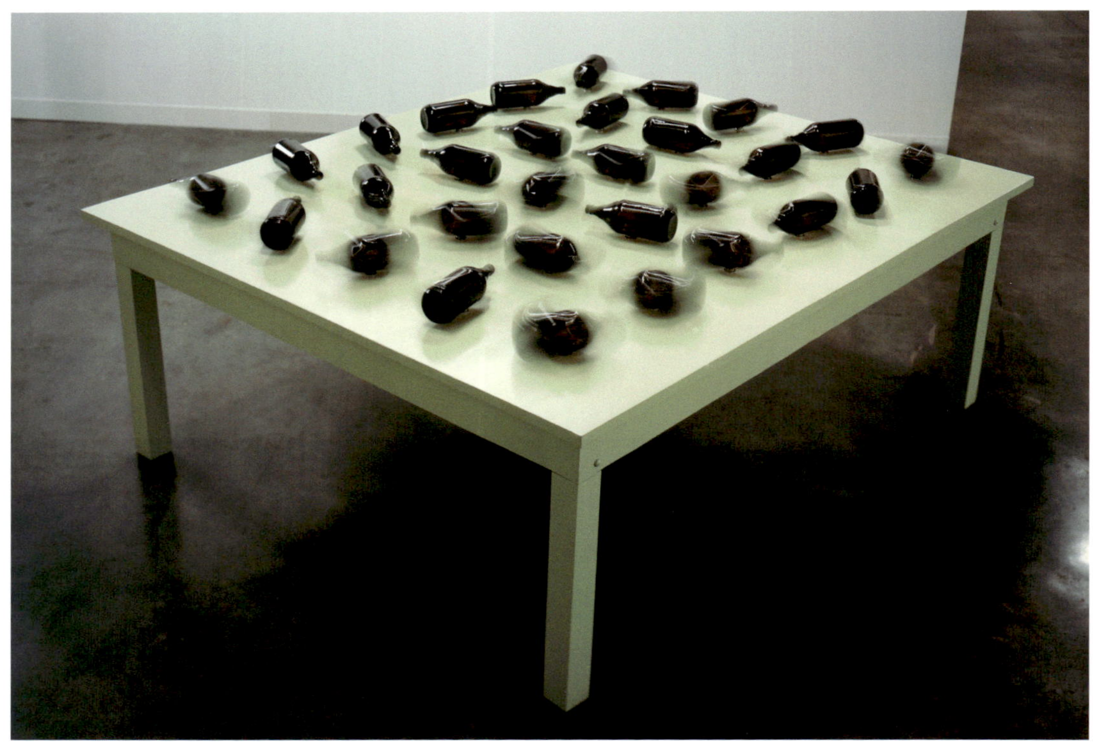

Installation views, Galería OMR, at Art Basel, Miami Beach, 2004

STANDARDS AND DOUBLE STANDARDS 2004

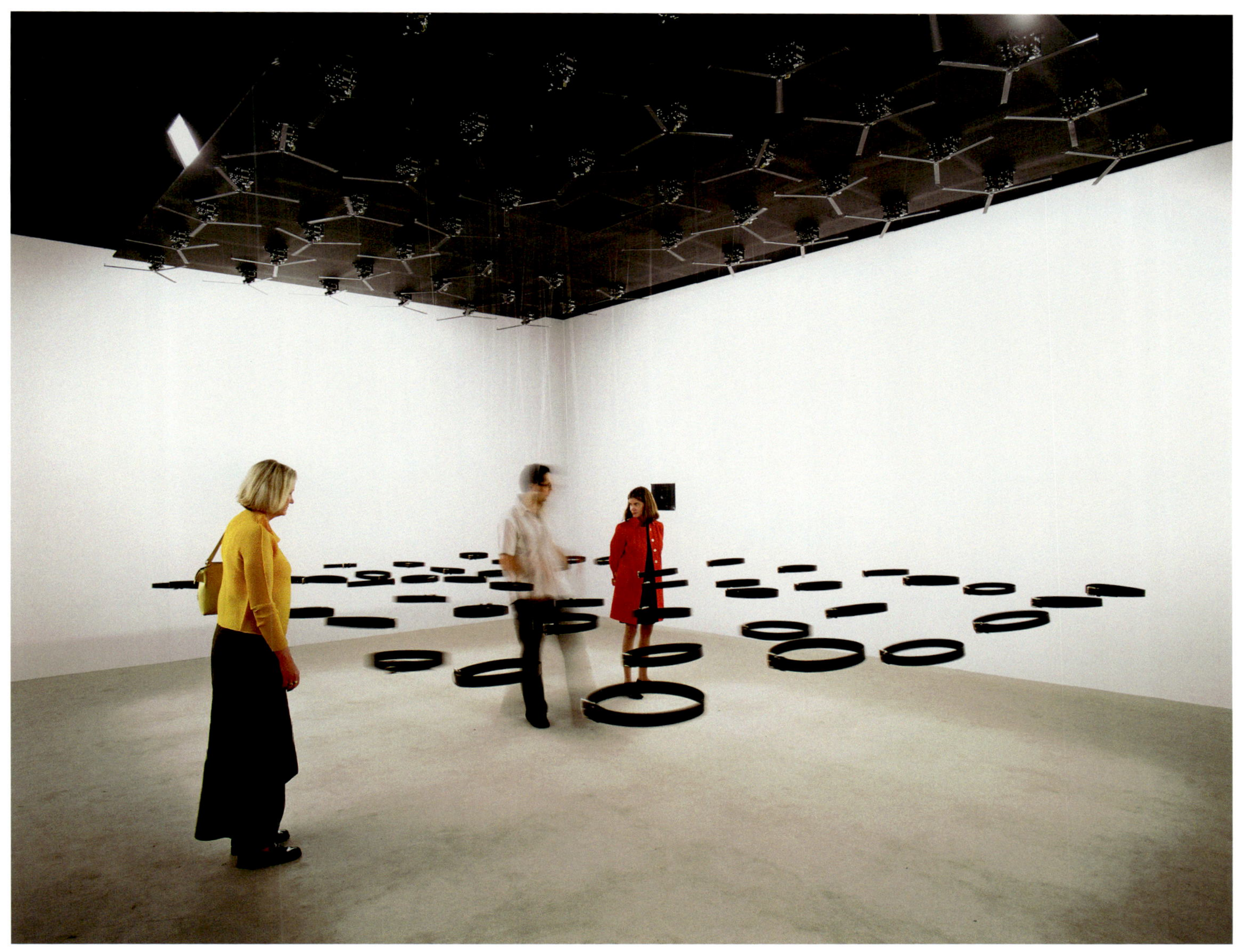

Installation view, Galería OMR, at Art Basel, Switzerland, 2004

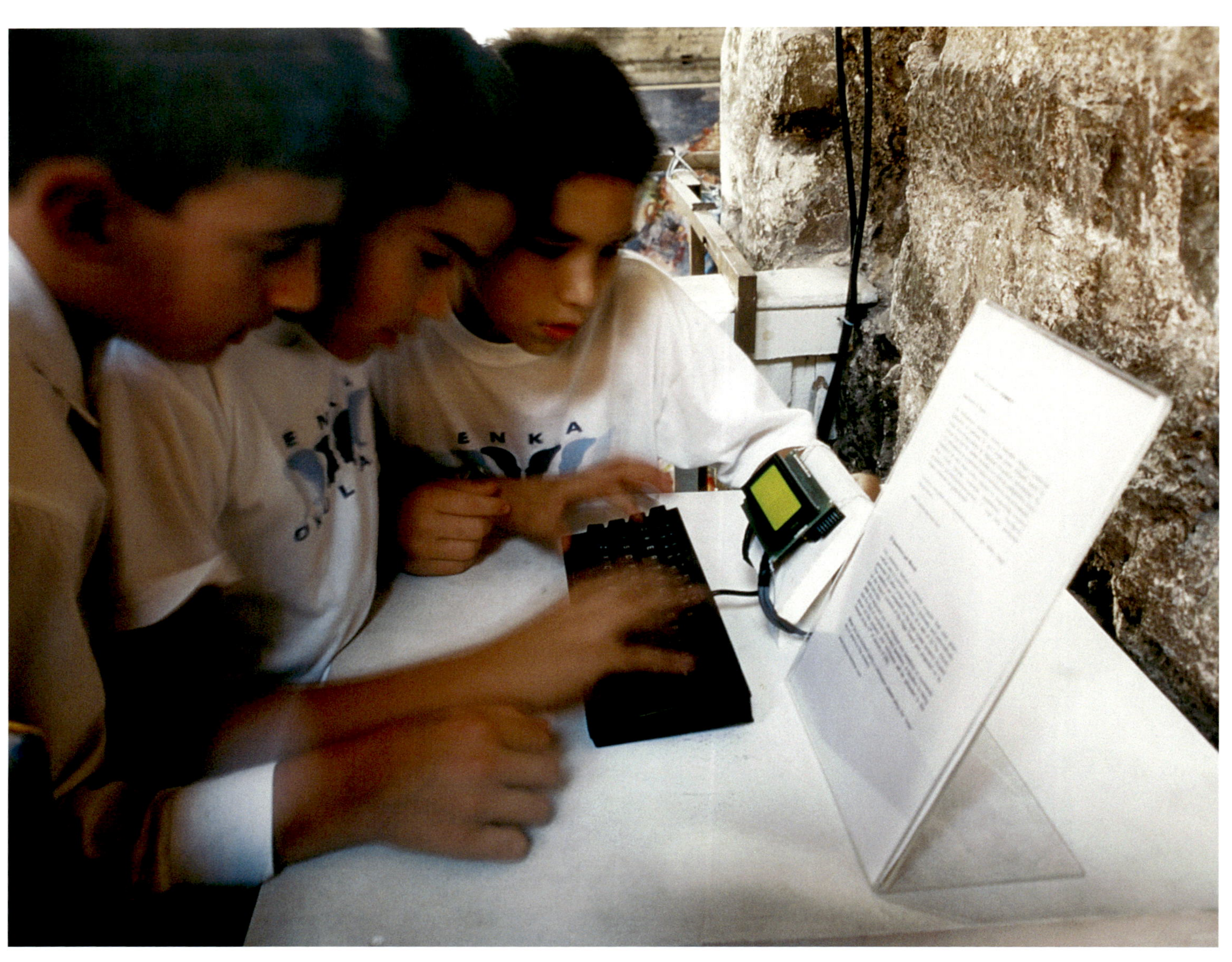

ALGORITHMIC BEHAVIOR

No hay tal cosa como la neutralidad o como la tabula rasa.
("There's no such thing as neutrality or tabula rasa.")
—Rafael Lozano-Hemmer, 2015

CODING IDENTITY

Vital to the questions that Rafael Lozano-Hemmer has consistently raised over the past three decades is not how artists have turned to newer formats of media technology to update modernist paradigms of representation, but how representation itself demands radical recalibration.[1] Pointing to the ways that it is no longer defined by medium or format, Lozano-Hemmer instead models how representation has become fundamentally conditioned by the protocols of storage media, including software and algorithms. By exploring this notion, he reveals the mutual embeddedness of media and identity.[2] With unparalleled intensity, his works reinforce the primacy of interfaces over medium in our experience of contemporary art. The artist also reminds us that data—like visual media—is never neutral, benign, or objective, but remains deeply conditioned by human behaviors and habits.

Lozano-Hemmer's artworks frame the complex relationship between models and systems (spatial, conceptual, and computational) of emancipation, access, and disruption and their inverses: the mechanisms of control, discipline, propriety, and other forces that maintain the social status quo. In particular, *33 Questions per Minute* (2000; see page 18); *Tape Recorders* (2011; see page 56), *Voz Alta* (Out Loud, 2008; see page 40), and *Vicious Circular Breathing* (2013; see page 78) all combine sophisticated computerized tracking systems, customized software, and sensors with workaday hardware supplies to generate real-time systems that pivot around ordinary human gestures, creating complex social dynamics. These works align with 1960s North American Conceptualism (itself informed by the agitprop precedents of the European avant-garde), which sought to adapt models introduced by the emerging fields of the

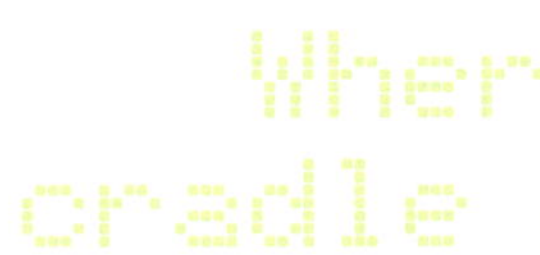

33 Questions per Minute, 2000. Installation view, Istanbul Biennial, Hagia Eirene, Turkey, 2001

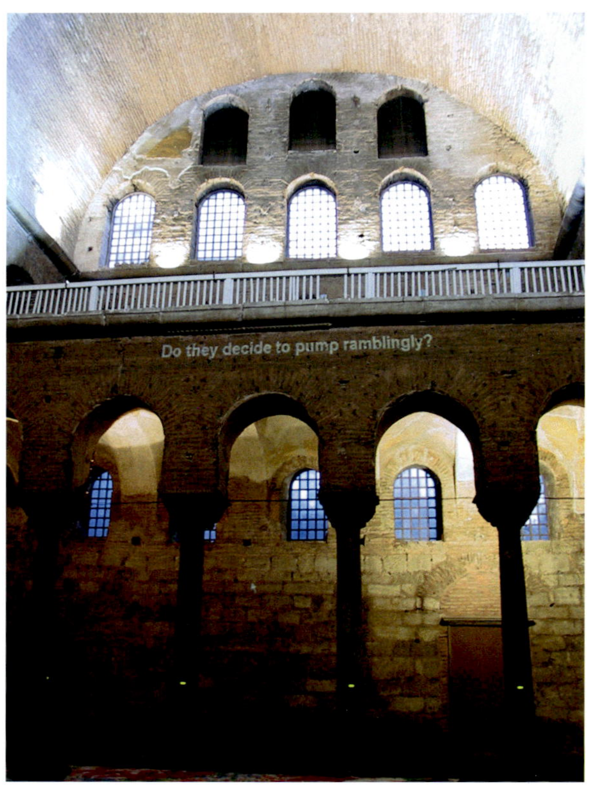

period—digital technology, communication theory, cognitive psychology, and psycho-analysis—as well as literary theory in order to generate new frameworks for visual art. Importantly, Lozano-Hemmer updates and expands upon these methodologies by introducing critical issues of translation and transposition (linguistic, computational, and cultural) to complicate—and to interrogate—the often-empty rhetoric of the terms agency, exchange, and participation, which occupy much of the discourse on contemporary art. In doing so, Lozano-Hemmer breathes new life into often-overlooked cultural contexts and histories, as he does with Mexico's 1968 Tlatelolco student massacre in *Voz Alta*. More circuitously, *33 Questions per Minute*, *Tape Recorders*, and *Vicious Circular Breathing* deploy novelty technology or software to expose the disci-plinary frameworks that often define and condition bodies and control speech—protocols these technologies normally obscure. These works recall the way that artist Marta Minujín's early media environments, produced throughout Latin America and Europe between 1965 and 1968, did not merely convert technology into aesthetic objects, but remained embedded within the very networks—social and political—they sought to make visible.[3] Diverse and diffuse in their own right, Lozano-Hemmer's works discussed here point to algorithmically enhanced systems of pattern recognition—scientific and social.

THRESHOLDS OF LEGIBILITY

33 Questions per Minute (2000; page 62 and fig. 8) consists of an adaptable meshwork of twenty-one palm-sized, greenish LCD screens, the type that adorn self-service ticket vending machines that direct you to "make your selection" or "insert your ticket" in dimly lit type. These seemingly innocuous screens have become ubiquitous within

Figure 8
33 Questions per Minute, 2000
Projector, computer, custom electronics, and custom software written in Delphi
Dimensions variable
Installation view, Istanbul Biennial, Hagia Eirene, Turkey, 2001

urban public transportation systems that seek to expedite human movement through automation. More often than not, the devices engender the opposite effect, eliciting frustration, confusion, and panic even in those versed in the local language or innately familiar with the customs of riding *el metro, le métro,* or MUNI—not to mention the difficulties they create for people with impaired vision. Locals and tourists alike are equally powerless to hasten passage through a turnstile flashing the message "please swipe again." In *33 Questions per Minute,* the individual LCD screens are stripped from their plastic casings and tethered by long black cables to a central computer running software that combines words from a databank to generate trillions of unique, if disquietingly odd, automated questions.[4] These resulting queries are displayed on the connected LCD monitors at a rate of thirty-three per minute—what the artist refers to as the "threshold of legibility"—for viewers to decode within the space of the exhibition.[5] If the integrated computer is connected to the Internet, the questions can be mirrored to a URL and accessed online in real time, thus generating an exponentially larger audience within a media landscape that tests not only the limits of legibility, but all aspects of focus and attention as well. To supplement the work's auto-generated questions, visitors may type their own interrogatives into an attached keyboard. In 2000, when the project was installed at the Centro de Arte Contemporáneo Wifredo Lam as part of the seventh Bienal de la Habana, Internet access was tightly restricted by the Cuban government. When visitors typed their sentiments, "rang[ing] from concern over the fate of the planet to ruminations on the consequences of being gay in Cuba," into the keyboard, the resulting phrases were instead posted on the artist's own robust Web platform, www.lozano-hemmer.com, creating an open source in an otherwise closed system.[6]

While online viewers may encounter the interrogative aphorisms outside of their initial public exhibition context, the variability and pace of the Web environment accentuates how the speed of the questions themselves thwarts any possibility for registration, let alone contemplation. Reconsidering *33 Questions* in 2019 also underscores the rise and predominance of translation algorithms such as Google Translate, a statistical translation machine introduced five years after Lozano-Hemmer created this artwork. Its nonsensical questions mimic how translation software infers language pairings by prioritizing numerical frequency over any semblance of signification and expression. More broadly, the relentless quest for accuracy demanded by such machines has reduced the interpretative nature of the translator's endeavor into a procedural one of "find and replace," devoid of the idiosyncrasy of cultural context. Equally disconcerting is how the capacity to grasp subtle, yet important qualities, such as ambiguity, instability, and indeterminacy, is not only diminished by translation software, but engineered to become defunct. Lozano-Hemmer's *33 Questions* thus portends the disappearance of mixed vocabularies and languages and, by extension, hybrid forms of cultural identity.

Initially created between the execution of two of the artist's more renowned works, *Vectorial Elevation* (1999; fig. 9) and *Body Movies* (2001; fig. 10), *33 Questions per Minute* articulates pivotal concerns that have occupied the artist's entire practice.[7]

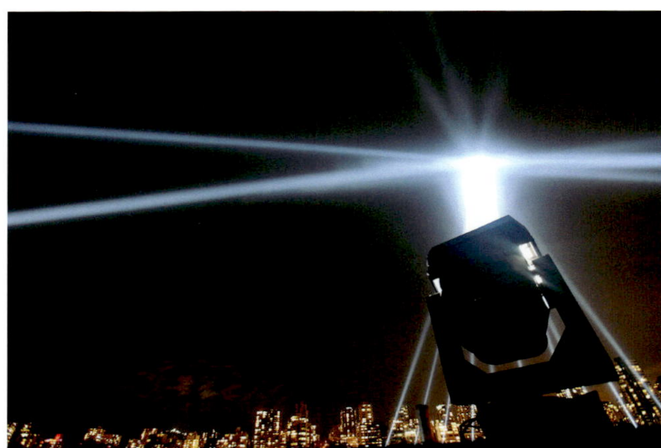

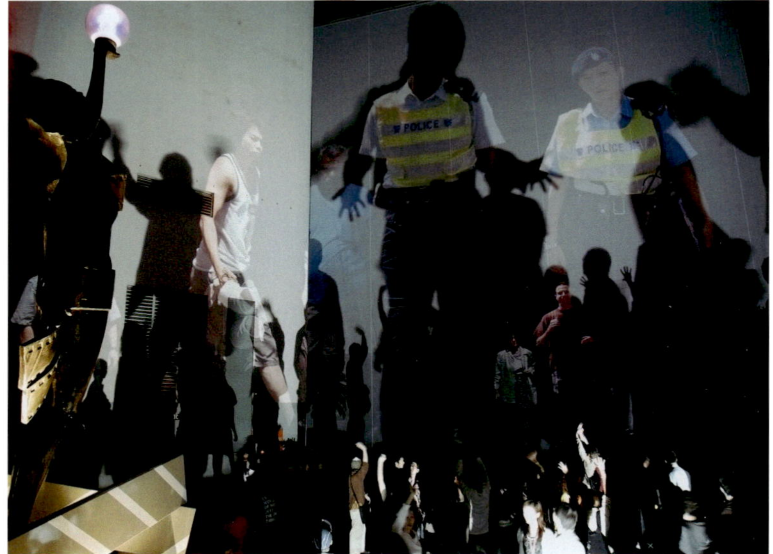

Lozano-Hemmer reminds us that translation is an act of constant transposition and nuanced exchange between languages (human and computer) that are inflected by the specificities of localities and bodies, and that are subject to patterns and mechanisms.

SPEECH ACTS: TRANSLATION AND TRANSPOSITION

When *33 Questions per Minute* was installed in the 2001 Istanbul Biennial, curated by Yuko Hasegawa, the cables of the LCD screens snaked around the rough-hewn stone columns of a former church. Viewers had to stand close to the glowing screens in order to decipher the nonsensical questions, such as "How slowly does it lure spitefully?" and "Does everyone disfigure impalpability?" Biennial goers could contribute their own questions by typing words, phrases, and sentences on a keyboard set up at a computer station within the exhibition. In addition to flashing immediately on the interlinked LCD screens as well as being projected onto the surrounding built environment, the terms viewers entered "became part of the program's database, expanding its vocabulary ad infinitum," according to Lozano-Hemmer.[8] As such, the project synched up with Hasegawa's curatorial aim for the Istanbul Biennial to examine issues of "collective consciousness, collective intelligence and co-existence" through the melding of both minds and machines.[9]

If, in 2001, Lozano-Hemmer pointed to the impossibility of discerning between human and machine sources, *33 Questions per Minute* gained another accretive layer in 2005 when it was installed in Berlin's Potsdamer Platz, embedded within the SPOTS media façade sponsored by HVB Immobilien AG. Utilizing the eleven-story glass curtain wall as a giant programmable screen, the project ushered in new inquiries of scale and scalability along with the scrolling questions that, despite enhanced visibility, remained purposefully incomprehensible. Like Jenny Holzer's *Truisms* (begun 1977),

Figure 9
Vectorial Elevation, 1999
Robotic searchlights, webcams, Linux servers, GPS, and Java 3-D DMX interface
Dimensions variable
Installation view, Cultural Olympiad, English Bay, Vancouver, 2010

Figure 10
Body Movies, 2001
Projectors, robotic rollers, 1,200 transparencies, computerized tracking system, plasma screen, and mirrors
Dimensions variable
Installation view, Hong Kong Museum of Art, Hong Kong Arts Development Council, 2006

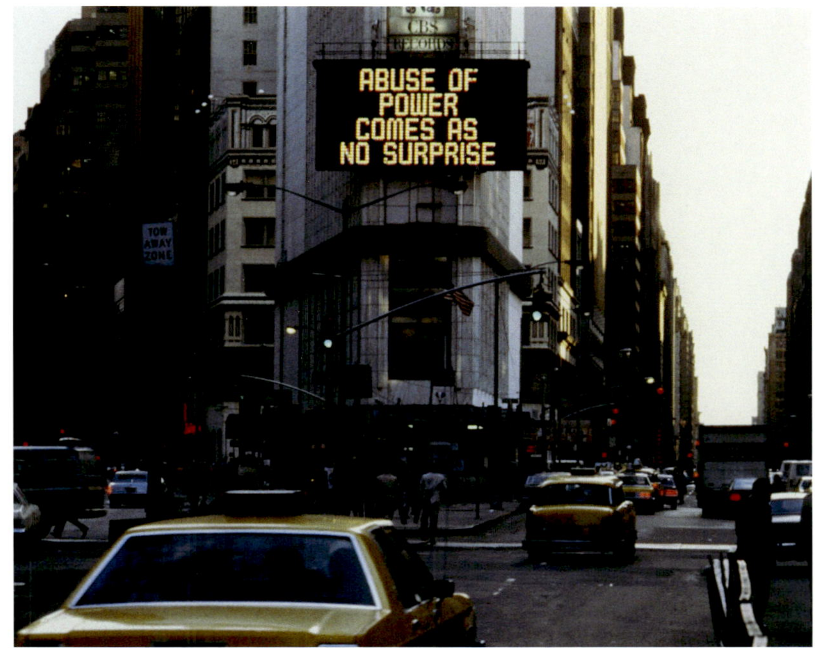

which can be sized from the printed page to architectural-scale projections—as when
it was displayed on the Spectacolor board of New York's Times Square in 1982 as
part of the series *Messages to the Public,* organized by the New York Public Art Fund
(fig. 11)—Lozano-Hemmer's *33 Questions per Minute* accesses both private speech and
techniques of corporate messaging. The work thereby heightens self-awareness in a
manner that curator Johanna Burton has called "direct address."[10] Both Holzer's and
Lozano-Hemmer's projects use media to reveal patterns of power and control while
inverting the relationship that tends to give more space, airtime, and bandwidth to
privileged voices. By streaming Lozano-Hemmer's unedited, machine-generated questions across the façade of the building in Berlin, the shift in scale within *33 Questions
per Minute* not only engages a physically larger space but also operates via one of the
very modes of public address it seeks to critique. In Holzer's case, by appropriating
slogans and making up statements in equal measure, *Truisms* offers a feminist critique of authorship. Her now-canonical *Truism* "Abuse of power comes as no surprise,"
for example, points to the elliptical way media operates, and has now become a *cri de
coeur* of the #MeToo movement. In this spirit, Lozano-Hemmer's works emphasize the
fact that algorithms, like identity, are always political.

ALGORITHMIC OPPRESSION AND HABITUAL MEDIA

Viewed as part of *Rafael Lozano-Hemmer: Unstable Presence,* traveling between the
polyglot cities of Montreal, Monterrey, and San Francisco, *33 Questions per Minute* now
figures against a cultural background in which search engines are the default mode for
accessing all forms of human knowledge. Indeed, "keywords" and "autofill"—concepts
that might retroactively be applied to *33 Questions*—have infiltrated every aspect of
communication. The ubiquity of the search function itself has transformed the process
of learning across all academic fields and disciplines, since the very functionality of
"search presumes that, (a) with the right phrase, any question can be answered and

Figure 11
Jenny Holzer, from *Truisms,* 1982
Spectacolor electronic sign
20 × 40 ft. (6.1 × 12.2 m)
Organized by Public Art Fund, Inc.
Installation view, Times Square, New York, 1982

(b) that the answers lie within the database," further eroding our comfort with indeterminacy.[11] As scholar Wendy Hui Kyong Chun compellingly argued in 2016, "our media matter most when they seem not to matter at all, that is, when they have moved from the new to the habitual."[12] Chun reminds us that while search engines have become the default means of knowledge acquisition, they are also conditioned by the same type of human habits—gender bias and racism—that have resulted in what scholar Safiya Umoja Noble has deftly outlined as "algorithmic oppression," referring to the way that women and people of color, in particular, are not only tagged, categorized, and scripted within search functions, but subsequently imaged, identified, and defined.[13] Amid such encoded bias, Lozano-Hemmer's *33 Questions per Minute* asks whether we can differentiate between machine and human sources. It also casts doubt on the relevance of such distinctions if both people and network technologies remain equally subject to the same types of prejudice that drive discrimination. As Lozano-Hemmer's works in the current exhibition communicate, the ability to discriminate—to make distinctions—remains critical. Yet this is not a neutral process, but an ideological one.

HUMAN/MACHINE BEHAVIOR

Tape Recorders offers metrics for how individuals act in public space, enumerating the often invisible ways that bodies are influenced by how others react—or choose not to—and rendering more legible the social dynamics at play within our current body politic. Paradoxically, *Tape Recorders* uses empirical tools to record and document (often irrational) behaviors. Here, standard Stanley PowerLock twenty-five-foot tape measures—obtainable from any hardware store—are held taut by a custom metal armature with a roller mechanism and mounted in a neat row along the length of the museum's white wall. As individuals enter the exhibition space, a computerized tracking system overhead records the duration and position of visitors' movement through the gallery. Instantaneously, yellow measuring tapes literally inch upward against the wall, recording the length of the visitor's stay until gravity brings the aluminum tape down with a loud, metallic slap, and the strip retracts back into its casing. The more bodies that enter the space, the louder and more frenetic the strips become, setting off a reaction pattern among the visitors who move to avoid the falling strips. The total number of minutes spent by visitors per hour is noted and time stamped on a narrow roll of paper tape that slowly spools from the wall—like the receipt after a sales transaction or the strip chart produced by an EKG machine monitoring vitals. *Tape Recorders* can be read as a human/machine interface that relies on sensory information to generate a real-time feedback mechanism. These seemingly evidenced-based instruments recording objective information reveal the way that mechanical and computational systems interface with human and social ones in a manner that exposes their inherent dualities. Are they recording human behavior, or are they influencing it?

PROTOTYPES

If in *Tape Recorders* the silent actions of the visitors' bodies trigger a cacophony of noise, clatter, and recorded information, the 2008 site-responsive public artwork *Voz*

Alta paradoxically hinged on the role of silence and the suppression of documented evidence. It was commissioned specifically to mark the fortieth anniversary of Mexico's Tlatelolco student massacre, an event defined by the violent suppression of a student uprising on October 2, 1968, ten days before the world's cameras were trained on Mexico City for the Summer Olympics. An act of public commemoration, *Voz Alta* also functions as a synecdoche—a marker of the contested ways that the flow of information and access to archives can be curtailed by both authoritarian and democratic regimes.

Central to the work is an electric megaphone. A tool often used to amplify the human voice for public address and to convey information out in the open across vast distances, the mechanism takes on a symbolic resonance in the case of *Voz Alta* by focusing the viewers' attention on the simple power of carrying individual voices across time and through history. Within the exhibition *Rafael Lozano-Hemmer: Unstable Presence*, Lozano-Hemmer's *Voz Alta* has been transposed into an installation that restages the original megaphone apparatus and displays video documentation of the 2008 event. Referred to as a "prototype" by the artist, the installation version provides a historical test case. It presents video documentation of an act of vocal protest over government suppression of facts regarding state violence. *Voz Alta and Prototype* also models an iterative process for civic engagement and correction to the historical record.

In the public event in 2008, Lozano-Hemmer mounted the megaphone on a simple stand on the Plaza de las Tres Culturas, the site of the 1968 massacre, where eyewitness accounts citing the murder of hundreds of student citizens contradicted the government's original report that only four people had been killed by its military force. The plaza itself remains a contested site. It was designed by Mario Pani, whose modernist *multifamiliares* (multifamily homes) symbolized the inequity of Mexico City's urban development policies, which prompted the initial student uprising. The plaza stands on the site of the 1521 Aztec massacre by Hernán Cortés and is also home to the Spanish Catholic church of Santiago de Tlatelolco. Calling the site the "Plaza of Three Cultures" can be read as an attempt to compress both time and geography by layering colonial conquests atop the oppression of Indigenous people in order to produce a distinctly modern environment.[14]

As people gathered in 2008 to mark the anniversary of the massacre in the plaza, they spoke through Lozano-Hemmer's megaphone, which was connected to a 10kW searchlight that automatically interpolated vocal sounds into a series of beams of light that corresponded in volume and reach with the power of the speaker's voice. Documentation of this event plays a decade later on a screen within the *Voz Alta and Prototype* installation, adding a charged historical layer to the original context of the work. Seen in Montreal, Monterrey, and San Francisco, the blinding light—now incorporated directly into the modified megaphone—can be read as the "light of interrogation," according to Lozano-Hemmer. "The light that blinds, the light of migration police pursuing migrants on the border . . . it's the light that ties in with Goethe's proposition: the brighter the light, the darker the shadow."[15] And while the recorded voices in the

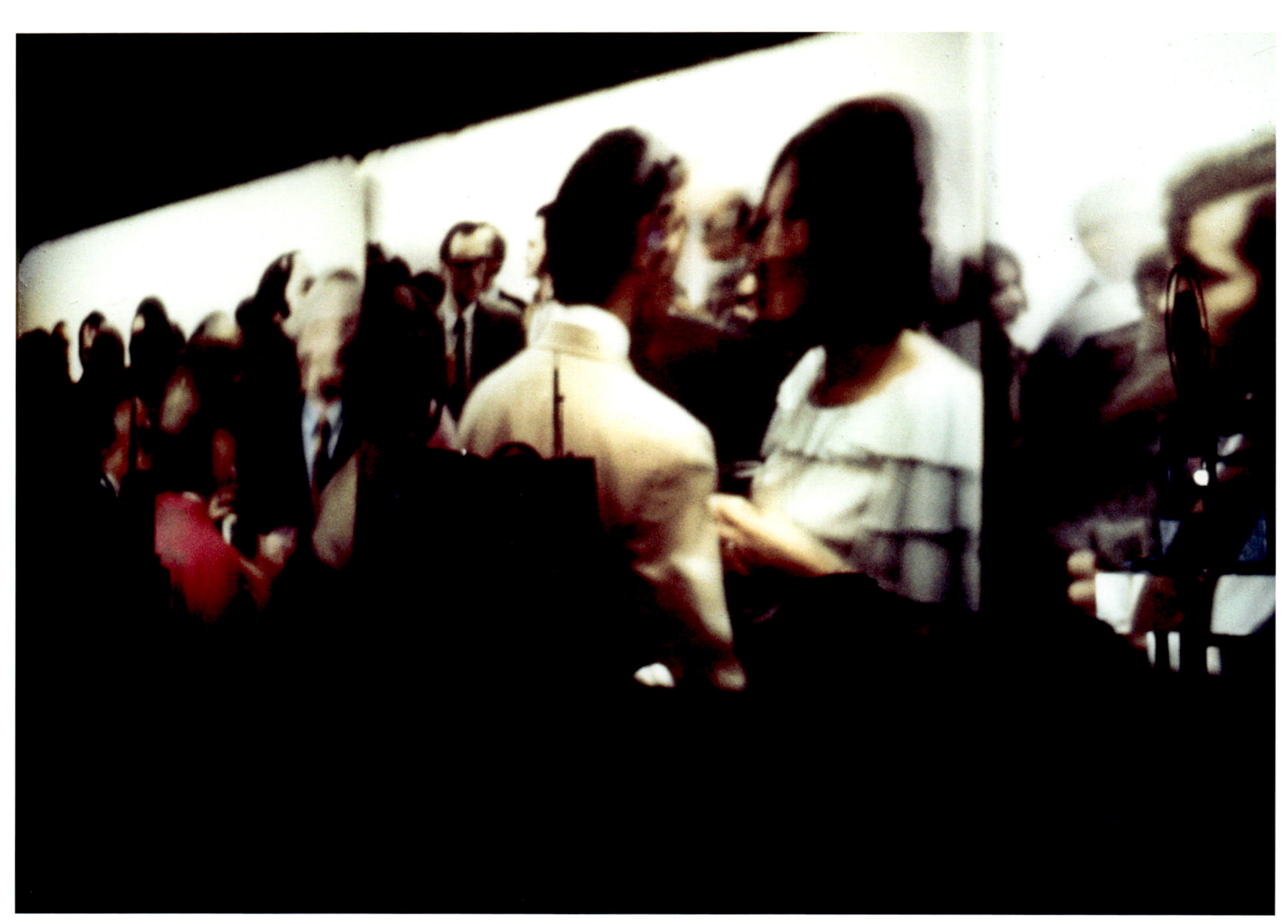

video trigger the searchlight's blinking pattern when installed in the museum, *Voz Alta and Prototype* offers a salient reminder that making a public outcry is the most basic form of civic debate, central to shedding new light on dark moments of public history.

In 2020, *Voz Alta and Prototype* reflects our own social habits back at us—revealing how we relate not just to others but to ourselves in the age of neoliberalism, in which the civic arena of public debate has been supplanted by the habits of online commerce and social media. Remotely amassing "active users" and "followers" has replaced the type of direct civil disobedience fostered through grassroots activism that first gave rise to the student uprisings at the Universidad Nacional Autónoma de México in the months preceding the 1968 Tlatelolco massacre.

By inviting participants to step up to the megaphone on the open plaza in 2008, the artist essentially asked individuals to subject themselves to the potential for public scrutiny. By including the video documentation from 2008 with the installation more than a decade later, Lozano-Hemmer now asks the public to scrutinize the political conditions that continue to frame this project. In both cases, the public artwork and the installation, *Voz Alta* uses seemingly straightforward gestures to elicit a panoply of human emotions (anger, fear, playfulness, empathy) that are contingent on status—how one relates to the social and political power dynamics on display. In this way Lozano-Hemmer's work points to the specificity of subjectivity, in addition to the specificity of site, in generating a compelling experience.

As noted previously, these works collectively recall the important artistic prototypes established earlier by Marta Minujín. Her pathbreaking 1960s multimedia environments, including *Importación-exportación* (Importation-Exportation, 1968), *Simultaneidad en simultaneidad* (Simultaneity in Simultaneity, 1966), and *Circuits* (1967) offered complex commentaries on issues of international exchange and cultural transmission between North America, Europe, and Latin America. These works critiqued the conventions of data manipulation through a pointed and prescient use of information technology and broadcast media (radio and television), as well as newspapers, polls, and questionnaires that generated real-time demographic and economic data drawing attention to their sources. In particular, *Minucode* (1968; fig. 12) combined live social events with documentation of staged episodes to critique the networks of art, commerce, media, and politics that connected the Cold War agendas of the Rockefeller family and the Center for Inter-American Relations. The work took up the "notion of the quotidian as a possibility for resistance" by using techniques such as exaggeration and humor to highlight the absurdity and intensity of the period, just as Lozano-Hemmer's *Voz Alta and Prototype* now does in the space of the museum.[16]

Like all of Lozano-Hemmer's works outlined here, Minujín's social-scientific environments often turn on a willingness to subject oneself to unfamiliar, awkward, or even dangerous situations. The flyer distributed to accompany Minujín's *La Menesunda* (Mayhem, 1965), for example, promised sensory environments that aimed to generate "difficult / strange / embarrassing / situations / for those who are willing to accept

Figure 12
Marta Minujín, *Minucode*, 1968
16mm, color, silent
Dimensions variable
Installation view, Center for Inter-American Relations
(now the Americas Society), New York, 1968

them."[17] Lozano-Hemmer lays out a similarly controversial proposition for visitors in *Vicious Circular Breathing*, a hermetically sealed apparatus that invites museumgoers to breathe recycled air, filtered not through machines, but through the bodies of other humans. Like a darker iteration of Minujín's flyer, warning signs point to the possibility of asphyxiation, contagion, and panic. *Vicious Circular Breathing* incorporates various individual components: a glass chamber with two sliding doors, two emergency exits, carbon dioxide and oxygen sensors, motorized bellows, an electromagnetic valve system, and sixty-one ordinary brown paper lunch bags affixed to the ends of clear plastic medical respiration tubes, which "constitute 5 octaves—the typical range of the musical organs that inspire the design."[18] Labored breathing—crumpling paper bags filling with the air exhaled by visitors and deflating as it recirculates into the sealed chamber—generates the work's distinctive soundtrack.

While organ music may be the intended allusion, the work itself sounds the perils of diminishing and unequal resources, the pervasiveness of VOCs (volatile organic compounds—carbon-based chemicals that encompass a variety of molecules emitted by humans), and the introduction of micropollutants in the air. Breath may be, as Lozano-Hemmer remarks, both "the source of life" and a "metric of our polluted environment." In *Vicious Circular Breathing*, it is also a vehicle for pheromones, potential toxins, and viruses passed from one human to another. "When air enters our lungs, public space, the common good, becomes private, intimate," offers Lozano-Hemmer, who adds, "when our blood is oxygenated and then, through breathing, our body generates carbon dioxide and we exhale, our private space once again becomes public."[19] *Vicious Circular Breathing* is also a reminder that since 1963, with the passage of the Clean Air Act in the United States, the chemical composition of outdoor air has been regulated, with penalties for polluters. Yet that does very little for Americans, who spend on average more than 90% of their time indoors, where the air contaminated by "the combined emissions of humans and their daily activities—cooking, cleaning, metabolizing—is more interesting, and potentially more lethal, than anyone had imagined."[20]

Ultimately, each of these four distinct works, *33 Questions per Minute, Tape Recorders, Voz Alta,* and *Vicious Circular Breathing,* does not pivot on technological impulses alone but isolates them to highlight distinctly human ones. They point to the mutable ways that surveillance, biometrics, and closed systems can be read as forms of oppression that are not only imposed from outside systems, but also can emanate from internal ones. Each one underscores the unsettling ways that, through habitual use, we instinctively mimic the patterns of our machines—incessantly tracking, updating, and linking, not to mention rebooting and refreshing—all in an anxious attempt to stave off our own built-in obsolescence.

Epigraph: Rafael Lozano-Hemmer, quoted in José Luis Barrios et al., eds., *Rafael Lozano-Hemmer: Pseudomatismos/Pseudomatisms* (Mexico City: Museo Universitario Arte Contemporianeo, 2015), 25; English translation, 187.

1. For a consideration of the historical stakes of modernist abstraction and relevant issues of spectatorship and reception, see Alexander Alberro, *Abstraction in Reverse: The Reconfigured Spectator in Mid-Twentieth-Century Latin American Art* (Chicago: University of Chicago Press, 2017).

2. See the contribution by Rafael Lozano-Hemmer and Guillermo Gómez-Peña, "Tech-illa Sunrise (.txt con Sangrita)," a performative text that fully articulates and frames the linguistic and computational tropes of coding identity, in *Transmedia Frictions: The Digital, the Arts, and the Humanities*, ed. Marsha Kinder and Tara McPherson (Berkeley: University of California Press, 2014), 330–37.

3. While Marta Minujín has been deeply influential throughout Latin America—especially in Argentina, where her experiments in combining video recording, playback projections, and live events at the Instituto Torcuato Di Tella during the mid-1960s became pivotal to visual art's broader adoption of media technology—she has received a delayed reception in the art historical discourse within North America. For a corrective account and an overview of her significance, not only within Latin American contexts but in global contemporary art, see Ana Longoni and Mariano Mestman, "After Pop, We Dematerialize: Oscar Masotta, Happenings, and Media Art at the Beginnings of Conceptualism," in *Listen, Here, Now! Argentine Art of the 1960s: Writings of the Avant-Garde*, ed. Inéz Katzenstein (New York: Museum of Modern Art, 2004), 156–72. See also Zanna Gilbert, "Mediating Menesundas: Marta Minujín from Informalismo to Media Art," in *Marta Minujín Reloaded* (New York: New Museum, 2019), the catalogue accompanying the 2019 reinstallation of *Menesundas* at the New Museum, on view from June 26 to September 29, 2019.

4. Currently, the work includes databases in English, Spanish, French, and German and operates (if possible) in the local language of the venue.

5. Lozano-Hemmer, *Pseudomatismos*, 128.

6. Grady T. Turner, "Sweet Dreams: The Seventh Havana Biennial Addressed the Theme of Communication, Which Many Artists Interpreted in Terms of Escape or Migration," *Art in America* 89, no. 10 (October 2001): 75, http://www.lozano-hemmer.com/33_questions_per_minute.php.

7. For brief context on this chronology, see Tina Rivers Ryan's review of *Rafael Lozano-Hemmer: Unstable Presence* at the Musée d'art contemporain de Montréal, *Artforum International*, September 2018.

8. Lozano-Hemmer, *Pseudomatismos*, 128.

9. Yuko Hasegawa, "Next Emergence from the Edge of Chaos: Istanbul," in *Egofugal: From 7th International Istanbul Biennial* (Istanbul: Istanbul Foundation for Culture and Arts, 2001), 13 and 41.

10. Johanna Burton, "Cultural Interference: The Reunion of Appropriation and Institutional Critique," in *Take It or Leave It: Institution, Image, Ideology*, ed. Johanna Burton and Anne Ellegood (Los Angeles: Hammer Museum, 2014), 24–25. Cited in Jenni Sorkin, "Patterns and Pictures: Strategies of Appropriation, 1975–85," *Burlington Contemporary*, May 2019, http://contemporary.burlington.org.uk/journal/journal/patterns-and-pictures-strategies-of-appropriation-197585.

11. Clemens Apprich, Wendy Hui Kyong Chun, Florian Cramer, and Hito Steyerl, *Pattern Discrimination* (Minneapolis: University of Minnesota Press, 2019), vii.

12. Wendy Hui Kyong Chun, *Updating to Remain the Same: Habitual New Media* (Cambridge, MA: MIT Press, 2016), 1.

13. Safiya Umoja Noble, *Algorithms of Oppression: How Search Engines Reinforce Racism* (New York: New York University Press, 2018), 4.

14. These details are drawn from Neil Sanzgiri, "Domesticating the Ghost: The Mobilization of History and Memory in Mexico, 1968," SmACT thesis, Art Culture Technology Program, MIT School of Architecture and Planning, Spring 2017. See also Sanzgiri's essayistic film *At the Top of Grasshopper's Hill* (single-channel video, 2016–17, 26:33), which presents overlapping narratives of the 1861 Second French Empire invasion of Mexico and the 1968 state-sponsored student massacre at Tlatelolco, https://www.suneilsanzgiri.com/the-reunion-1.

15. Lozano-Hemmer, *Pseudomatismos*, 199.

16. Gabriela Rangel, "May 1968 à la Minujín," in *Marta Minujín MINUCODEs*, ed. Alexander Alberrro, Ines Katzenstein, and Gabriela Rangel (New York: Visual Arts of the Americas, Americas Society, 2015), 8. Drawing on new primary information, curators Gabriela Rangel and José Luis Blondet restaged and reinstalled Minujín's *MINUCODE* in 2010 at the institution where it first appeared, the Center for Inter-American Relations in New York, now called the Americas Society, along with documentation from *Simultaneidad en simultaneidad* (Simultaneity in Simultaneity, 1966) and *Circuits* (1967).

17. Marta Minujín, "La Menesunda," trans. Marguerite Feitlowitz, in *Listen, Here, Now! Argentine Art of the 1960s: Writings of the Avant-Garde*, ed. Inéz Katzenstein (New York: Museum of Modern Art, 2004), 107. Cited in Catherine Spencer, "Performing Pop: Marta Minujín and the 'Argentine Image-Makers,'" in *Tate Papers*, no. 24 (Autumn 2015), https://www.tate.org.uk/research/publications/tate-papers/24/performing-pop-marta-minujin-and-the-argentine-image-makers.

18. Lozano-Hemmer, *Pseudomatismos*, 186.

19. Lozano-Hemmer, 186.

20. Nicola Twilley, "Home Smog: When It Comes to Air Pollution, Indoors May Be Worse Than Out," *New Yorker*, April 8, 2019, 35.

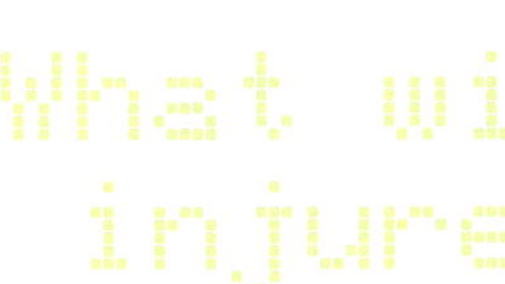

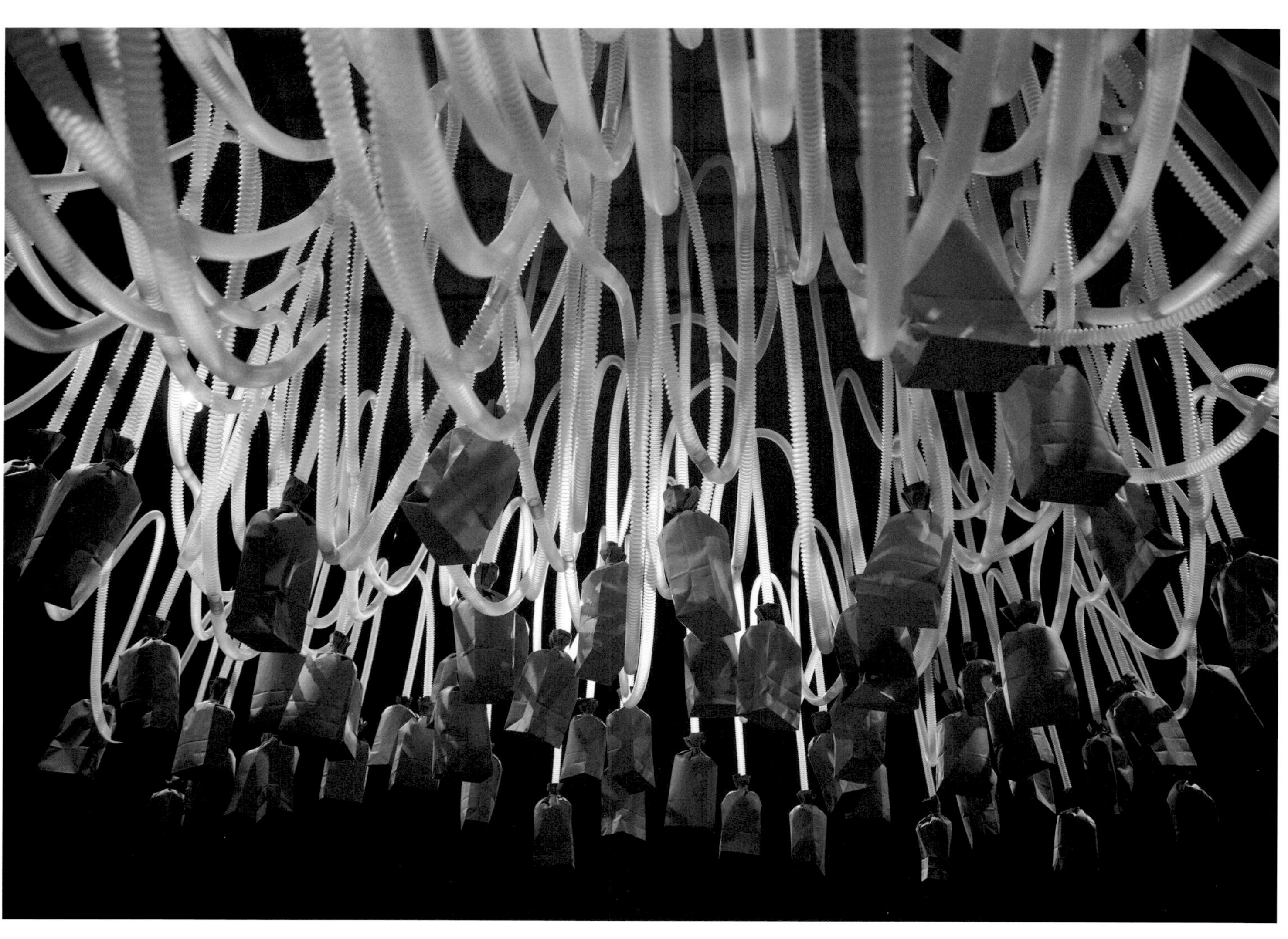

FRANÇOIS LETOURNEUX

ON VICIOUS CIRCULAR BREATHING

Rafael Lozano-Hemmer's visually assertive *Vicious Circular Breathing* (2013; see page 78) stands out as the artist's most sculptural work in scale, form, and materiality. In its parody of immersion and participation, it is also one of the most sinister. It limits the agency of the visitor to an all-or-nothing dare: to enter (or not) the hermetically sealed glass cubicle, sit still, and breathe air that other participants previously inhaled and exhaled. Nearby, a wall text warns of the serious risks of panic, contagion, and asphyxiation, and restricts entry only to healthy adults. The whiteness of the apparatus, the transparency of the glass cubicle and motorized bellows, and the electromagnetic valve system all suggest giant medical equipment; the sense of participating in a live, at-your-own-risk experiment only adds to the anxiety.

The enactment of a voyeuristic device around what essentially functions as an invitation to a "relatively gentle form of suicide"[1] constitutes an intriguing strategy—to say the least. Entering the cubicle, however, is really only about as dangerous as spending time in an elevator or an airplane. Still, *Vicious Circular Breathing* perpetuates a strange and compelling fiction in which the visitor's decision to participate (and their reaction during participation) is carefully set up to be observed by others.

Many scholars/writers have interpreted the piece as a commentary on neoliberalism's ambition to privatize natural resources at a time of global depletion, and the willful blindness to the systemic economic and technological violence of a culture that celebrates uncritical participation. But *Vicious Circular Breathing* should also be situated in the context of modern and contemporary art's engagement with the

Vicious Circular Breathing, 2013. Installation view, Museo de Arte Contemporáneo de Monterrey, Mexico, 2019

twentieth century's weaponization and industrialization of the atmosphere (extermination by gas; the sanitization, conditioning, and commercial design of air; immunological "bubbles," and so on).[2]

Like so many others in Lozano-Hemmer's output, the installation also functions as a memento mori, a temporary archive of bodily traces, stored here in suspended paper bags that inflate and deflate rhythmically, opposite the glass cubicle. Music as embodied language is another, related topic. *Vicious Circular Breathing* finds its origin in *Last Breath,* a serial work that uses similar equipment (at a much smaller scale, with a single paper bag) and could simply be described as a permanently activated, "hermetically sealed biometric portrait or recording."[3] The first iteration, produced for the 2012 Havana Biennial, was a portrait of Cuban singer Omara Portuondo, destined to act as a memorial after her passing.[4] *Vicious Circular Breathing* differs from *Last Breath* in the sense that it features a collection of indistinct, anonymous, and ephemeral breaths. In both pieces, however, individual presence appears subsumed into an abstract, automatically animated trace.

Many composers of the Western canon undergo a related transformation in Lozano-Hemmer's *Sphere Packing* series (2013–18; see page 110), which compresses individual pieces of music into a quasi-monotonic cacophony. A similar process applies to individual contributions in *Voice Array* (2011; see page 126). In fact, Lozano-Hemmer's oeuvre is rife with works that organize visitor output around elementary, biological signs. Beyond the poetic, playful, and connective aspects of the art, this anonymous "leveling" also relies on an undertone of violence—even, at times, with explicit totalitarian references. In stark contrast, *Level of Confidence* (2015; see page 104) and *Voz Alta* (Out Loud, 2008; see page 40) insist on the agency of active voices and discrete faces that refuse to disappear from the archive.

An interest in the tense relationship between the individual and the collective cuts across all of Lozano-Hemmer's production. It is central to *Vicious Circular Breathing,* where in using the instrumental motif of the organ (as embodied in the work's bellows mechanism), the artist invokes music and religion as distant forerunners in the cultural genealogy of co-presence. In this historical perspective, a bridge between the breath as vital sign and its function as support structure for embodied language (spoken and sung) connects individuals with each other and the metaphysical world.

The word for "soul" or "spirit" (Latin, *spiritus*) in many cultures is synonymous with "breath," and breath work is often a key component of religious practice. In Greek, the word for "breath" or "spirit" is *pneuma,* which gave birth to *neumes,* later (musical) "notes," and also, of course, to *pneumatic* ("containing or operated by air or gas under pressure"). Breath has been a staple of the technical and theoretical discourse on musical organs since antiquity (with common allusions, for instance, to their "lung capacity"). These instruments were often considered second in nobility only to the voice. As early as the fifth century CE, Prosper d'Aquitaine described organ pipes as being filled with the Word of God. And, as organs appeared in the churches of Late

Middle Ages Europe, a "vascular" argument was even made in their favor (according to which music made worshippers more receptive by dilating their hearts). Conversely, Calvinists have viewed the potential confinement of the "breath" in such machines with suspicion, and both the organ and the accordion have also been considered "diabolical" instruments, because of their mechanical nature.[5]

For Lozano-Hemmer, the breath is indeed "the ineffable and mysterious substance of our words, songs and sighs."[6] Many of his other works, such as *Babbage Nanopamphlets* (2015; see page 84), *Call on Water* (2016; see page 86), and *Volute 1: Au clair de la lune* (2016; see page 46), address the aerial transmission and (de/re)materialization of language over long stretches of time (with modern, poetic, and scientific references replacing the theological).

The sealing of the organ[7] in *Vicious Circular Breathing,* however, "vitiates" the transmission narrative and acts as a powerful signifier. It recalls the subsumptive effect that characterizes so many of the artist's other works. Yet it is not only the slow and willful eclipse of the singular subject that comes to mind here, but also, perhaps, that of the infra-individual, rhythmic substrate of language itself,[8] which the voyeuristic, clinical, and majestic aspects of the piece imbue with particular poignancy.

NOTES

1. Rafael Lozano-Hemmer, from a conversation with Kathleen Forde, in *Rafael Lozano-Hemmer: Pseudomatismos/Pseudomatisms*, ed. José Luis Barrios et al., exh. cat. (Mexico City: Museo Universitario Arte Contemporáneo, 2015), 96.

2. See Peter Sloterdijk, "Air Quake," in *Foams: Spheres Volume III: Plural Spherology*, trans. Wieland Hoban (South Pasadena, CA: Semiotext[e], 2016).

3. Rafael Lozano-Hemmer, from a conversation with Kathleen Forde, in *Rafael Lozano-Hemmer: Vicious Circular Breathing*, exh. cat. (Istanbul: Borusan Contemporary, 2013), 11.

4. Another version of the work, now in the collection of the San Francisco Museum of Modern Art, was done in collaboration with American accordionist Pauline Oliveiros.

5. Hugo Perina, "L'orgue italien de la Renaissance (1400–1550): Commandes artistiques, savoirs pratiques et usages liturgiques," PhD diss., EHESS, Paris, 2018. See also Nigel Wilkins, *La musique du Diable* (Sprimont, France: Pierre Mardaga, 1999).

6. Rafael Lozano-Hemmer, in Forde, *Pseudomatismos/Pseudomatisms*, 96.

7. *Vicious Circular Breathing* is described as a "sealed organ" in the warning wall text that accompanies the work.

8. Brian Massumi, "Relational Architecture: Rafael Lozano-Hemmer," in *Architectures of the Unforeseen: Essays in the Occurrent Arts* (Minneapolis: University of Minnesota Press, 2019).

VICIOUS CIRCULAR BREATHING ²⁰¹³

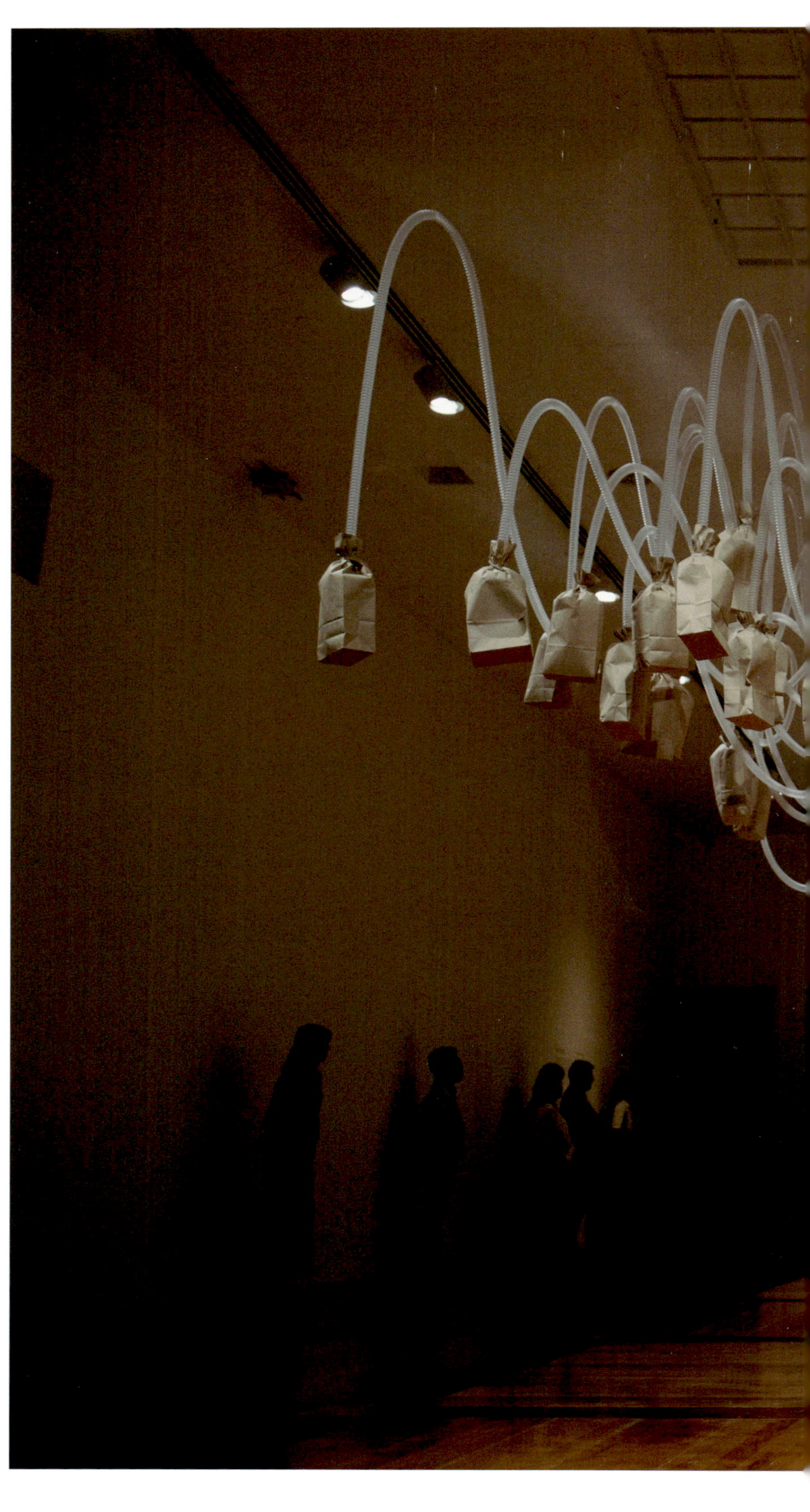

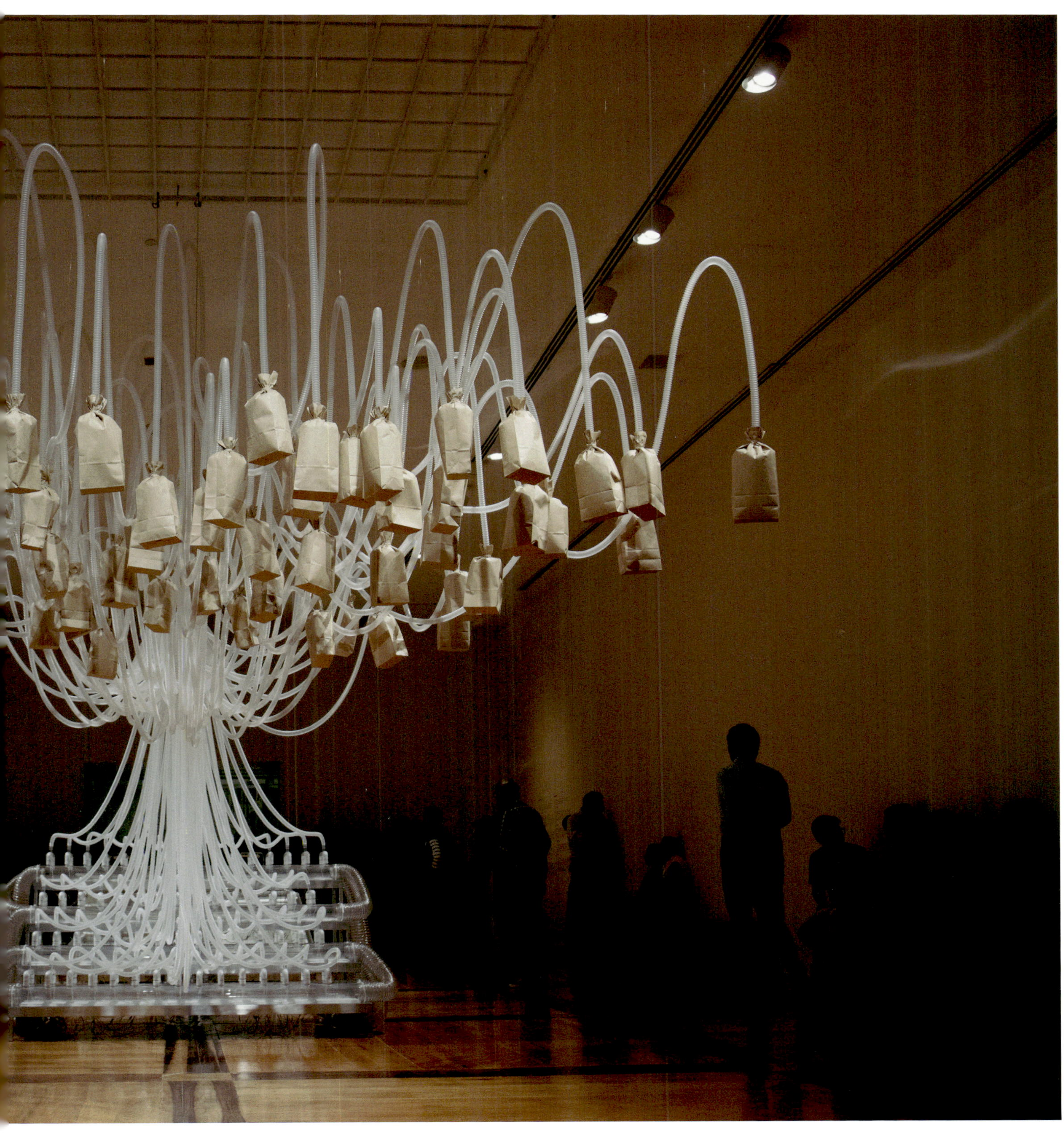

Installation view, Museo de Arte Contemporáneo de Monterrey, Mexico, 2019

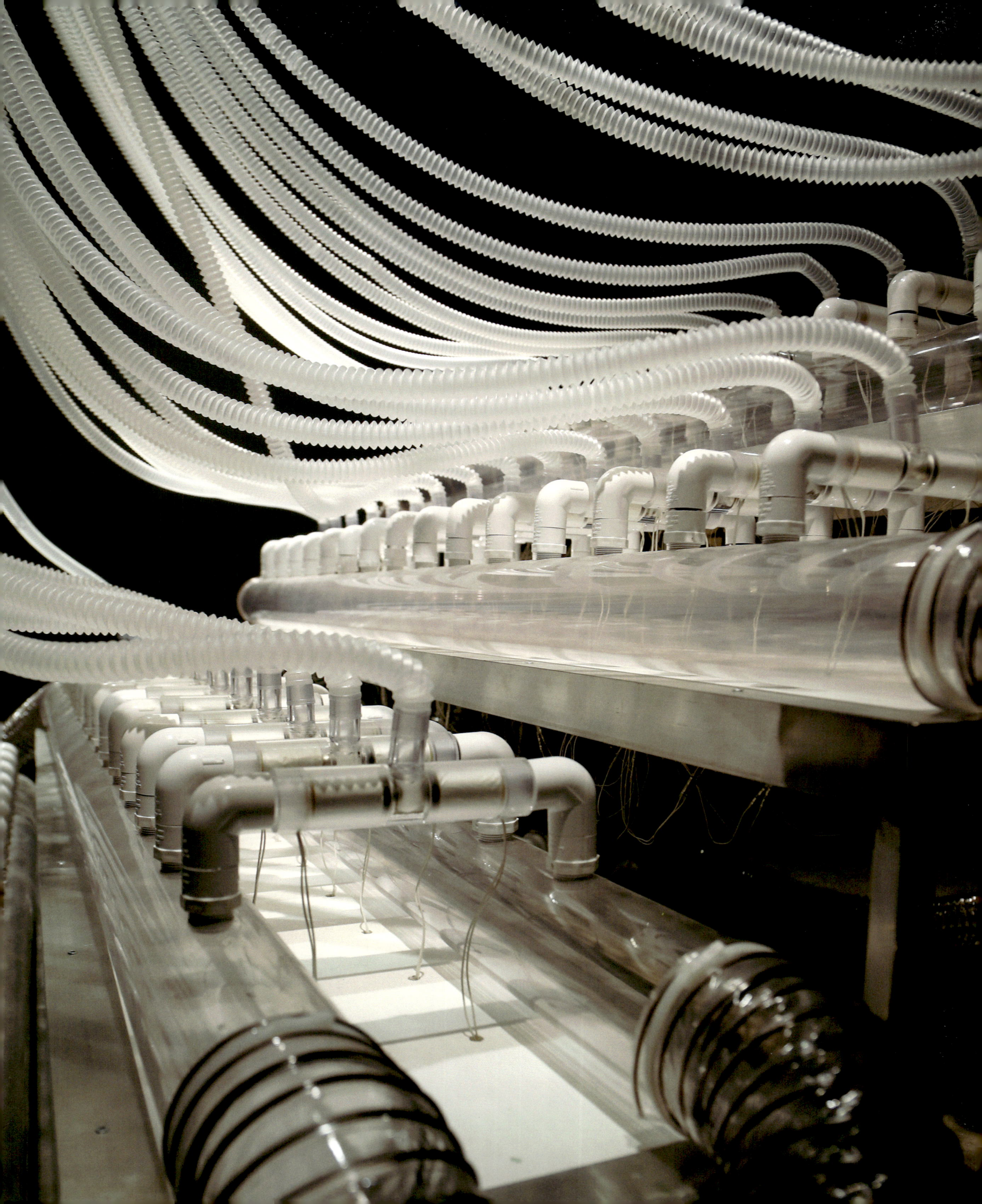

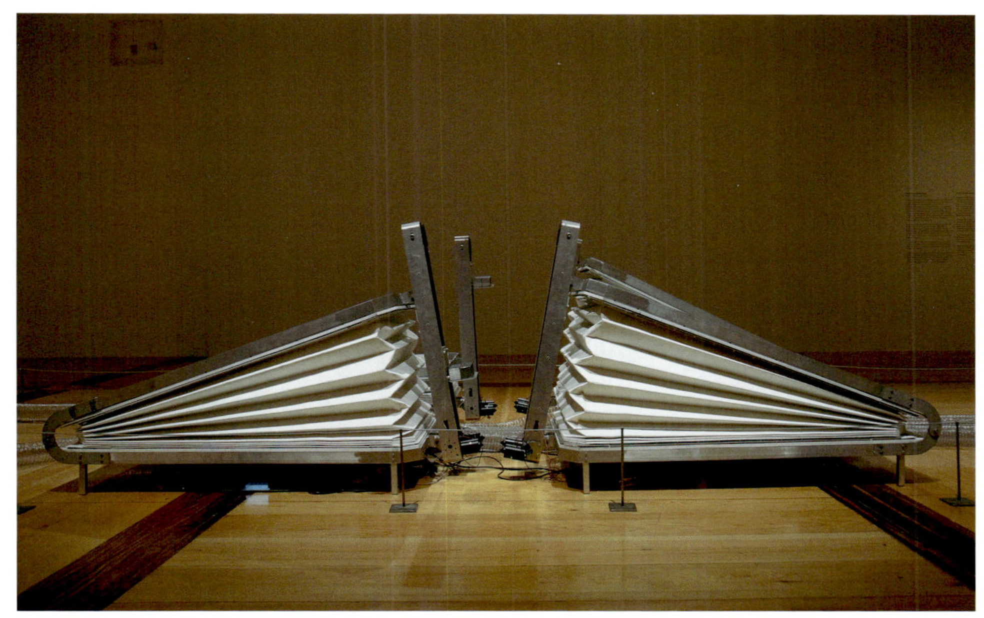

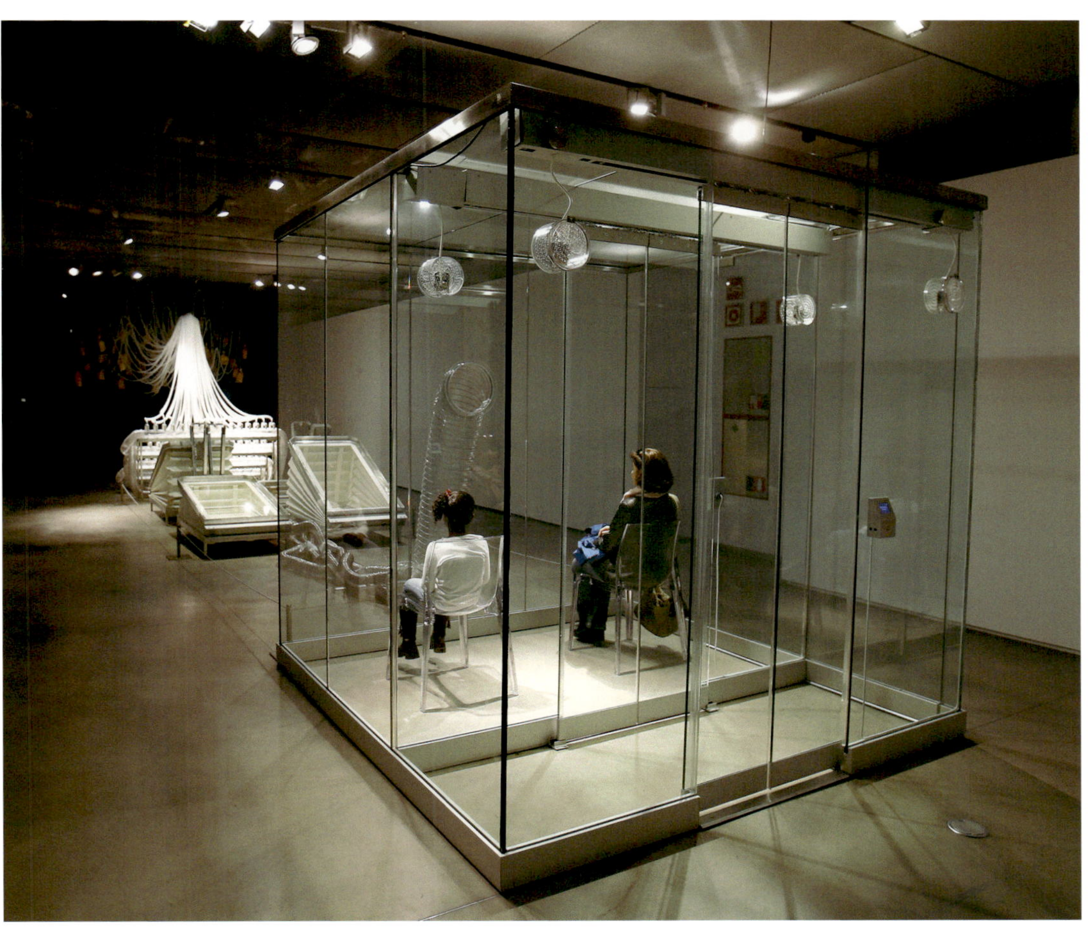

Installation views, Fundación Telefónica, Madrid, 2014 (left and right), and Museo de Arte Contemporáneo de Monterrey, Mexico, 2019 (top)

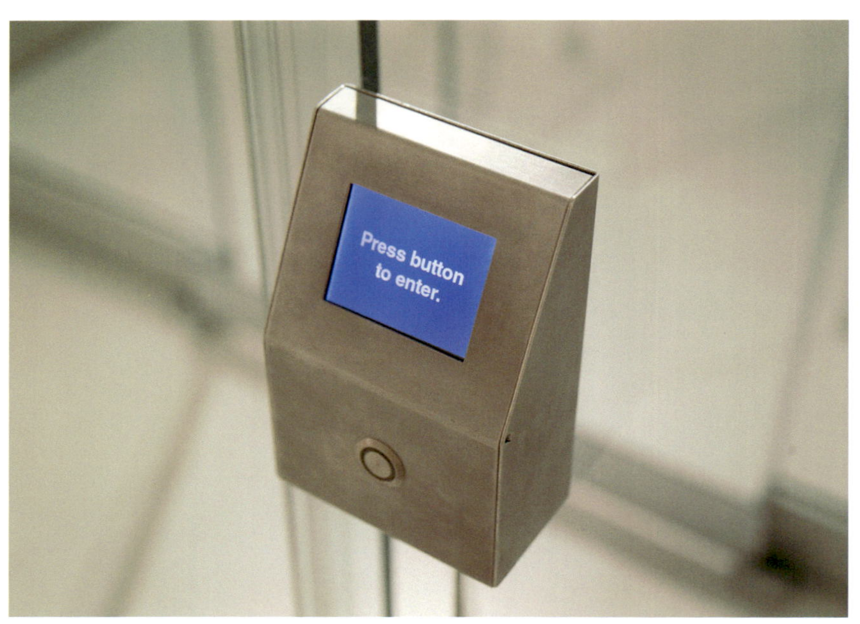
Press button
to enter.

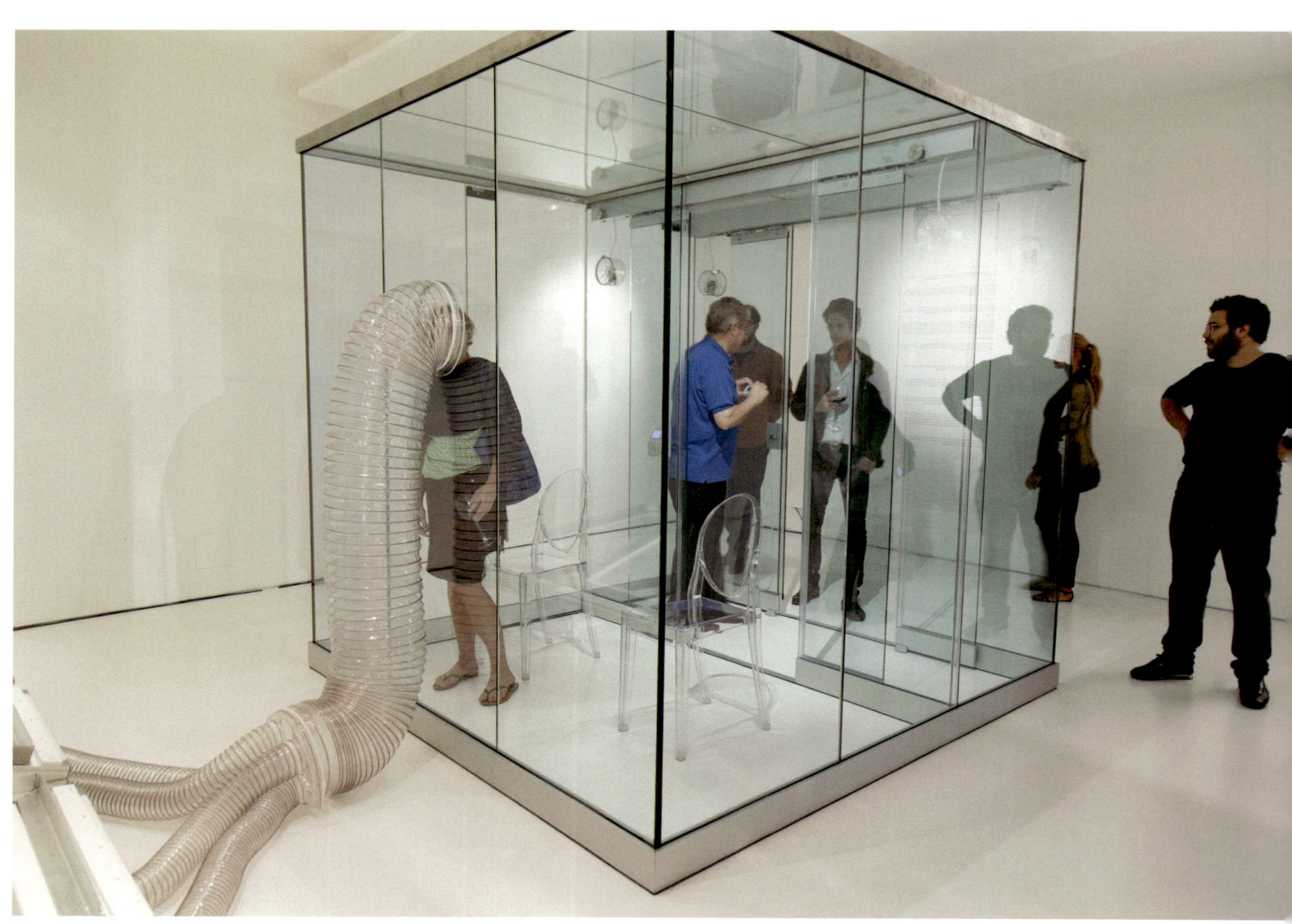

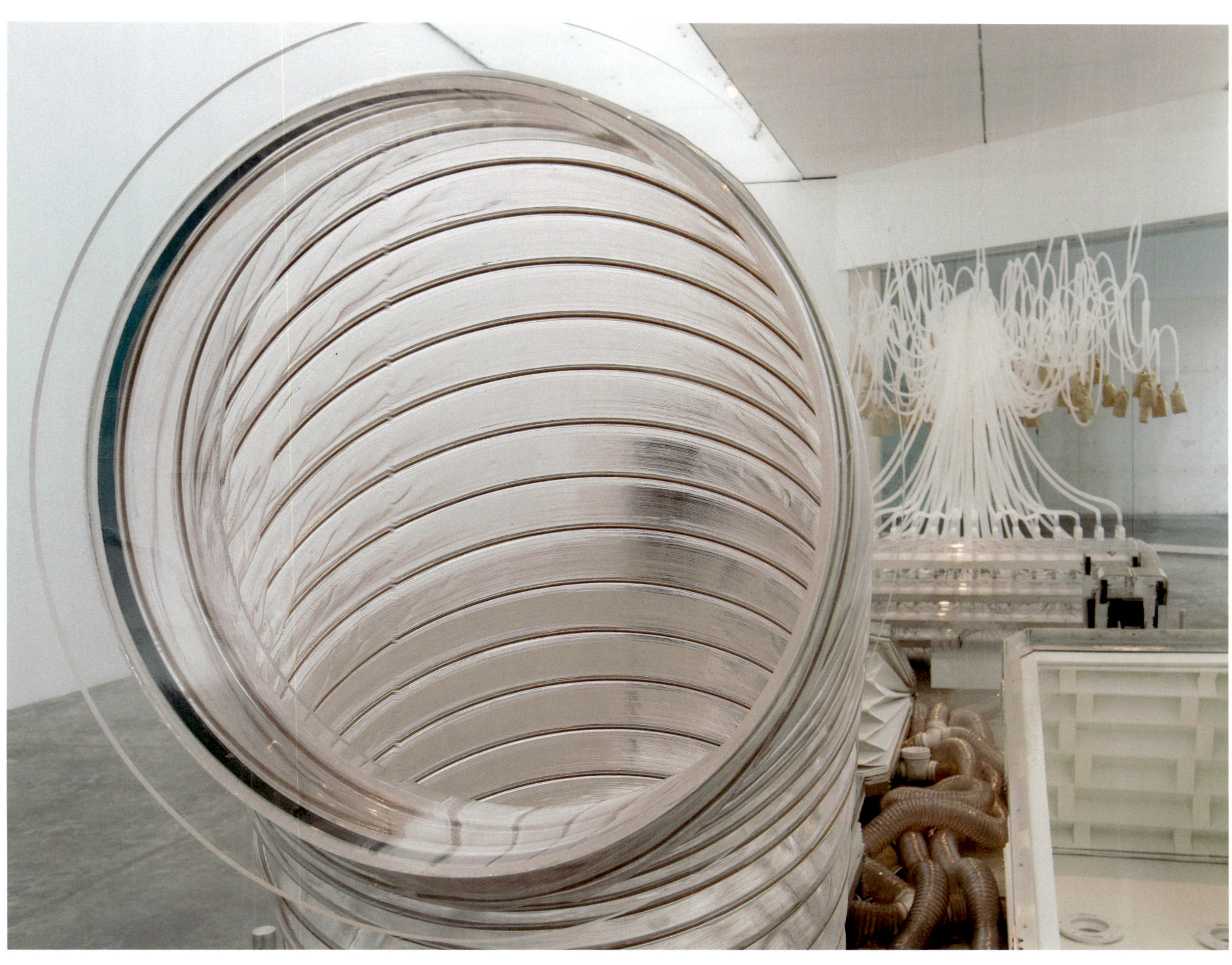

Installation views, Borusan Contemporary, Istanbul, 2013 (left), a d Museo Universitario Arte Contemporáneo, Mexico City, 2015 (above)

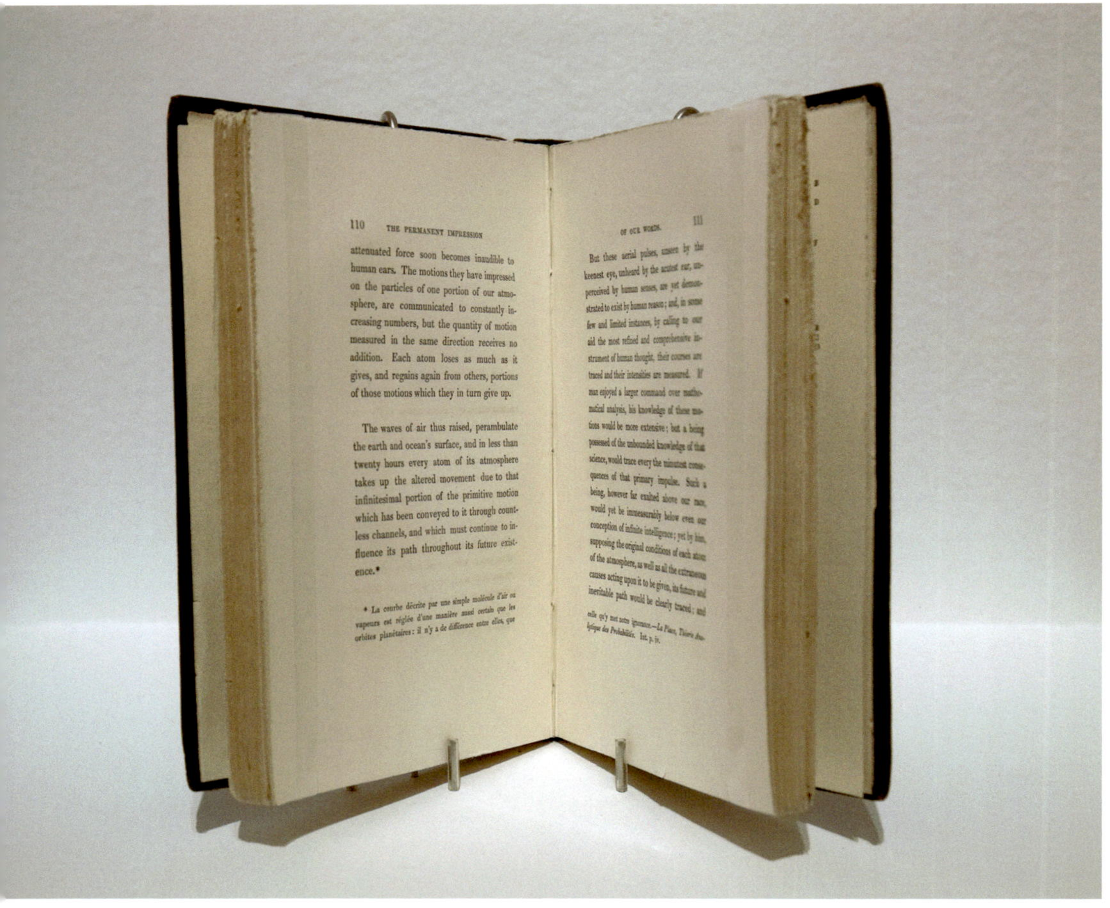

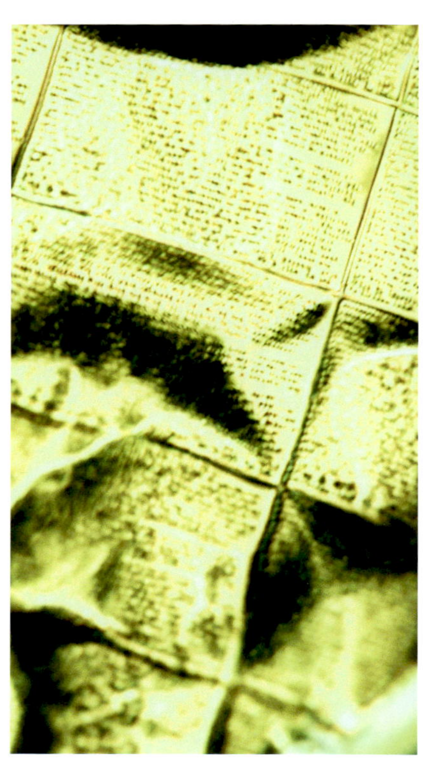

First edition of Charles Babbage's *The Ninth Bridgewater Treatise*, 1837, installation view, Museo de Arte Contemporáneo de Monterrey, Mexico, 2019 (left); electron microscopic image of gold nanopamphlets engraved with Babbage's text (right); installation view, Museo Universitario Arte Contemporáneo, Mexico City, 2015 (far right)

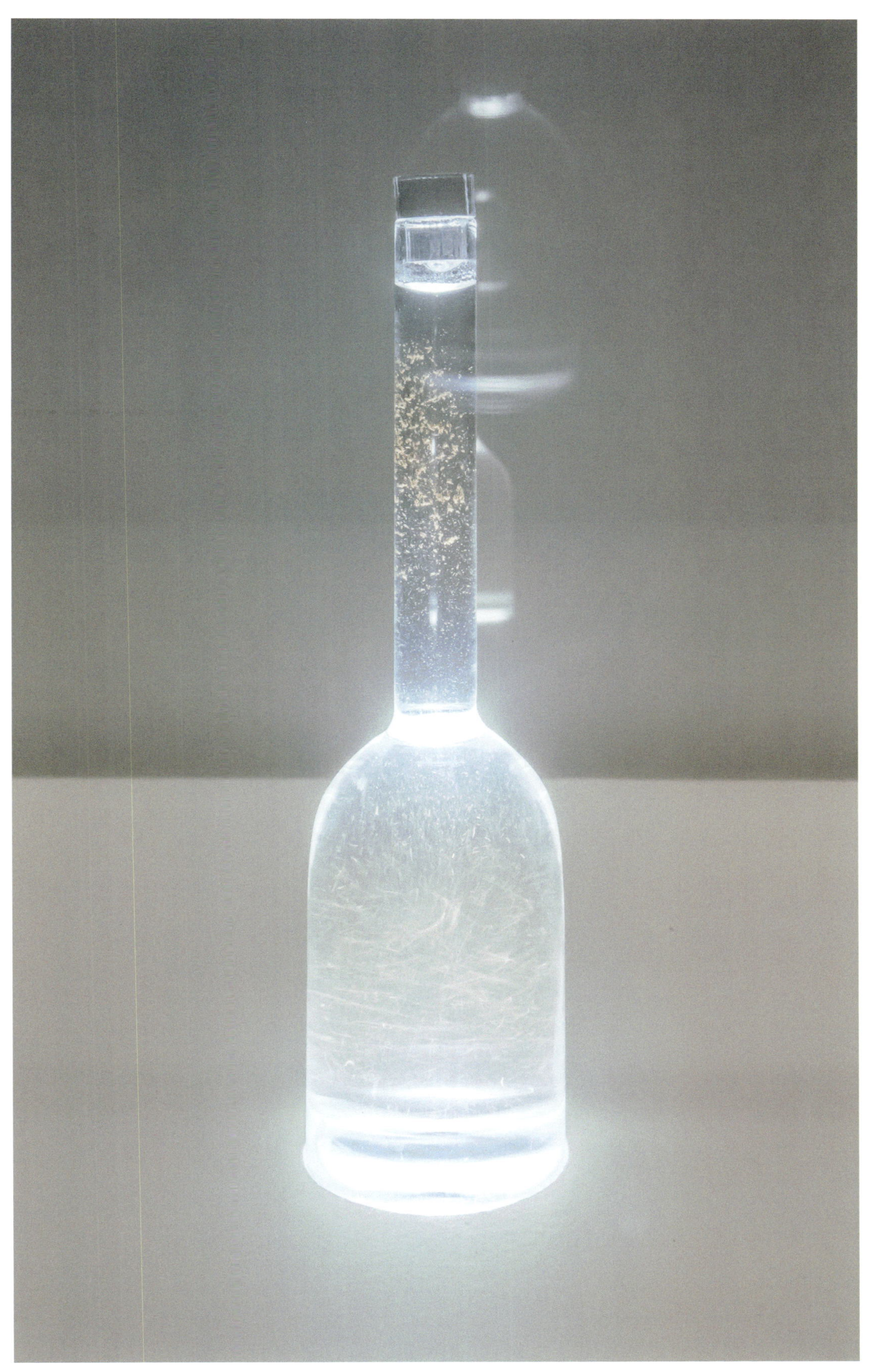

CALL ON WATER 2016

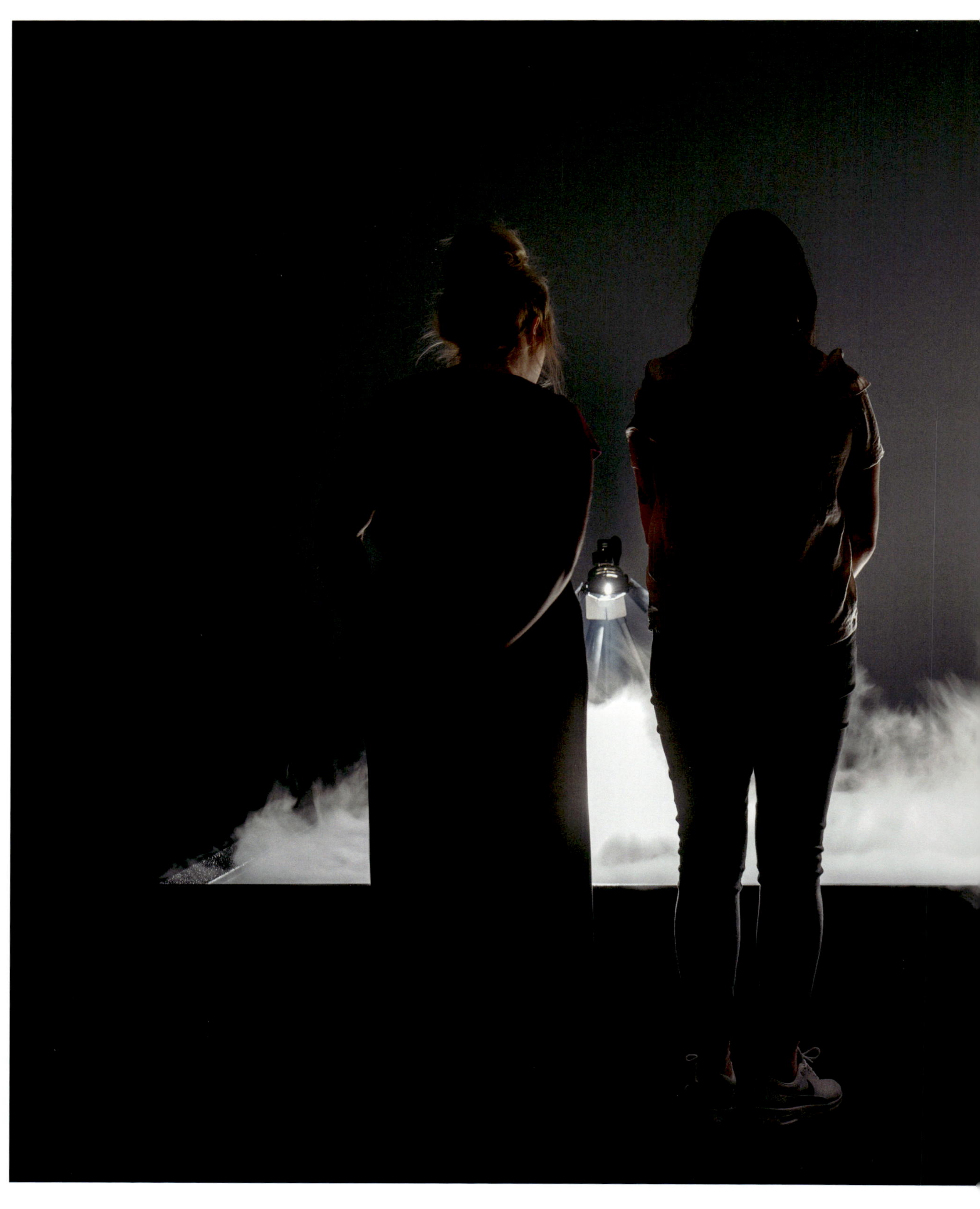

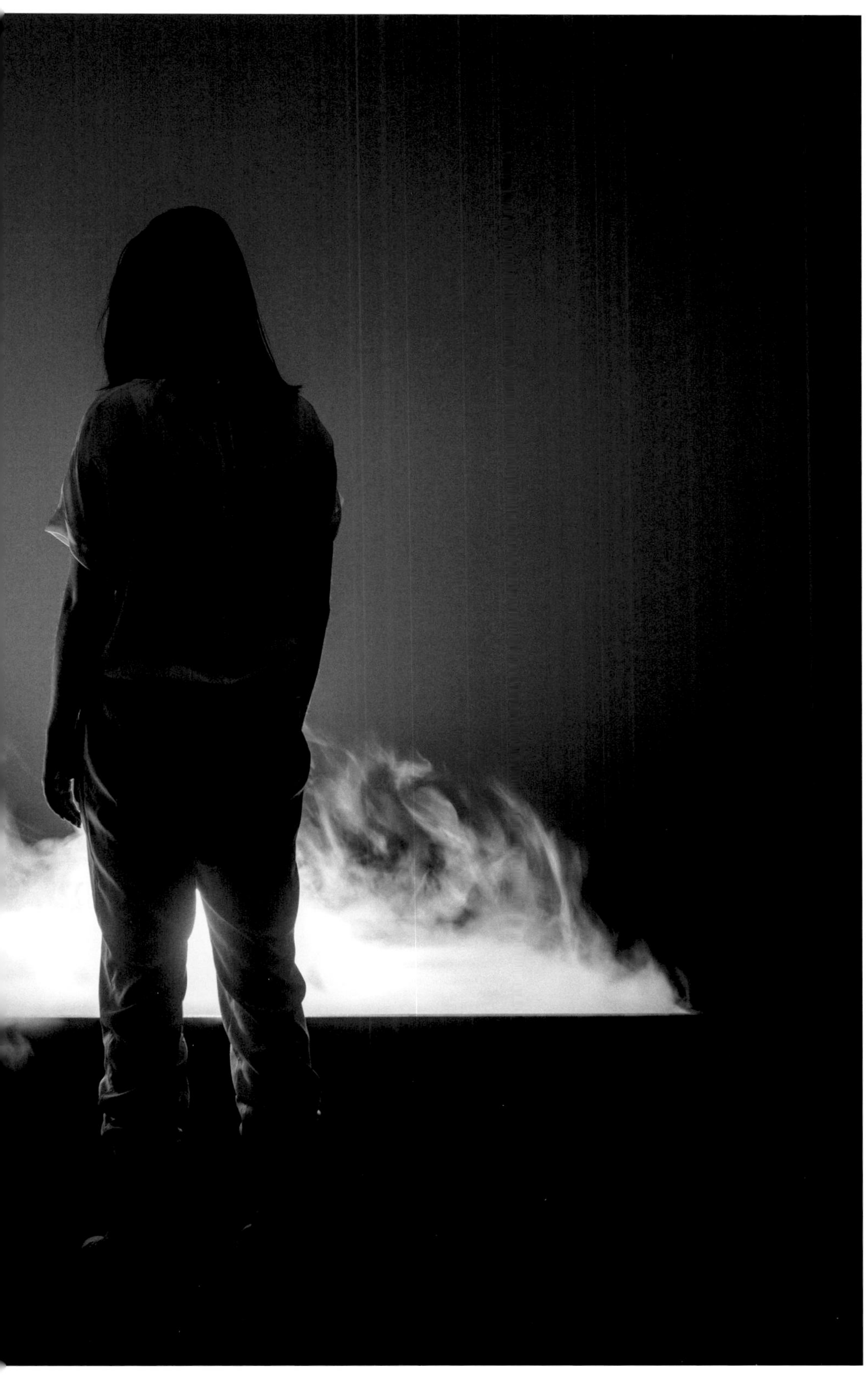

Installation view, Musée d'art contemporain de Montréal, 2018

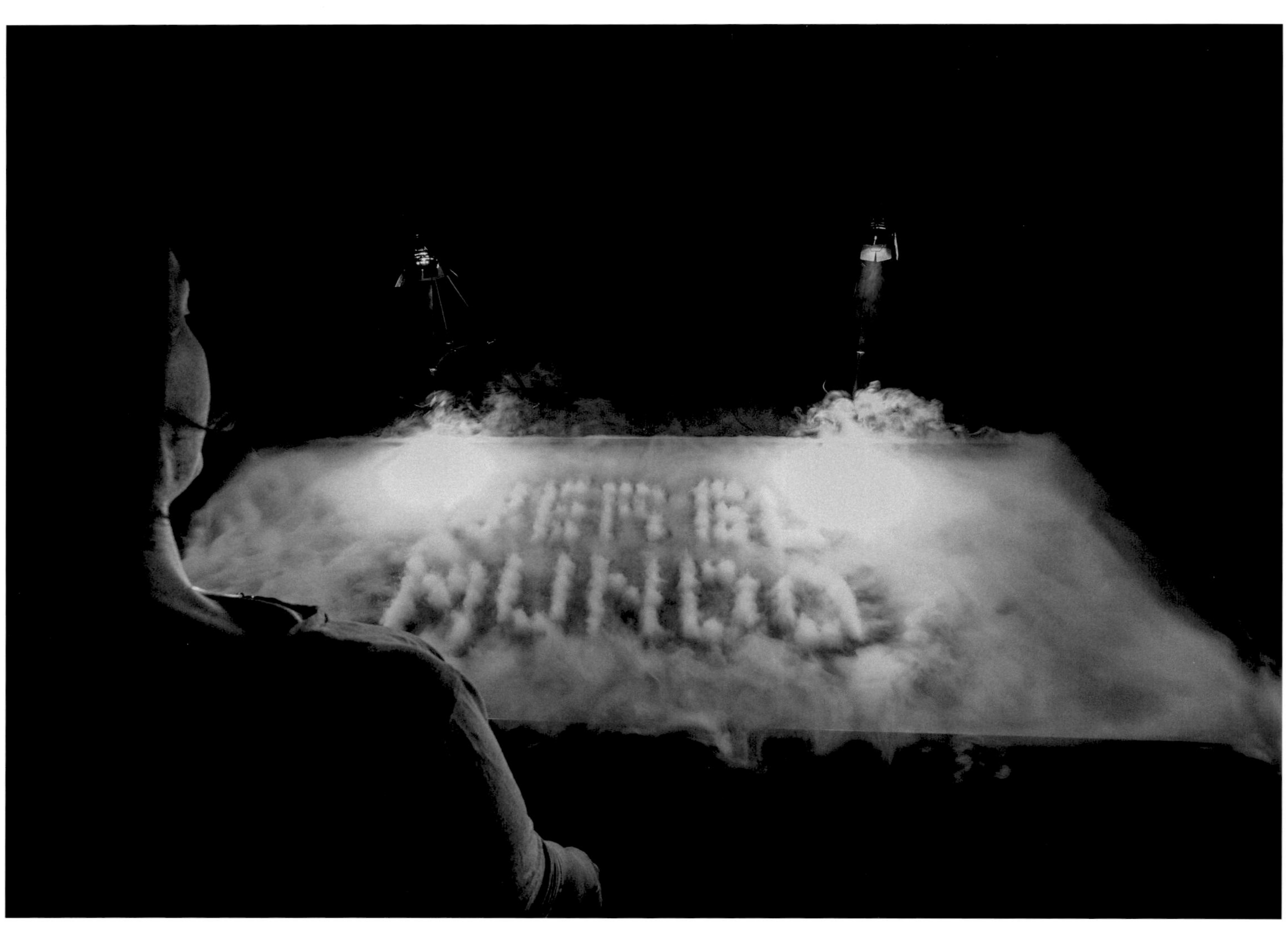

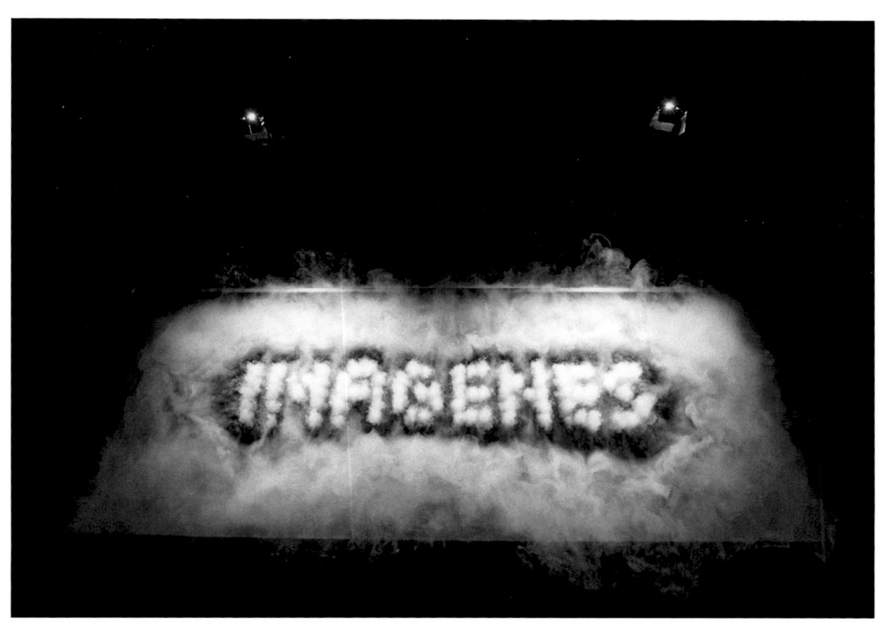

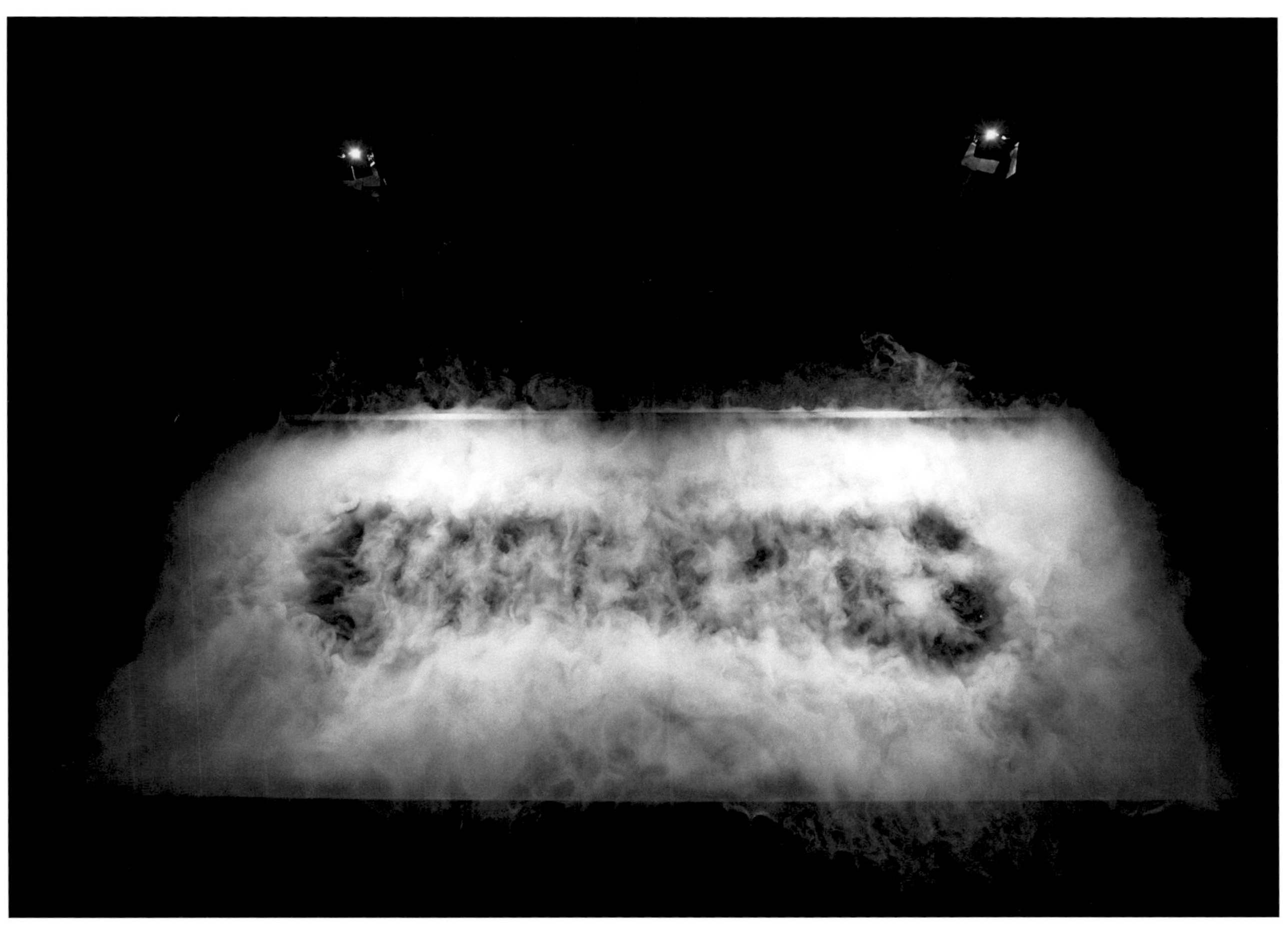

Installation views, Musée d'art contemporain de Montréal, 2018 (left), and Museo de Arte Contemporáneo de Monterrey, Mexico, 2019 (above)

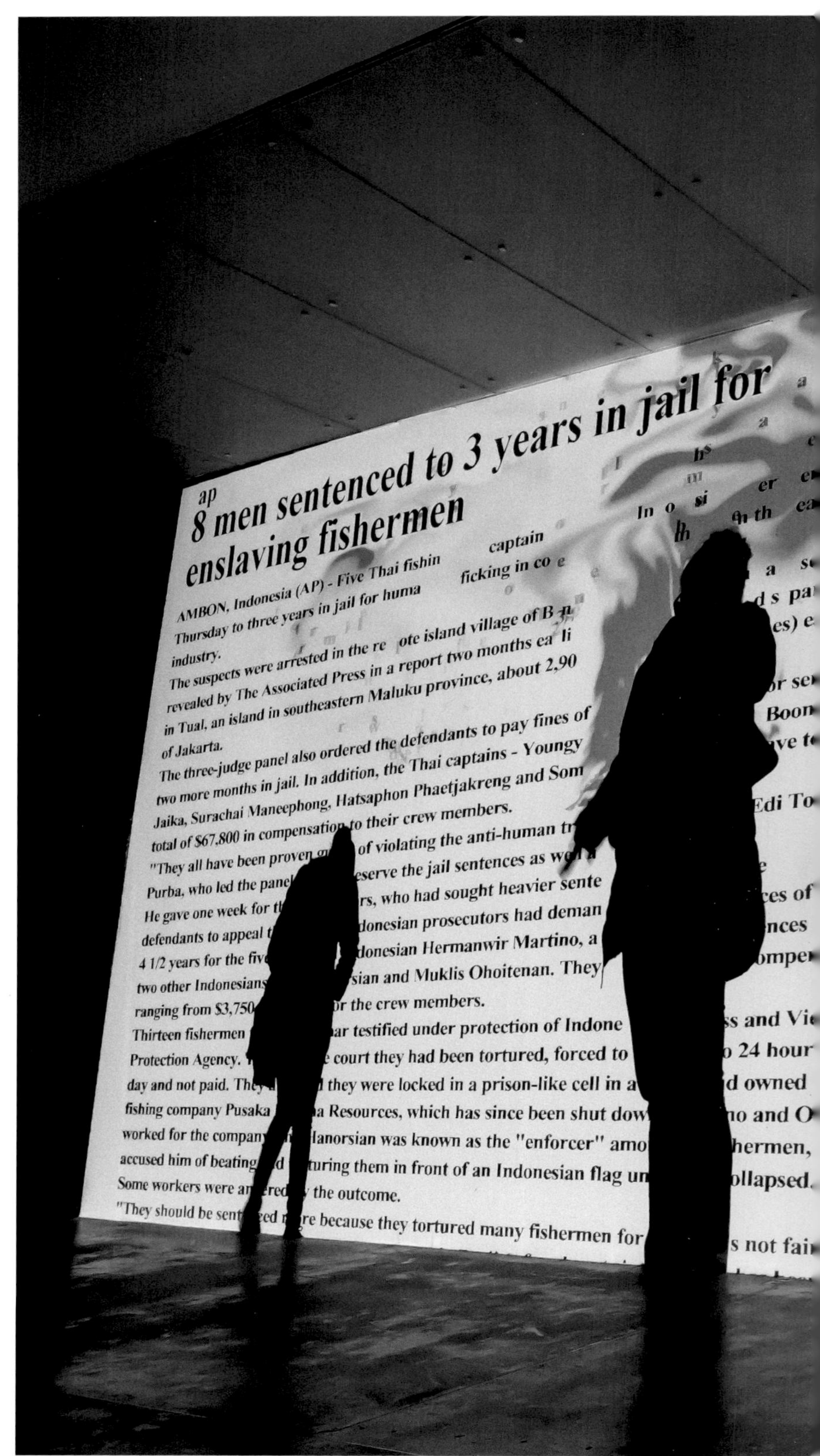
ap
8 men sentenced to 3 years in jail for enslaving fishermen
captain
ficking in co e
AMBON, Indonesia (AP) - Five Thai fishin
Thursday to three years in jail for huma
industry.
The suspects were arrested in the re ote island village of B
revealed by The Associated Press in a report two months ea li
in Tual, an island in southeastern Maluku province, about 2,90
of Jakarta.
The three-judge panel also ordered the defendants to pay fines of
two more months in jail. In addition, the Thai captains - Youngy
Jaika, Surachai Maneephong, Hatsaphon Phaetjakreng and Som
total of $67,800 in compensation to their crew members.
"They all have been proven g of violating the anti-human tr
Purba, who led the panel eserve the jail sentences as w
He gave one week for t rs, who had sought heavier sente
defendants to appeal donesian prosecutors had deman
4 1/2 years for the five donesian Hermanwir Martino, a
two other Indonesians sian and Muklis Ohoitenan. They
ranging from $3,750 r the crew members.
Thirteen fishermen ar testified under protection of Indone
Protection Agency. e court they had been tortured, forced to
day and not paid. The they were locked in a prison-like cell in a
fishing company Pusaka a Resources, which has since been shut dow
worked for the company lanorsian was known as the "enforcer" amo
accused him of beating uring them in front of an Indonesian flag u
Some workers were a re the outcome.
"They should be sent ed re because they tortured many fishermen for

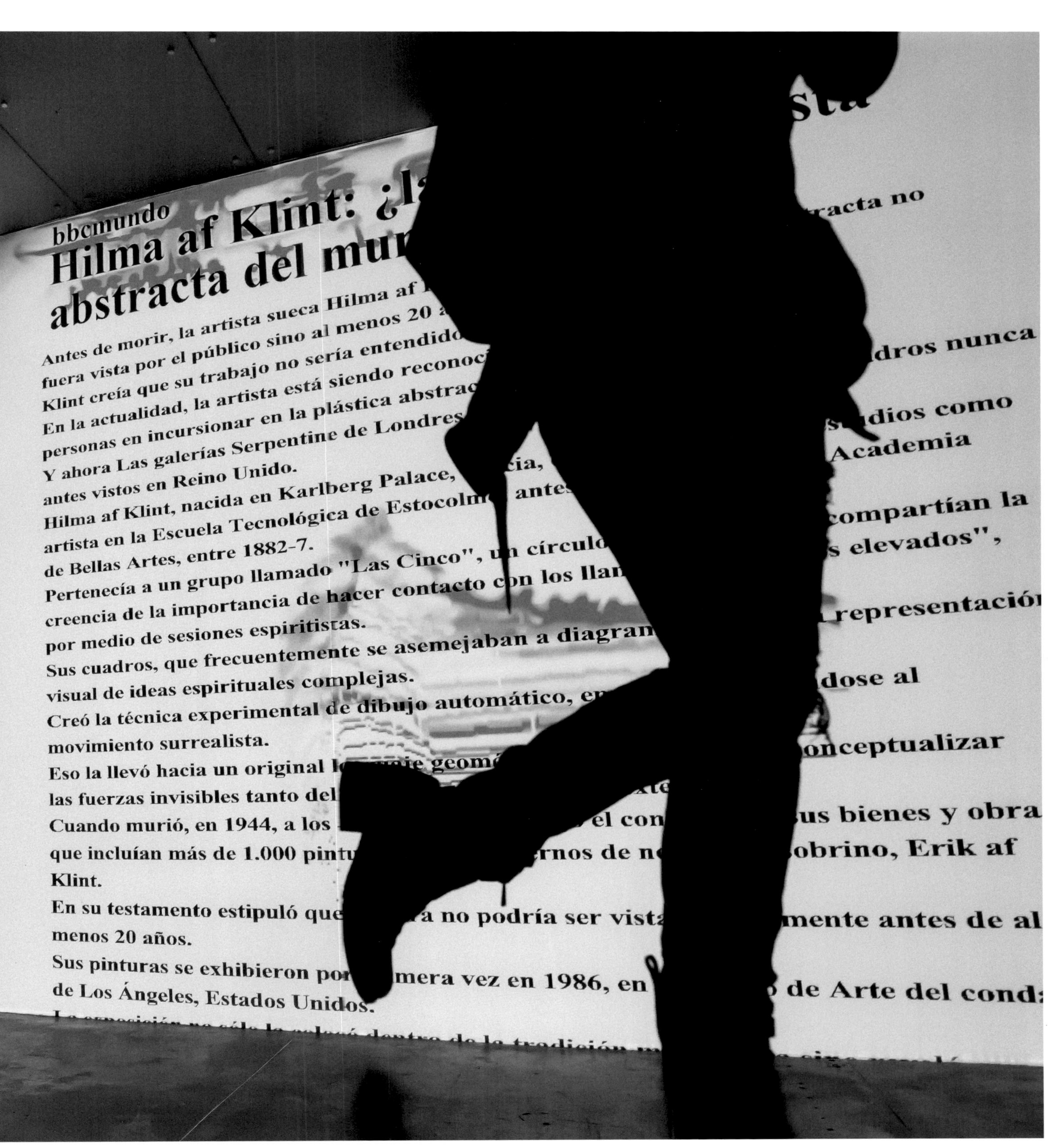

Installation view, Museo Universitario Arte Contemporáneo, Mexico City, 2015

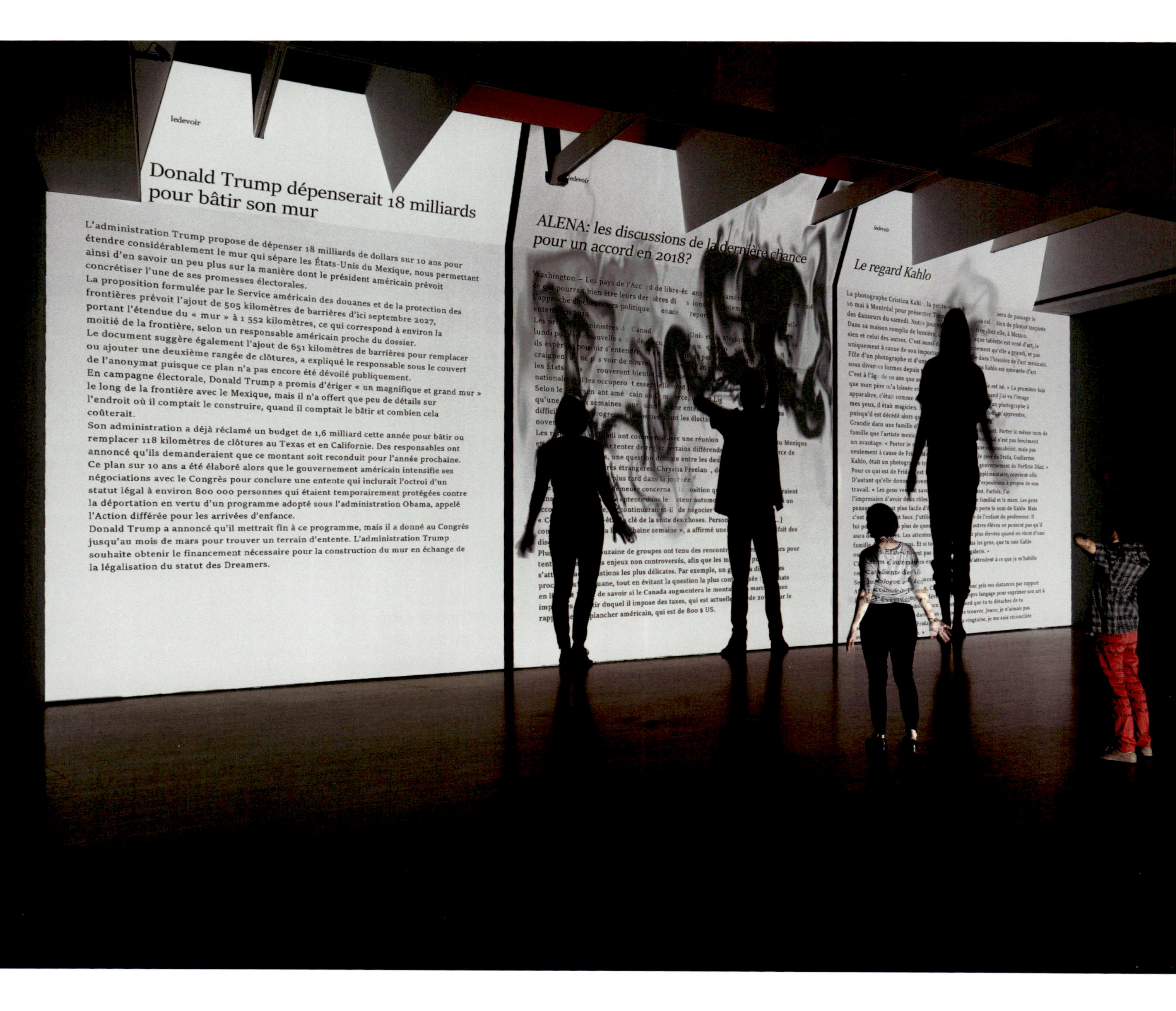

ledevoir

Donald Trump dépenserait 18 milliards pour bâtir son mur

L'administration Trump propose de dépenser 18 milliards de dollars sur 10 ans pour étendre considérablement le mur qui sépare les États-Unis du Mexique, nous permettant ainsi d'en savoir un peu plus sur la manière dont le président américain prévoit concrétiser l'une de ses promesses électorales.
La proposition formulée par le Service américain des douanes et de la protection des frontières prévoit l'ajout de 505 kilomètres de barrières d'ici septembre 2027, portant l'étendue du « mur » à 1 552 kilomètres, ce qui correspond à environ la moitié de la frontière, selon un responsable américain proche du dossier.
Le document suggère également l'ajout de 651 kilomètres de barrières pour remplacer ou ajouter une deuxième rangée de clôtures, a expliqué le responsable sous le couvert de l'anonymat puisque ce plan n'a pas encore été dévoilé publiquement.
En campagne électorale, Donald Trump a promis d'ériger « un magnifique et grand mur » le long de la frontière avec le Mexique, mais il n'a offert que peu de détails sur l'endroit où il comptait le construire, quand il comptait le bâtir et combien cela coûterait.
Son administration a déjà réclamé un budget de 1,6 milliard cette année pour bâtir ou remplacer 118 kilomètres de clôtures au Texas et en Californie. Des responsables ont annoncé qu'ils demanderaient que ce montant soit reconduit pour l'année prochaine.
Ce plan sur 10 ans a été élaboré alors que le gouvernement américain intensifie ses négociations avec le Congrès pour conclure une entente qui inclurait l'octroi d'un statut légal à environ 800 000 personnes qui étaient temporairement protégées contre la déportation en vertu d'un programme adopté sous l'administration Obama, appelé l'Action différée pour les arrivées d'enfance.
Donald Trump a annoncé qu'il mettrait fin à ce programme, mais il a donné au Congrès jusqu'au mois de mars pour trouver un terrain d'entente. L'administration Trump souhaite obtenir le financement nécessaire pour la construction du mur en échange de la légalisation du statut des Dreamers.

ALENA: les discussions de la dernière chance pour un accord en 2018?

Le regard Kahlo

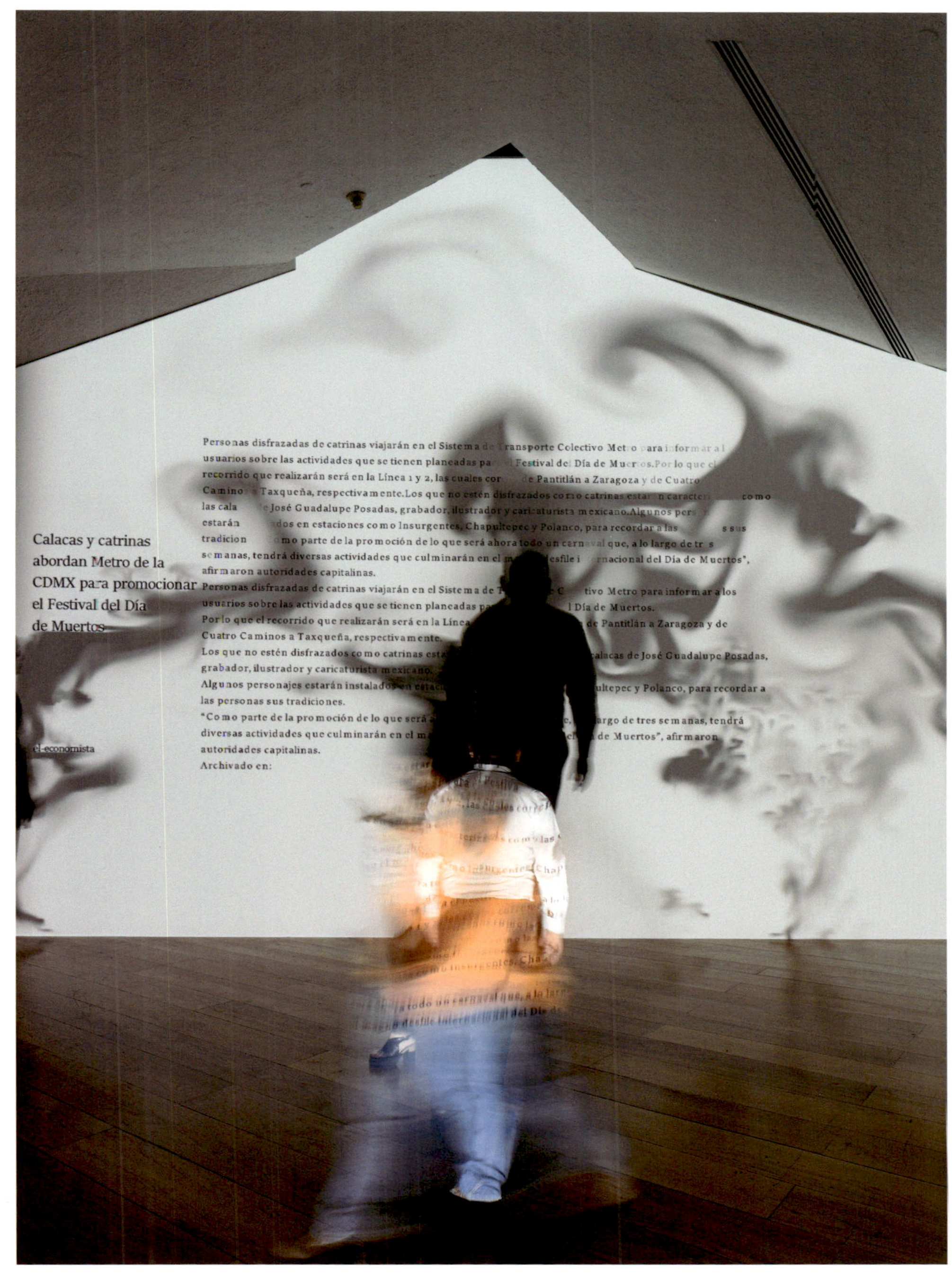

Installation views, Musée d'art contemporain de Montréal, 2018 (left), and Museo de Arte Contemporáneo de Monterrey, Mexico, 2019 (right)

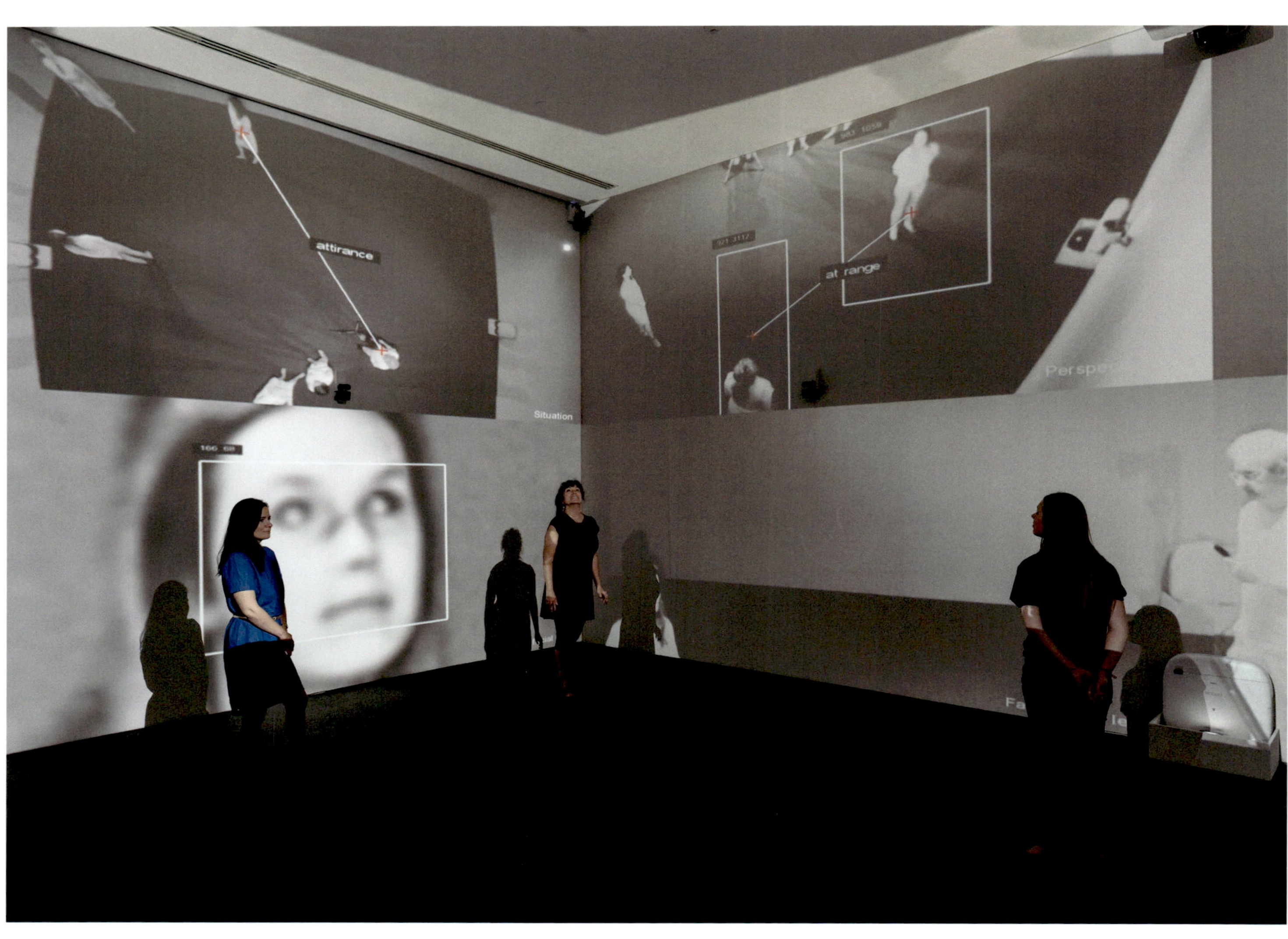
attirance
at range
Situation
Perspe
166
Fa

FRANÇOIS LETOURNEUX

ON ZOOM PAVILION

Immediately upon entering Rafael Lozano-Hemmer's *Zoom Pavilion* (2015; see page 98), visitors experience a simultaneous sense of envelopment and openness. The space feels comfortable, airy, and luminous. Images of visitors' bodies are captured and projected on the gridded walls and ceiling, sliding by in clusters, and at various scales and angles. Infrared lights confer a graphic, almost abstract quality to the environment, making the pale, grayscale figures look ghostly.

A sense of suffused anxiety also accompanies the installation. The equipment used to detect and track participants (computerized cameras employing facial recognition, background subtraction, and machine-learning algorithms) is repurposed and exposed surveillance technology. *Zoom Pavilion* has often been compared to a giant microscope; the work engages a kind of predatory flipping of the traditional subject-object relationship, with the work looking at the visitor, instead of the reverse. The pavilion itself, as architectural form, may refer to the cosmopolitan culture of leisurely pleasure in aristocratic societies as much as to the captivating showcase of technological feats in modern world fairs. Yet the intrusive reduction of optical distance and use of the visitor as object of experiment in *Zoom Pavilion* provides another echo of technology's capacity to fascinate and its codependent power of subjection.

Surveillance cameras have been a staple of Lozano-Hemmer's oeuvre for many years, and *Zoom Pavilion* expands on works produced in previous moments of intensified surveillance, such as the 1991 Gulf War (*Surface Tension*, 1992) and the post-9/11 War on Terror (*Inspired by Real Events*, 2004; *Subtitled Public*, 2005, see page 148). Notions

Zoom Pavilion, 2015. Installation view, Musée d'art contemporain de Montréal, 2018

of automated surveillance as autonomous intelligence and machinic agency, already featured in such theoretical contributions as Manuel de Landa's *War in the Age of Intelligence Machines* (1991)[1] and addressed in these earlier works by Lozano-Hemmer, are revisited and updated in *Zoom Pavilion*.

The installation features up to three camera angles: an aerial, drone-like view (projected on the ceiling), a classic closed-circuit TV camera (as used in schools or prison yards), and a facial recognition apparatus (similar to the ones used in airports, police stations, or phones). The latter tracks faces with particular ruthlessness, matching any attempt to dodge capture. Crucially, *Zoom Pavilion* does not track individual visitors so much as their spatial relationships, evaluating the degree and quality of interactions ("potential," "interest," "remote," "perspective"), then drawing them out on the screens with annotated, flowing vectors.

The entrance (back) wall displays an archive of current and past visitors' faces, organized in twos, specifying how long the individuals were paired in the gallery, how far apart they remained, and when their assembly happened, underscoring that the monitoring of free association (or public assembly), rather than that of individual behavior, is the specific topic of *Zoom Pavilion*. The work is the result of collaboration between Lozano-Hemmer and Krzysztof Wodiczko, the celebrated pioneer of interactive social practice and projection mapping on public architecture and monuments (who himself was born during the 1943 Warsaw Ghetto Uprising and grew up under the surveillance regime of Soviet-dominated Poland). In his 1983 article on public projection, Wodiczko describes the social, architectural body as "a disciplined-disciplining body, allowing for both the multidirectional flow of power and the controlled circulation of the individual bodies," and the building as "a meta-institutional, spatial medium for the continuous and simultaneous symbolic reproduction of both the general myth of power and the individual desire for power."[2]

While sensations of abuse and surveillance dominate *Zoom Pavilion*, many visitors also interact playfully with the cameras, responding with their own intelligent devices, and creating "mediated" selfies that double down on the mirroring effect of the work, eventually plugging in to the network, webcasting live. *Zoom Pavilion* thus also comments on the current attention economy and correlated "experiential turn" in art, acknowledging forerunners such as Dan Graham's *Time Delay Room* (1974) and French Situationist Guy Debord's 1988 definition of "liberal democracy" as "integrated spectacle," fusing "concentrated spectacle" (European totalitarianisms) and "diffuse spectacle" (American capitalist entertainment).[3]

As such, the disturbing interlocking of surveillance apparatus and narcissistic gazes in *Zoom Pavilion* highlights the libidinal nature of the new economy and the fascination it elicits globally. With the work's documentation of bodies in space and the reciprocal digital recording by visitors of their own selves being watched, a great number of still and moving images begin circulating both inside the piece and out, many percolating online. Few of these could strictly be called selfies, as many include figures that are unknown to the "author" of the photograph. In this respect, *Zoom Pavilion* could be said to function as a kind of "group-portrait machine" for the age of integrated spectacle. Many of Lozano-Hemmer's interactive installations function as such, but most rely on partial, indexical processes and a certain degree of abstraction, whereas *Zoom Pavilion*'s use of exacting facial recognition software creates a wholly different context.

As a group-portrait machine, the work relates to a broader history of group portraits, hearkening back to early photography and even painting.[4] Like such precedents, it holds value as a sociological marker, with two additional, unusual traits. First, the piece is both site and situation specific, to borrow from Lozano-Hemmer's distinction of Wodiczko's methods from his own. *Zoom Pavilion* reflects both the situated interactions that occur inside it and the sites where it is exhibited, as its own ironic history readily illustrates: initially conceived for Beijing's Architecture Biennial but cancelled at the last minute by the authorities in Communist China, the installation traveled instead to Art Basel, Switzerland, the highest ground of the international art market. Second—though often unknown to visitors—like most of Lozano-Hemmer's works, it does not archive the visitors' presence permanently.

Therein lies *Zoom Pavilion*'s paradoxical nature: contrary to historical precedents, its form of group portraiture is, in fact, nomadic; viewers and figures merge in the piece, existing in a spatial and visual continuum from which they must eventually depart permanently. Because of this, the historical meaning of the work does not operate in relation to the documentation of its figures; it is rather the pure, mirror-like agency of the apparatus itself that remains, as a unique portrait of co-presence in our time.

NOTES

1. Manuel de Landa, *War in the Age of Intelligence Machines* (Cambridge, MA: MIT Press, 1991).

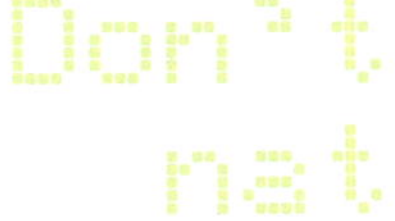

2. Krzysztof Wodiczko, "Public Projection," in *Canadian Journal of Political and Social Theory / Revue canadienne de théorie politique et sociale* 7, nos. 1–2 (Winter–Spring 1983): 185–87.

3. Guy Debord, *Commentaires sur la société du spectacle* (Paris: Gallimard, 1992), 21–25.

4. The modern group portrait could be considered to have made its entrance on the scene of Western painting at the height of Dutch economic and military might, during the sixteenth and seventeenth centuries. As the Austrian art historian Alois Riegl famously suggested in *The Group Portraiture of Holland* (1902), the new depiction of the powerful corporations of the day notably introduced a virtual, spatial, and optical continuum between viewers and figures, connecting their respective modes of attention and signaling an alignment of portraiture with contemporary, democratic values. Riegl's discussion of the group portrait is now considered the first example of an aesthetics of reception in art history, and could be said to have anticipated (long before the age of the "attention economy") contemporary art's foregrounding of relational and situated practices. See Wolfgang Kemp, introduction to *The Group Portraiture of Holland* by Alois Riegl (Los Angeles: Getty Publications, 1999); Catherine Soussloff, "The Birth of the Social History of Art," in *The Subject in Art: Portraiture in Art and the Birth of the Modern* (Durham, NC: Duke University Press, 2006); and Jonathan Crary, "Modernity and the Problem of Attention," in *Suspensions of Perception: Attention, Spectacle, and Modern Culture* (Cambridge, MA: MIT Press, 1999).

ZOOM PAVILION 2015

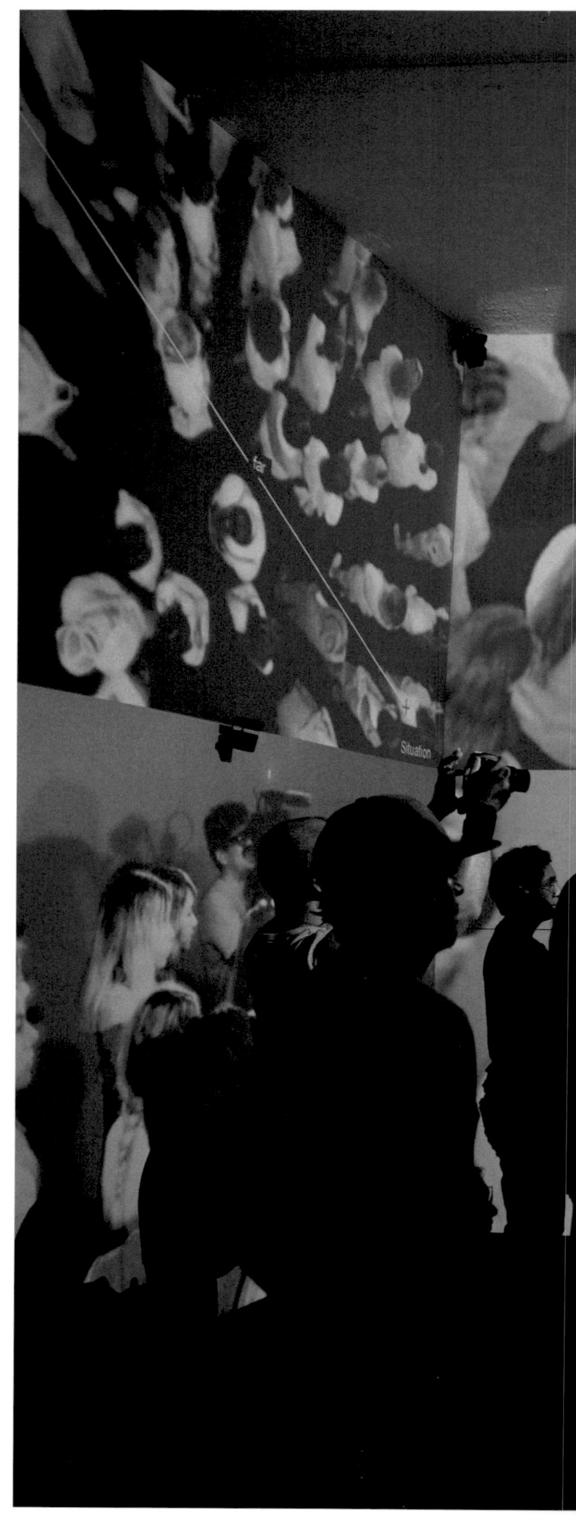

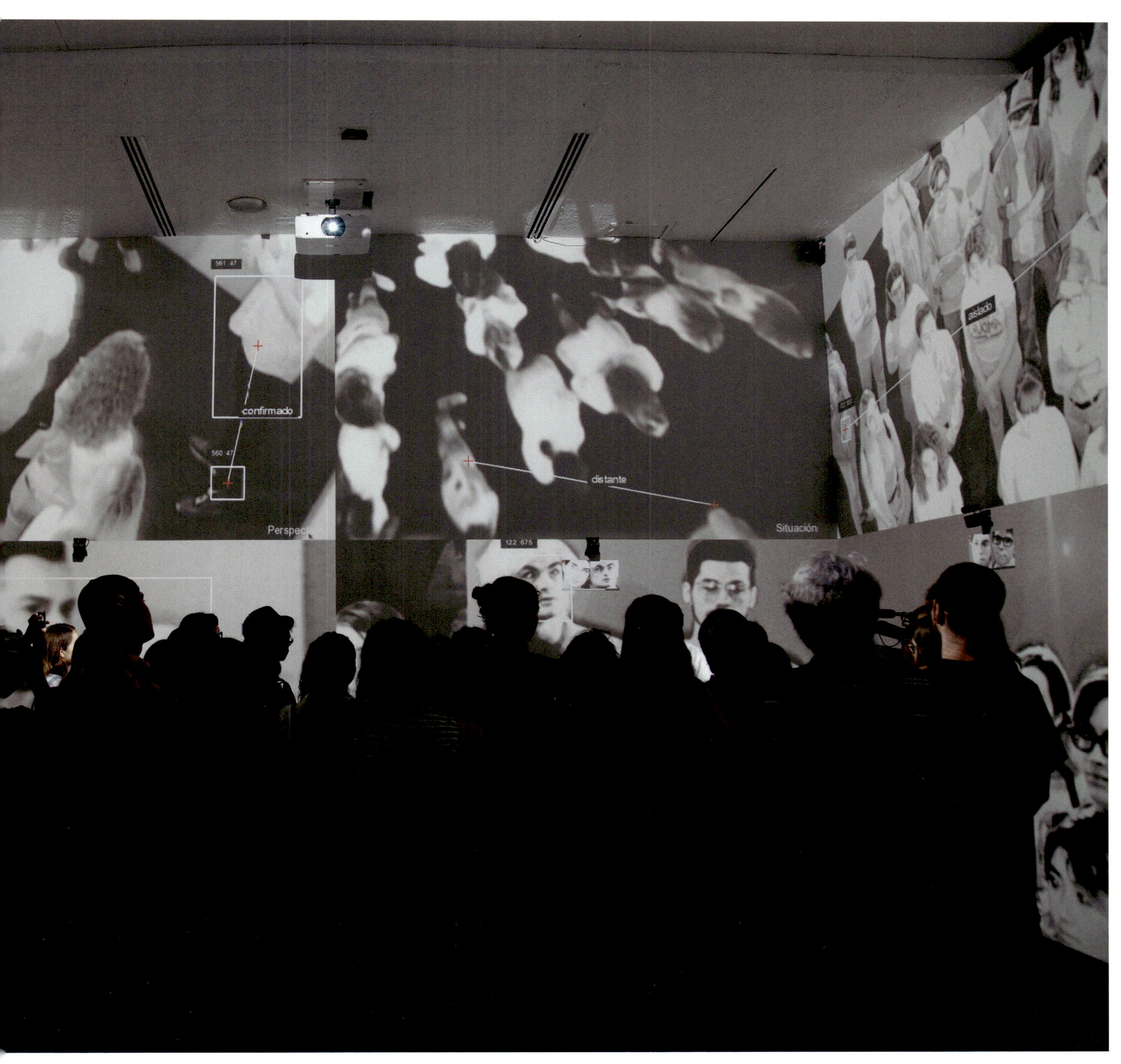

Installation view, Museo de Arte Contemporáneo de Monterrey, Mexico, 2019

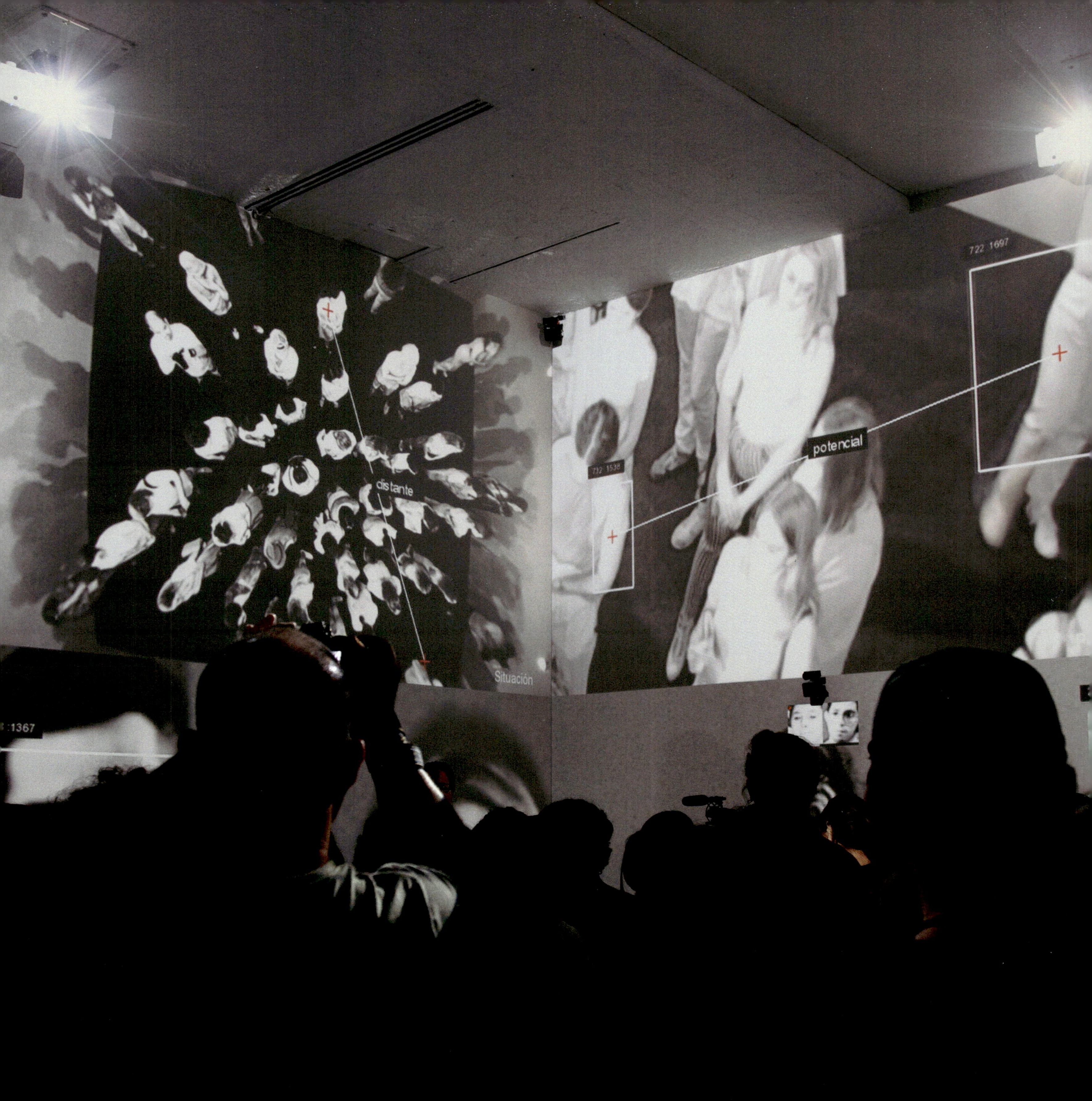

722 1697
distante
potencial
722 1538
Situación
:1367

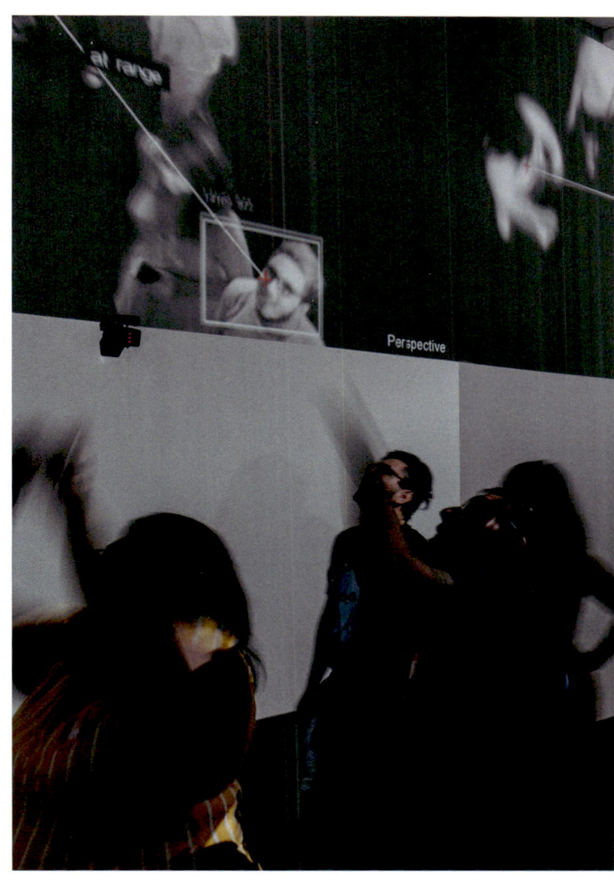

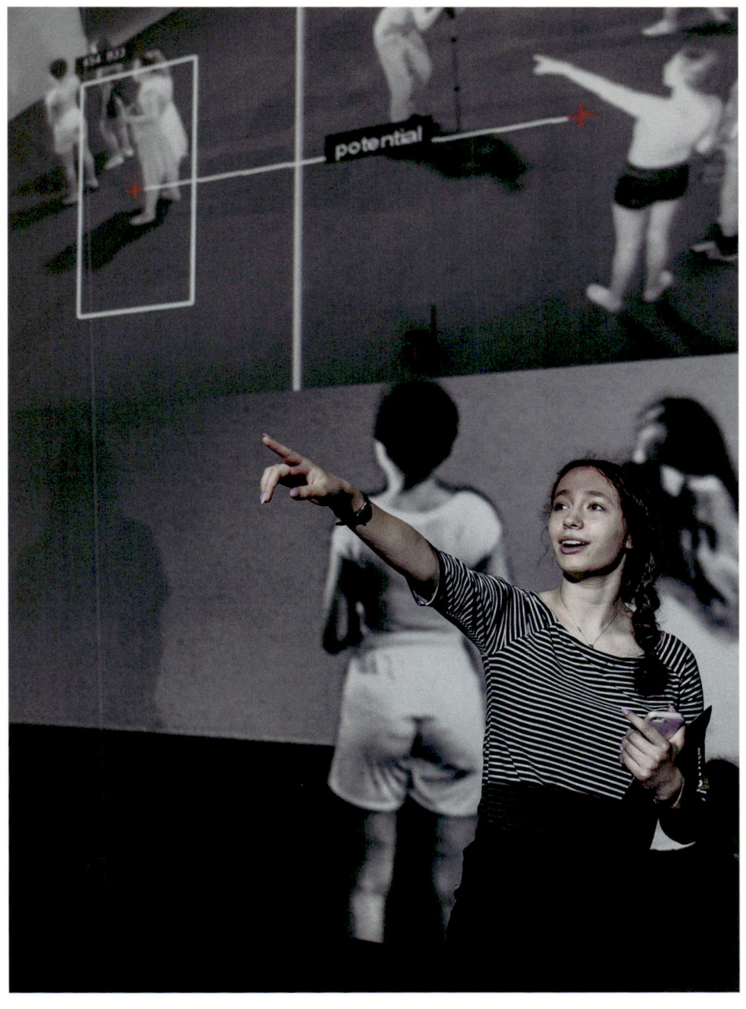

Installation views, Museo de Arte Contemporáneo de Monterrey, Mexico, 2019 (left and above), and Musée d'art contemporain de Montréal, 2018 (right)

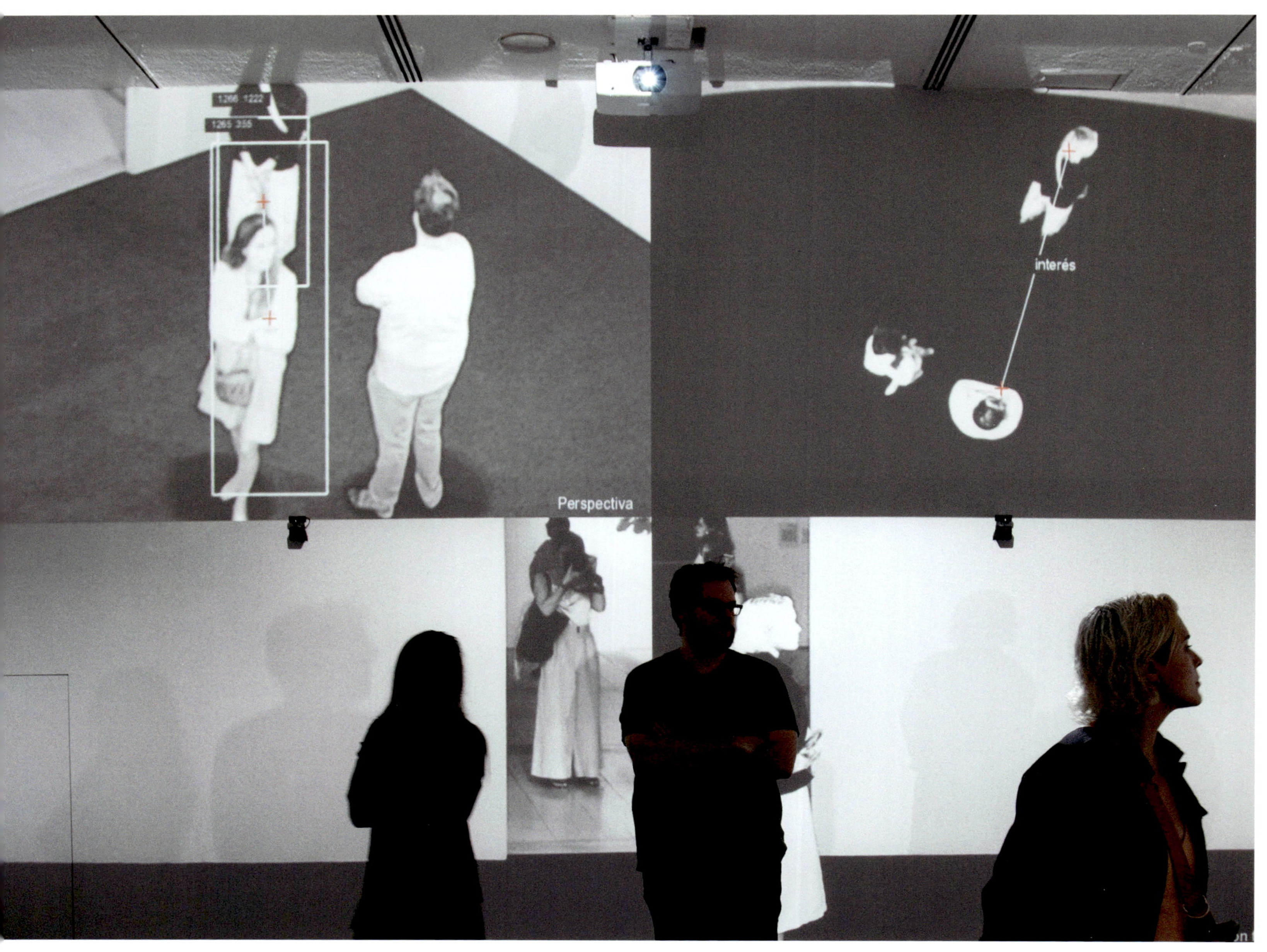
1266 1222
1265 355
Perspectiva
interés

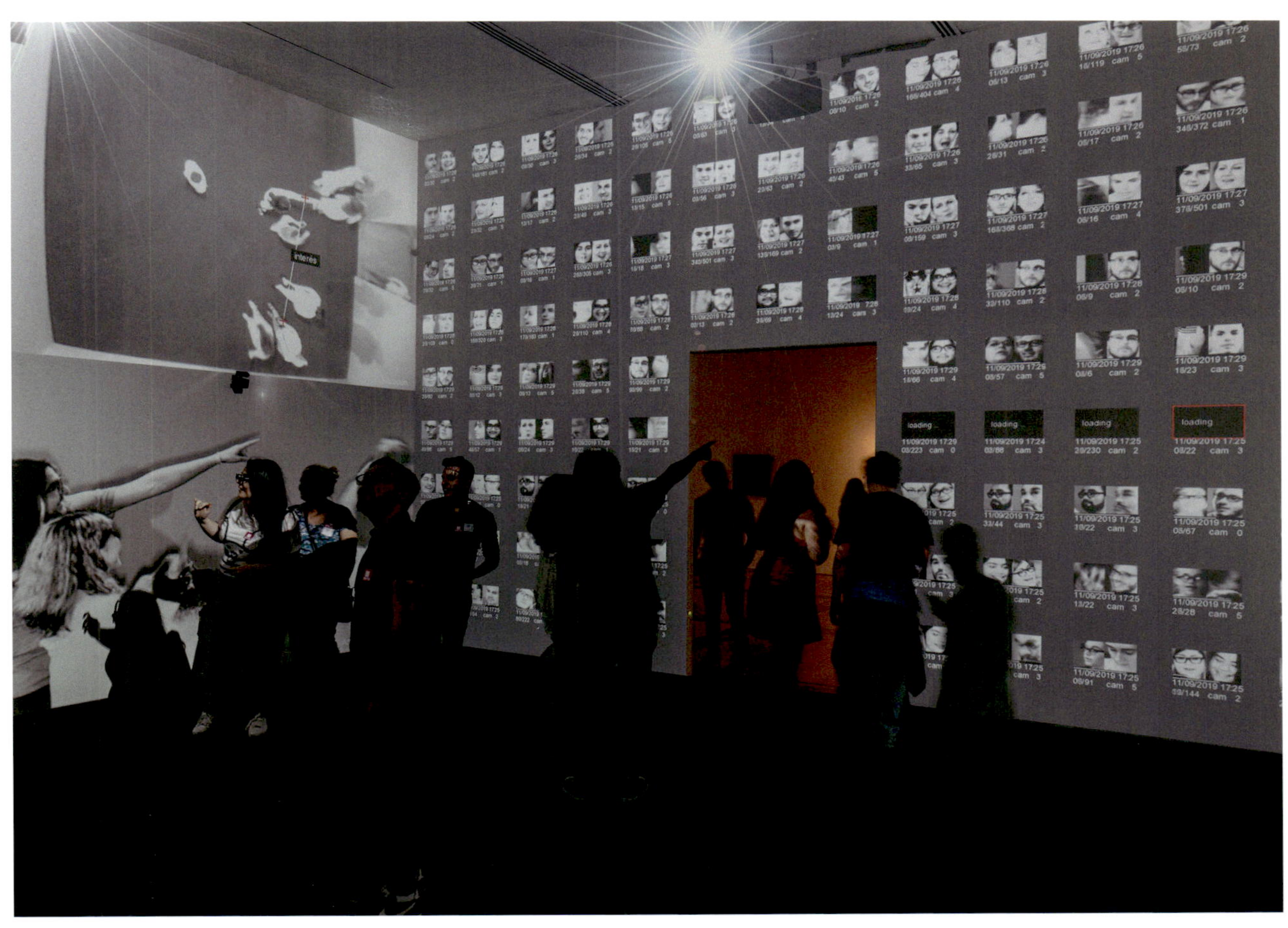

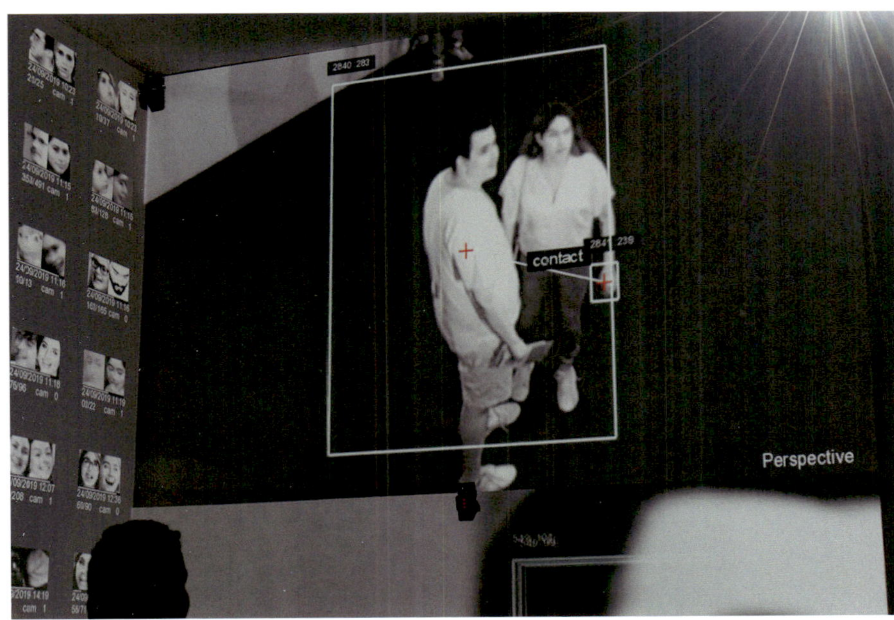

Installation views, Museo de Arte Contemporáneo de Monterrey, Mexico, 2019

LEVEL OF CONFIDENCE 2015

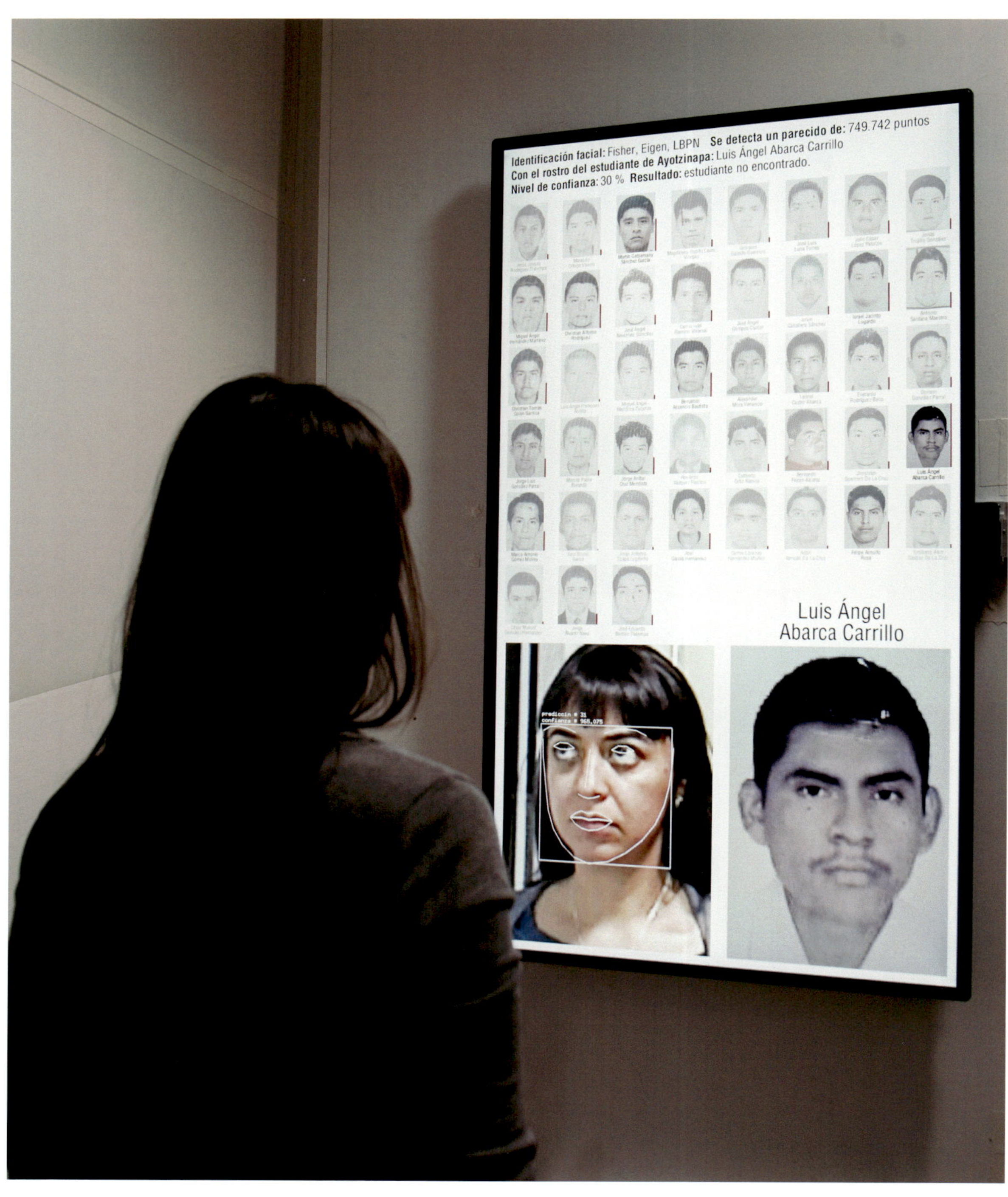

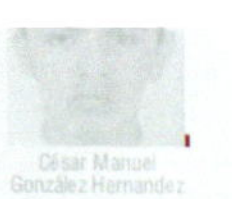

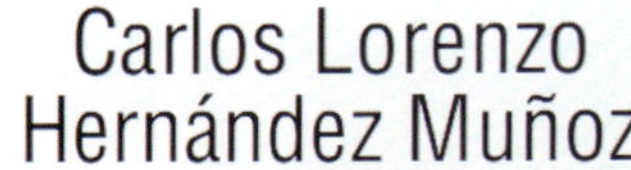

Carlos Lorenzo
Hernández Muñoz

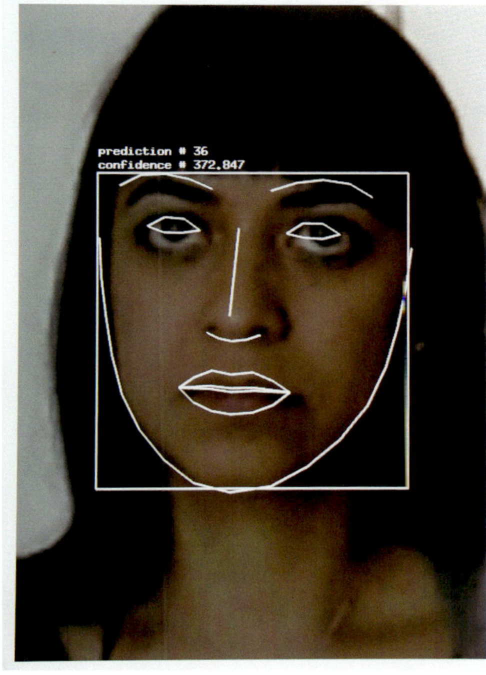

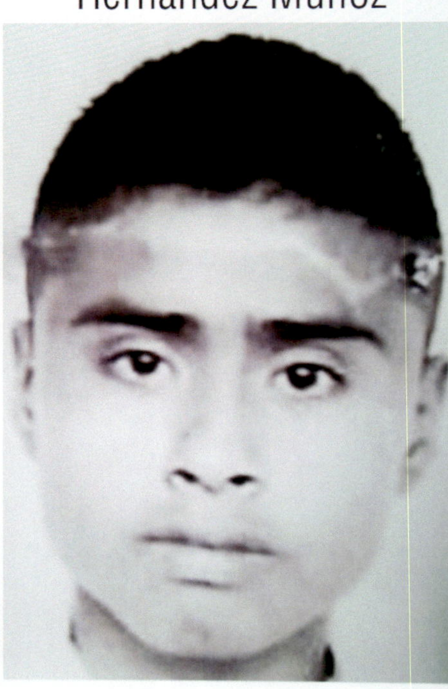

Facial recognition engine: Fisher, Eigen, LBPN   **Detected similarity score:** 334.692 points
With the face of disappeared Ayotzinapa student: Alexander Mora Venancio
Level of confidence: 16 % **Result:**

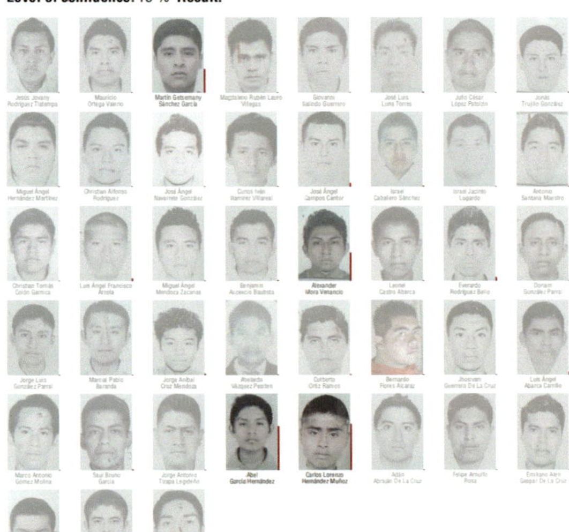

Alexander
Mora Venancio

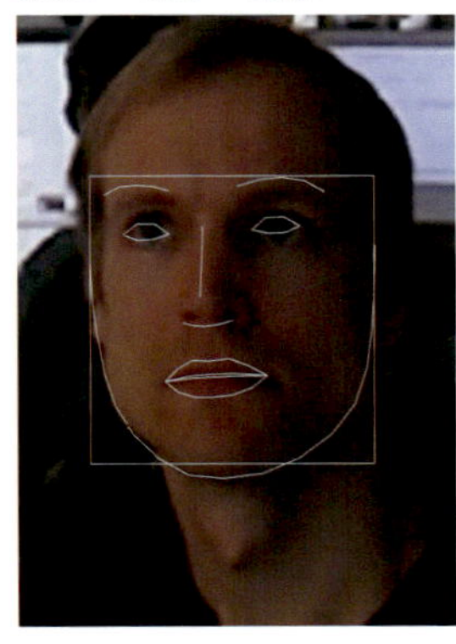
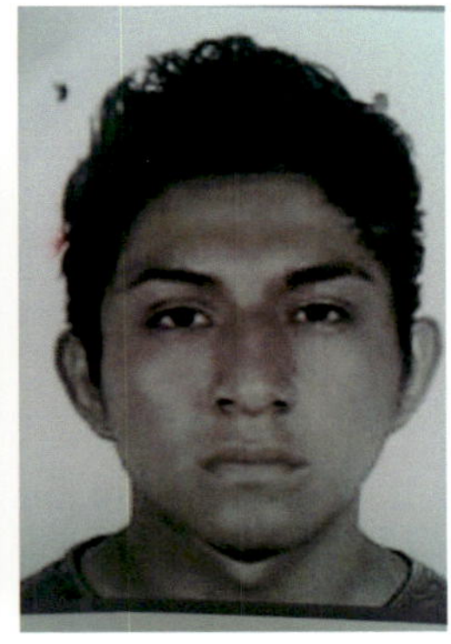

Installation views, Antimodular Research, Montreal, 2015

PAN-ANTHEM 2014

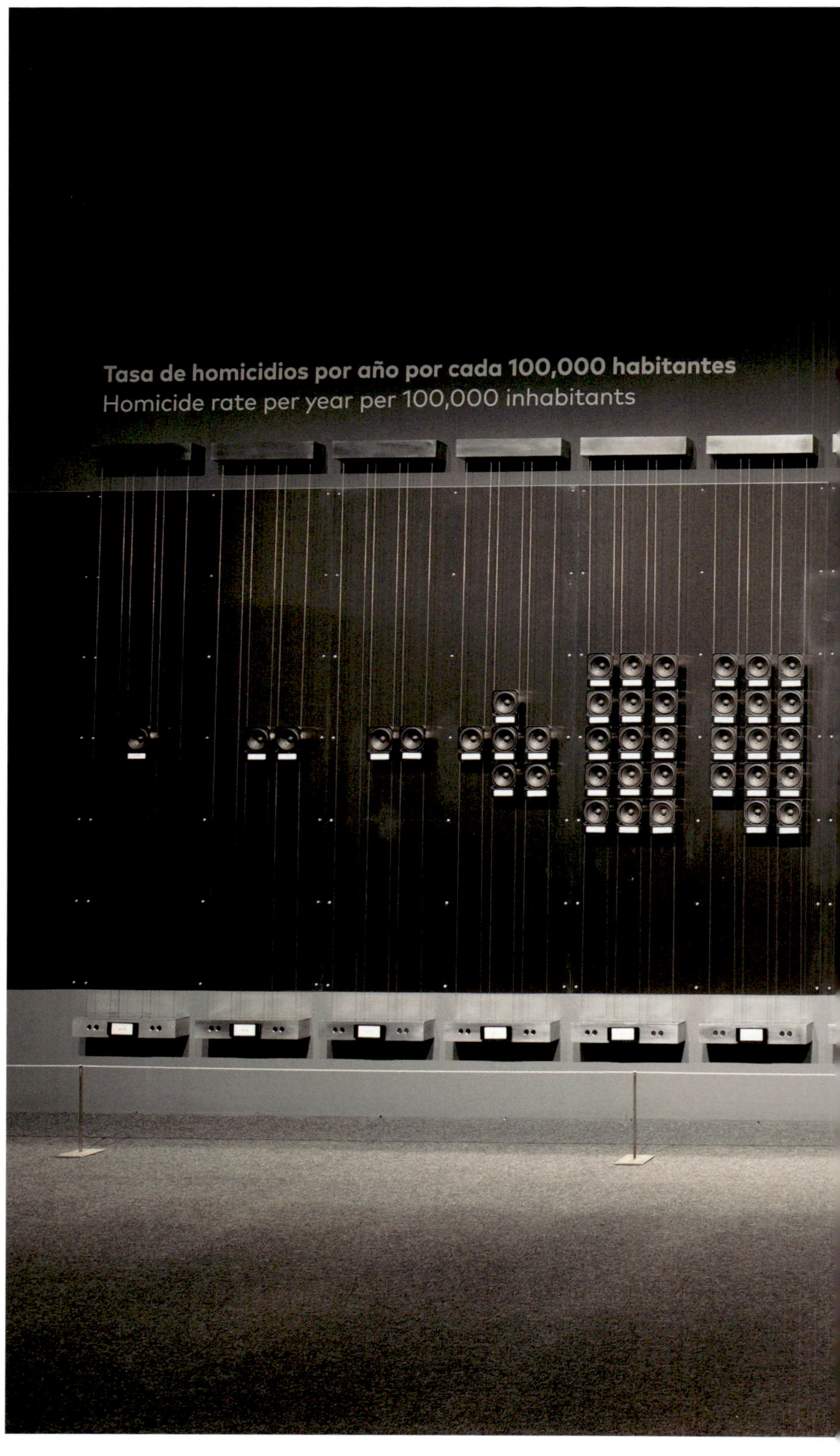

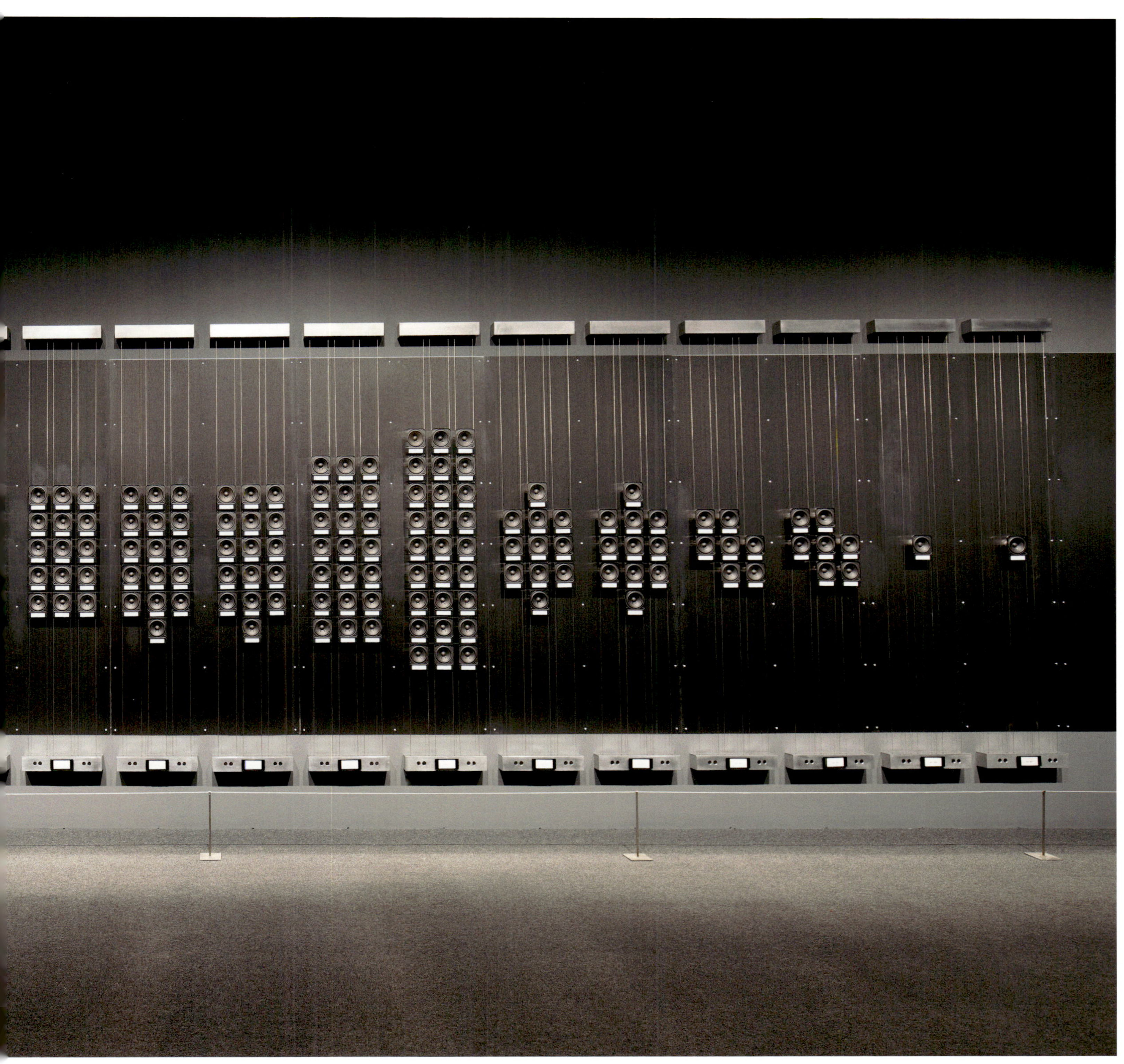

Installation view, Museo de Arte Contemporáneo de Monterrey, Mexico, 2019

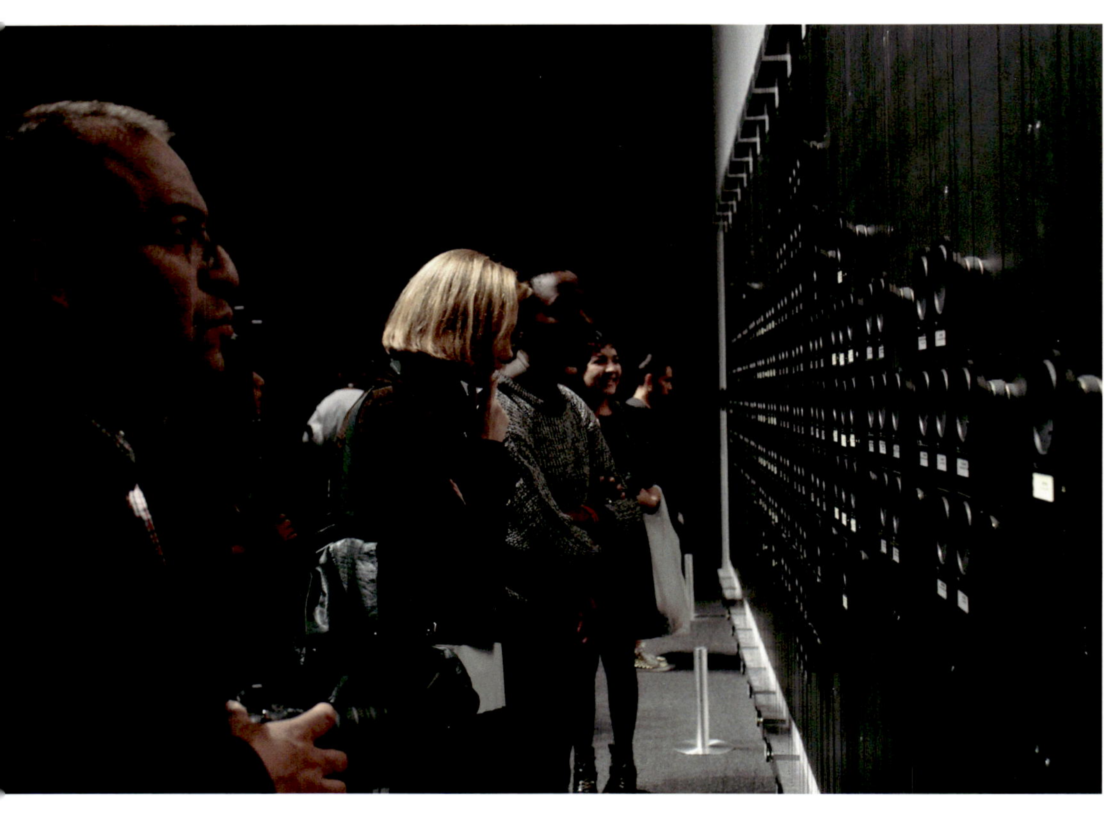

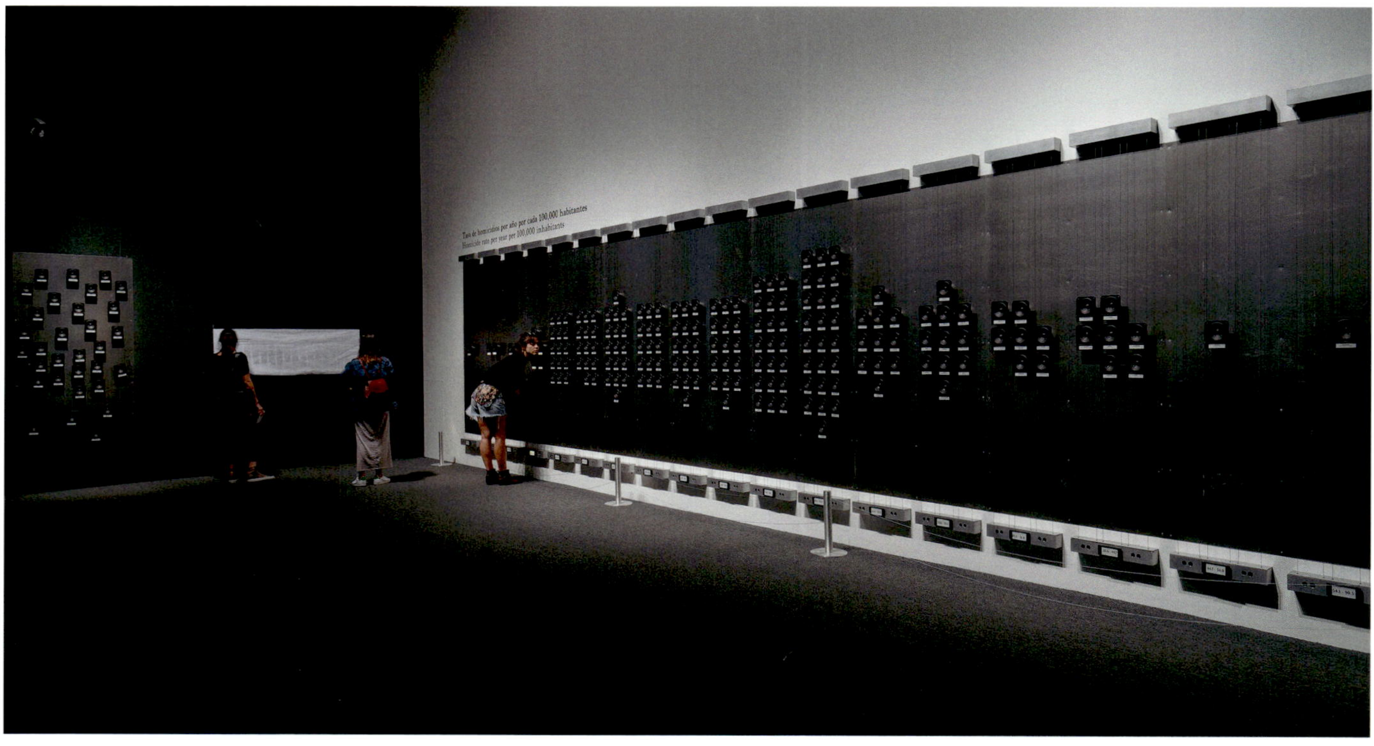

Installation views, Museo Universitario Arte Contemporáneo, Mexico City, 2015

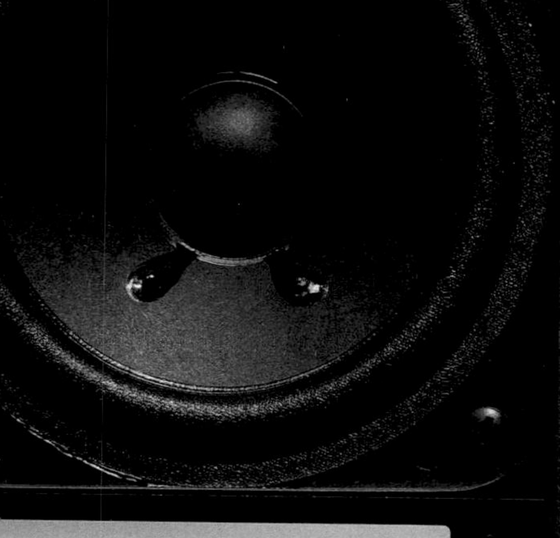

PHILIPPINES
Lupang Hinirang

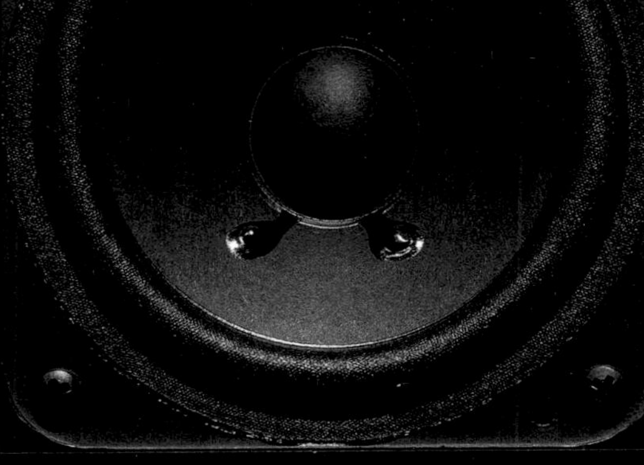

ANGOLA
Angola Avante!

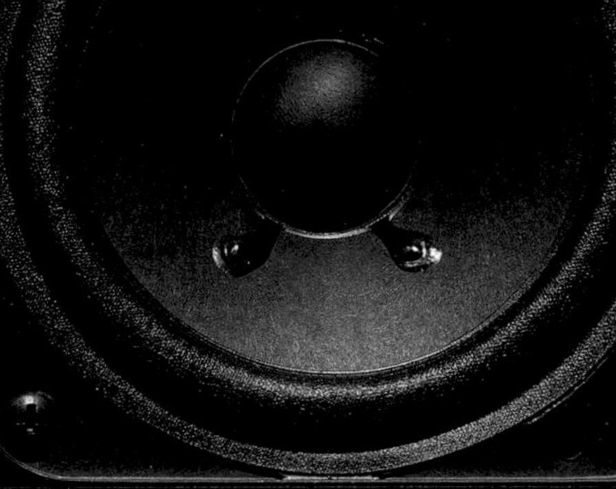

ZAMBIA
Stand and Sing of Zambia, Proud and Free

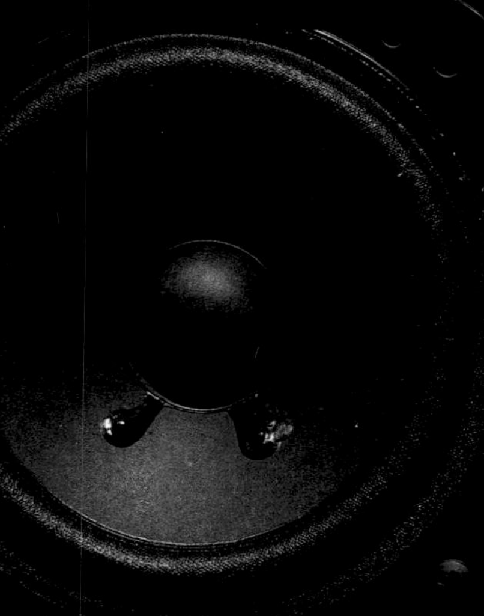

GUINEA-BISSAU
Esta É a Nossa Pátria Bem Amada

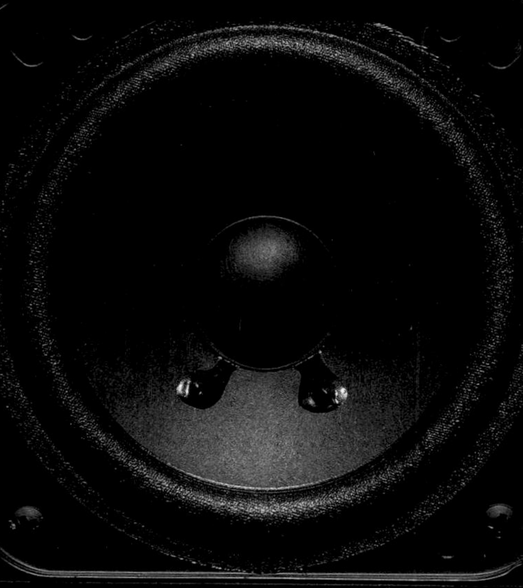

COMOROS
Udzima wa ya Masiwa

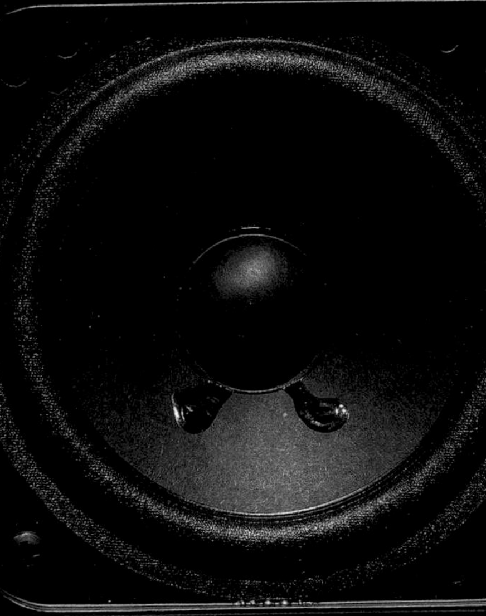

UGANDA
Oh Uganda, Land of Beauty

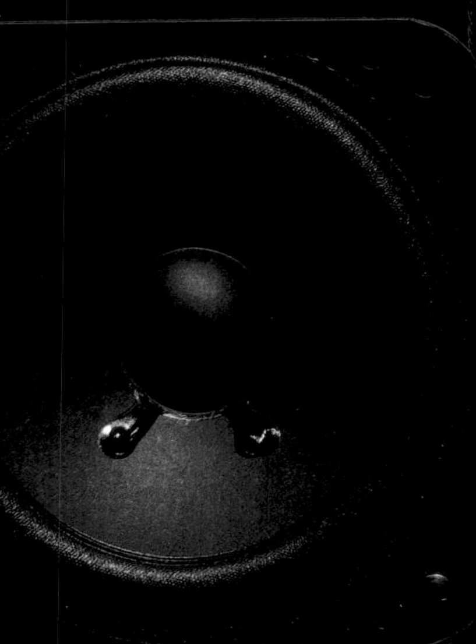

GABON
La Concorde

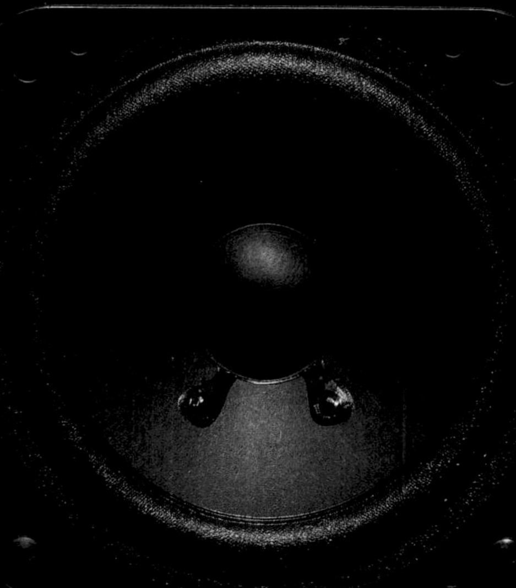

DJIBOUTI
Djibouti

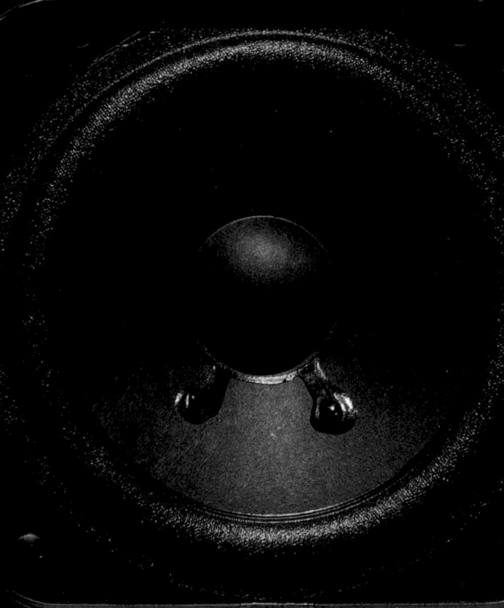

MADAGASCAR
Ry Tanindrazanay malala ô!

SPHERE PACKING: BACH 2018

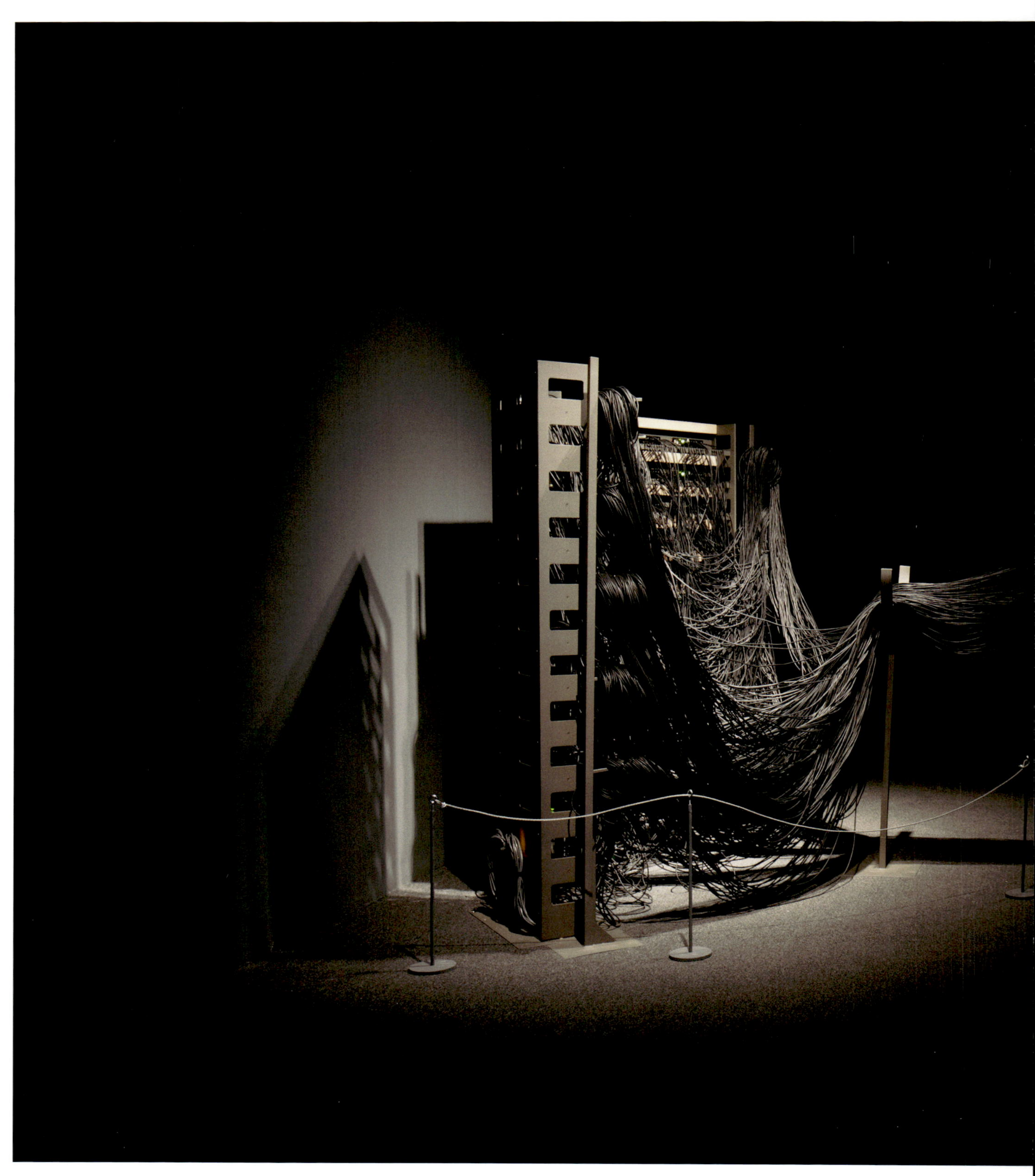

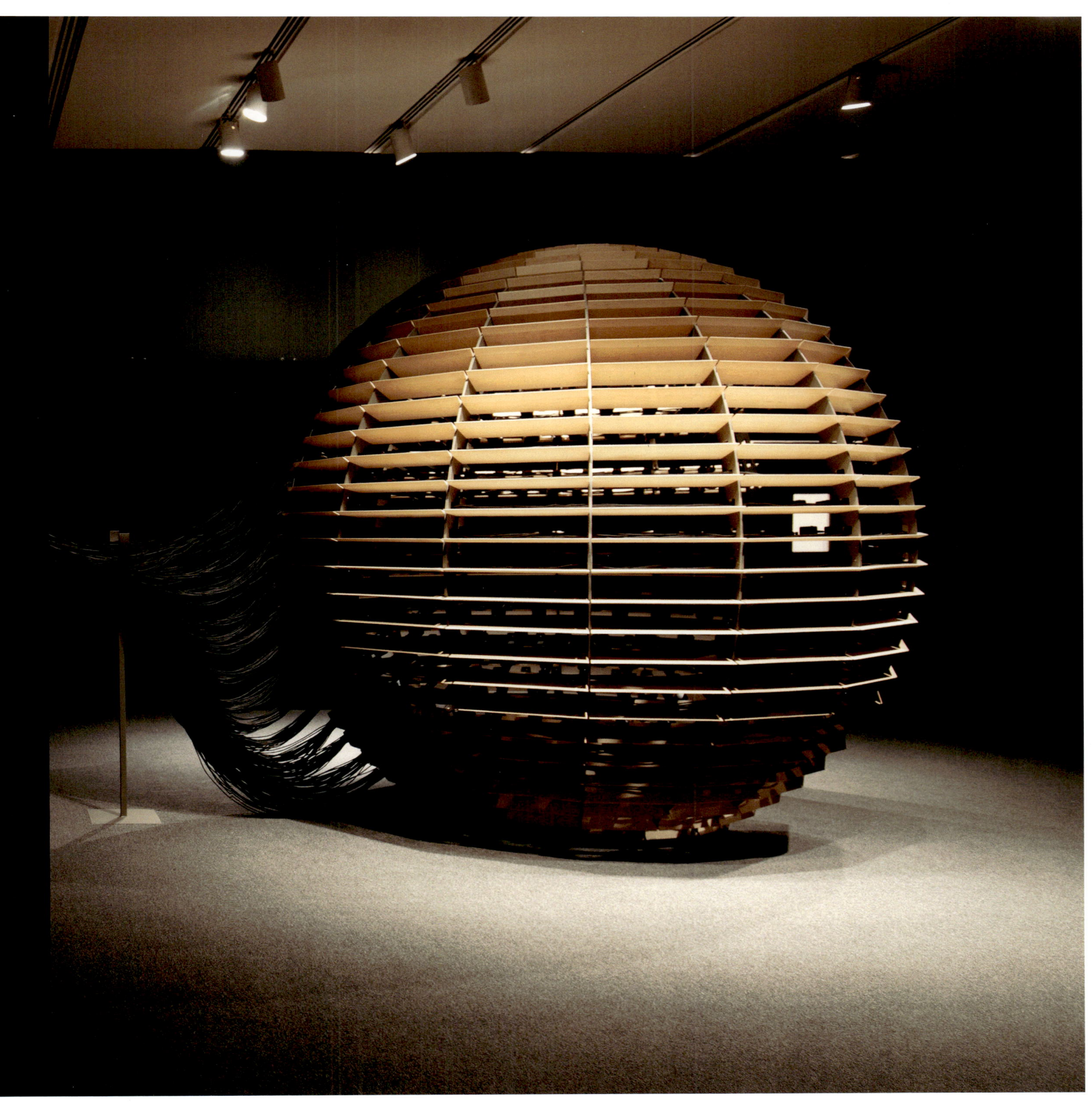

Installation view, Museo de Arte Contemporáneo de Monterrey, Mexico, 2019

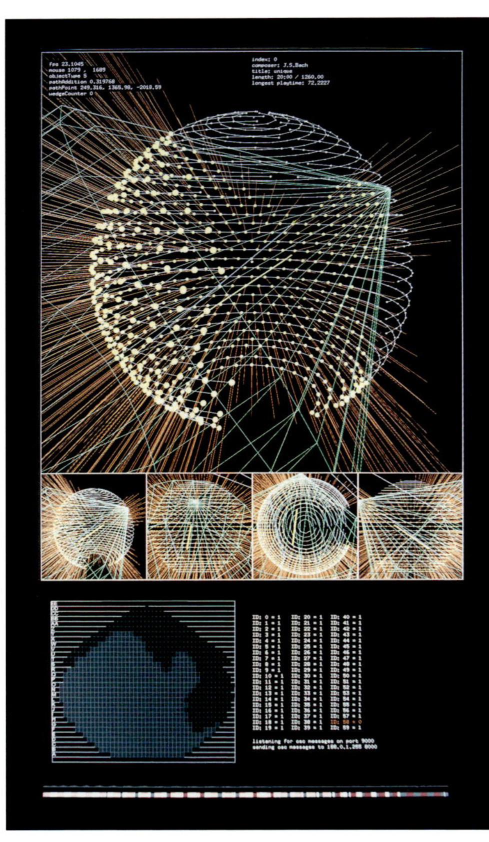

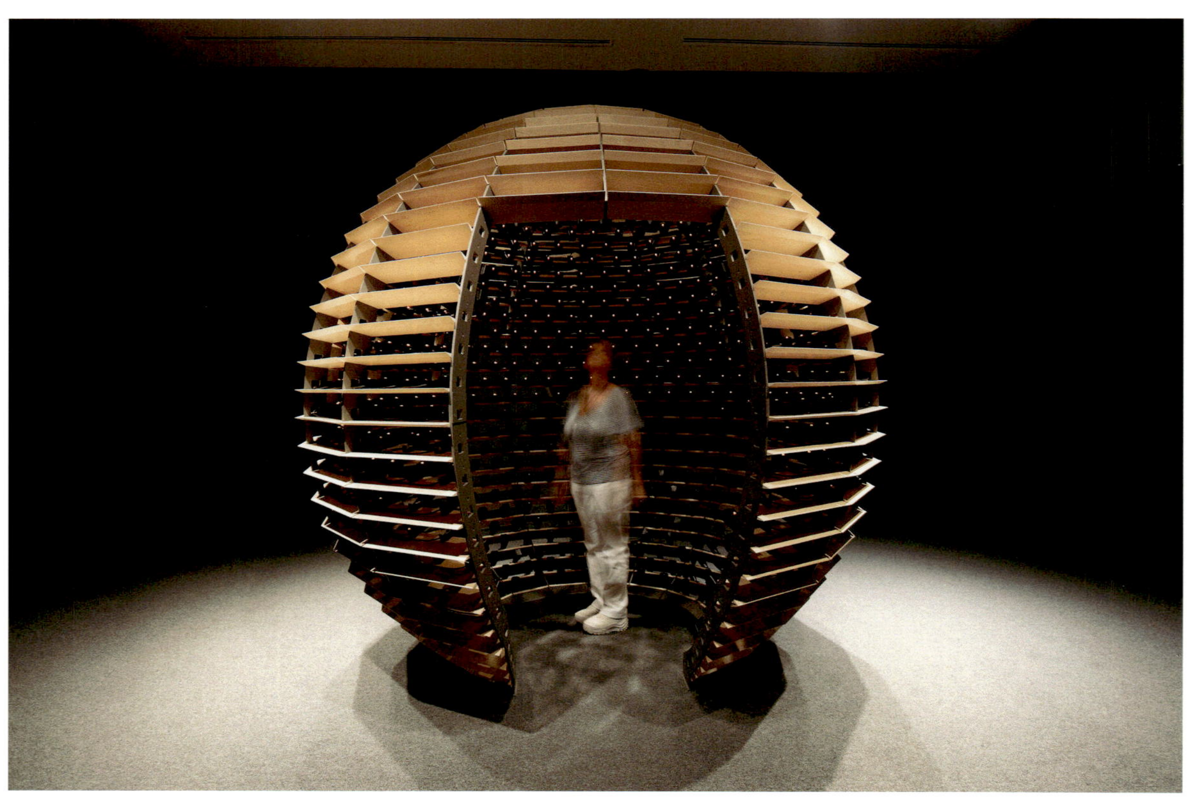

Custom software control panel for *Sphere Packing: Bach* (top); installation views, Museo de Arte Contemporáneo de Monterrey, Mexico, 2019 (above), and Musée d'art contemporain de Montréal, 2018 (right)

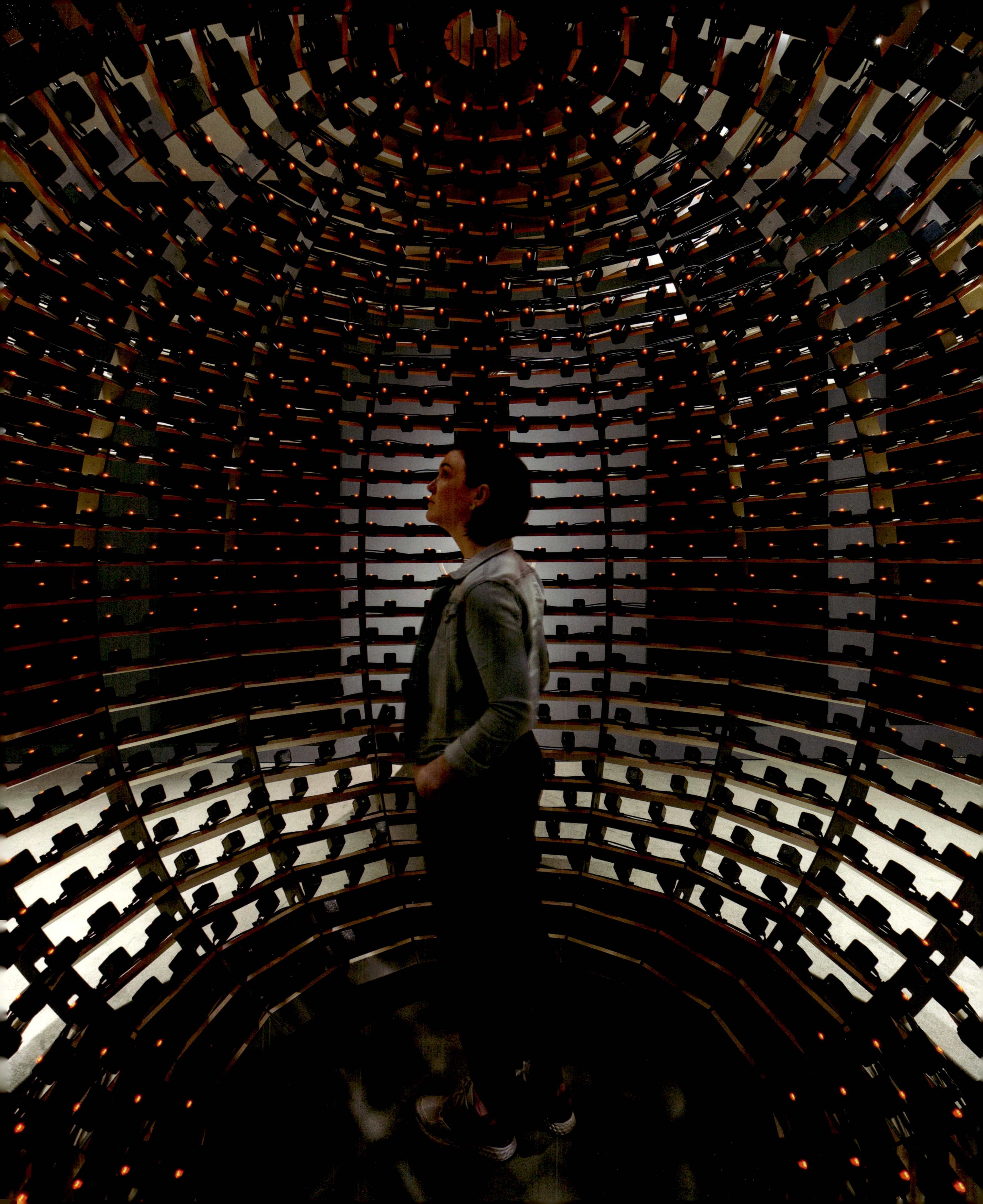

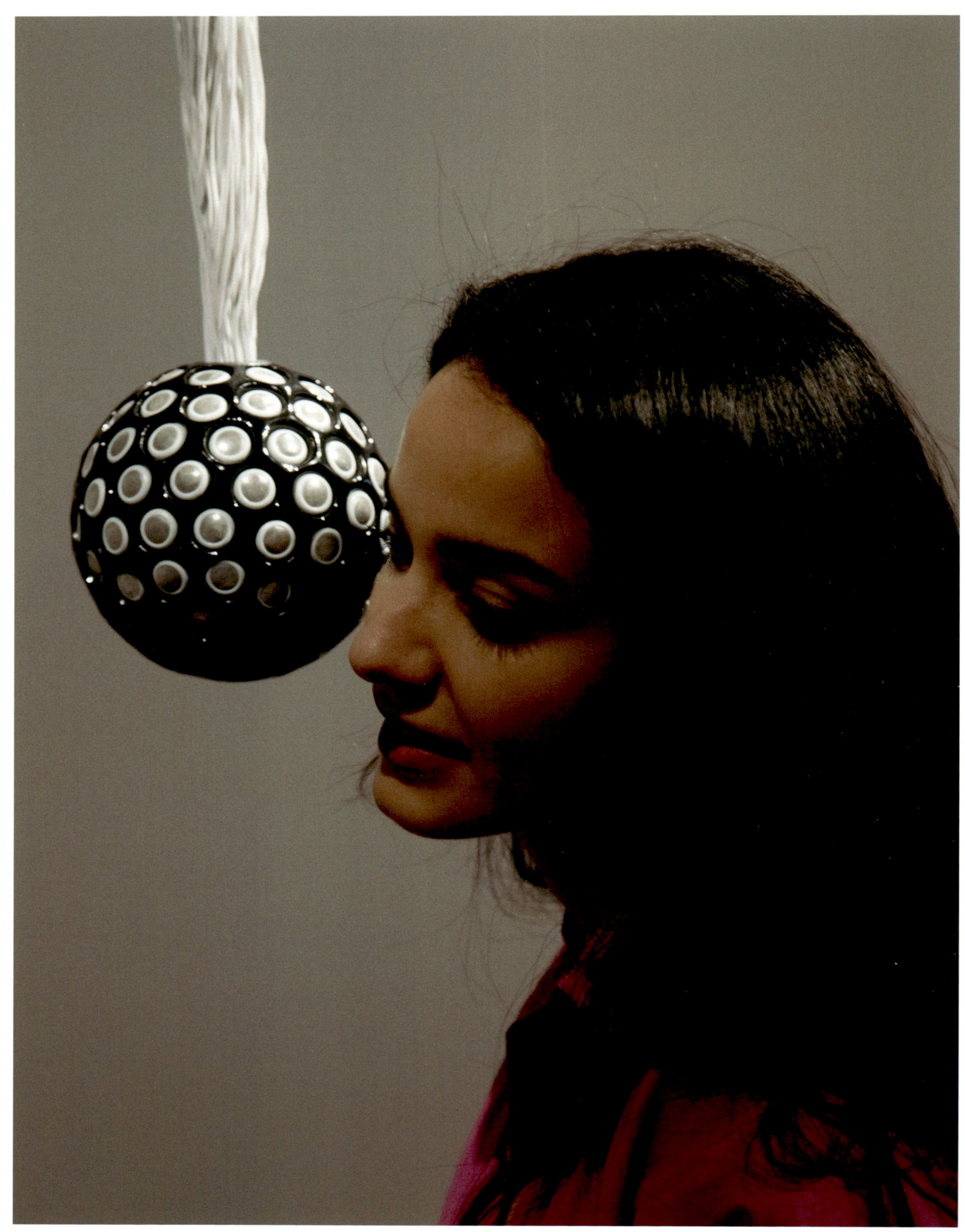

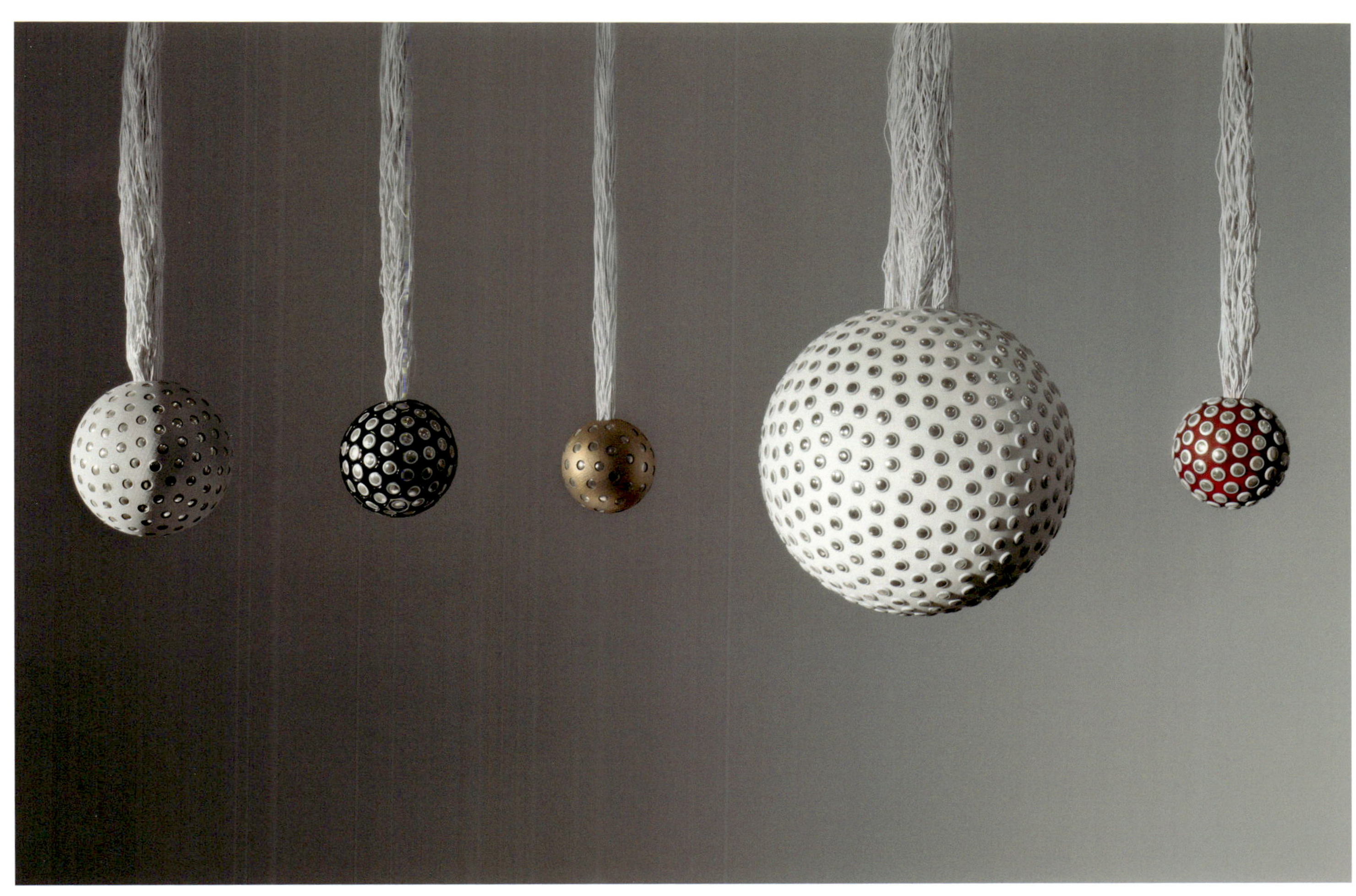

Sphere Packing: Wagner, 2013, insta lation view, Museo de Arte Contemporáneo de Monterrey, Mexico, 2019 (left); *Stockhausen*, *Wagner*, *Von Bingen*, *Mozart*, and *Górecki* (left to right), from the series *Sphere Packing*, all 2013, installation view, Antimodular Research, Montreal, 2014 (above)

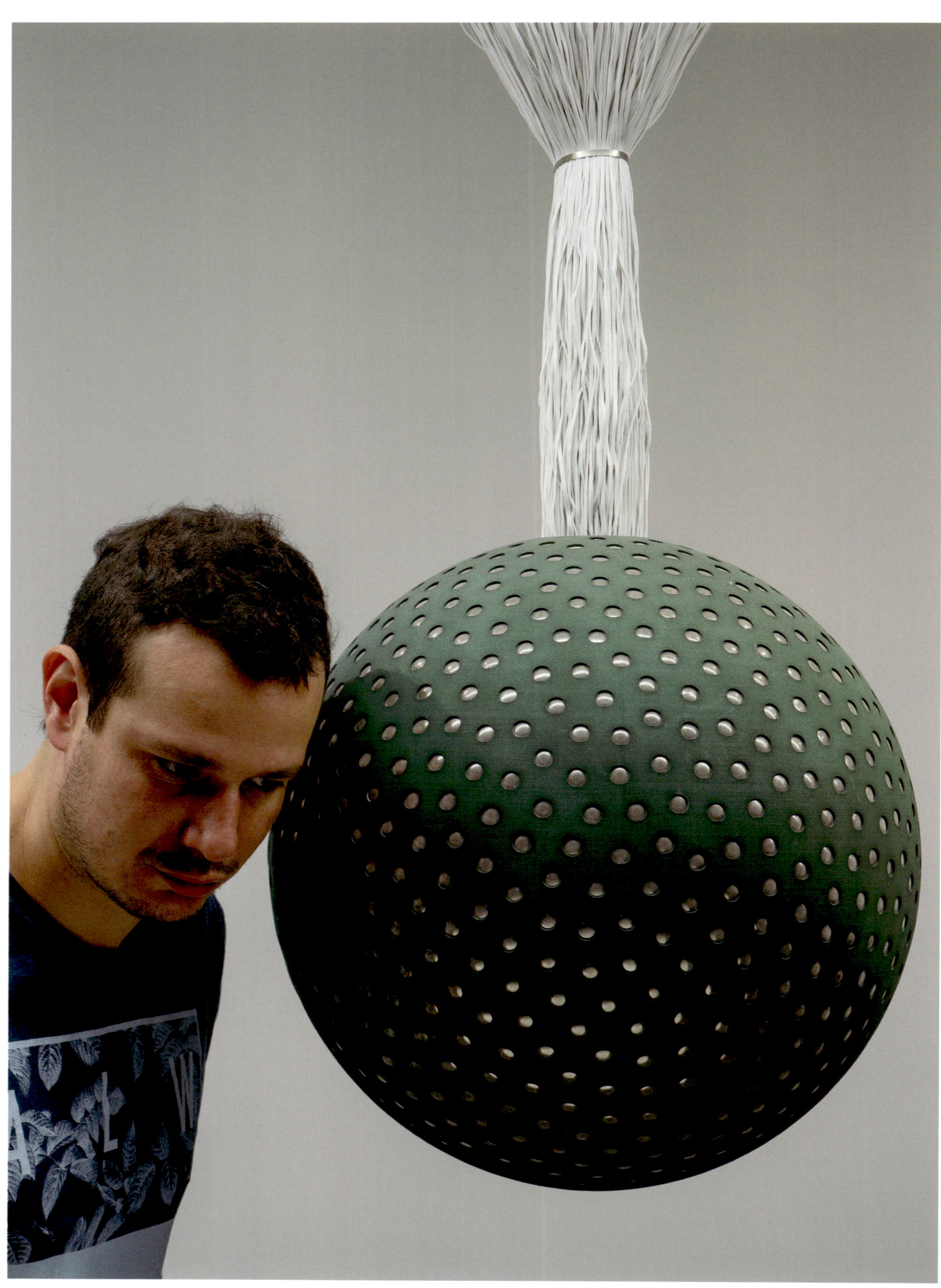

SEAN CUBITT

FUGUE

¿Irías a ser ciega que Dios te dio esas manos?
("Was it because you were to go blind that God gave you those hands?")
—Vicente Huidobro, *Altazor*

Several hundred of the works whose recordings play simultaneously in Rafael Lozano-Hemmer's *Sphere Packing: Bach* (2018; fig. 13 and page 110) are fugues. German philosopher Ernst Bloch sees in Johann Sebastian Bach's pious and well-tempered fugues an aesthetic of equanimity in the time when the ancien régime was dying and the new guard was still struggling to be born.[1] More recently, the programmatic elements of Bach's fugues became increasingly relevant for minimalist artists and electronic composers. The fugue performs a series of formal operations on an initial given, in much the way that databases constantly reorganize the data they start with into new relations. One of many inventions permeating Lozano-Hemmer's works is their fugal play with data, to which they return a sonic dimension.

In many respects, the fugue is the most technical of musical forms, the one that most closely cleaves to a set of variations prescribed by the initial motif—often only a handful of notes. Every permutation is worked through, in perfect harmony like a ringing circle of church bells. In practice, Bach's fugues frequently apply a second rule to avoid dissonance when the interval between two notes is not permitted in standard harmony, an adjustment that disappears into the intertwining melodies. The selection of moments when the extra rule applies might be the only freedom the composer has to intervene in a system that, once set up, runs on its own logic.

The Bach variant from Lozano-Hemmer's *Sphere Packing* series (the whole collection comprises spheres for seventeen composers, from Hildegard of Bingen to György Ligeti and Franz Schubert [opposite] to Henryk Górecki) is both typical of the series, which

Sphere Packing: Schubert, 2015
Plastic Formiga 3-D print, 998-channel audio, and custom electronics
17 ¾ in. (45 cm) diameter
Installation view, *Rafael Lozano-Hemmer: Pseudomatismos*, Museo Universitario Arte Contemporáneo, Mexico City, 2015

homes in on composers whose work in harmony distinguishes them, and particular to the challenge that the exhibition *Rafael Lozano-Hemmer: Unstable Presence* addresses: like the composer, the works in this exhibition invent systems. So important is the unfolding of the rule-governed procedure that Bach's late *Art of the Fugue* (ca. 1740s) does not even specify on which instruments it should be played. In *Sphere Packing: Bach,* however, Lozano-Hemmer does specify the "instruments" to be used—in this case, all the compositions credited to J. S. Bach. The artist's system plays through them with the same formal steadiness and complexity as are found in the composer's own fugal compositions; Lozano-Hemmer has handed over his creativity to the system in precisely the way Bach did. This relinquishing thus begs the question of the creativity of the system itself, of the *Geist* in the machine.

Underpinning the Bach *Sphere* is a massy yet elegantly crafted infrastructure of loudspeakers and power cables, wall sockets and audio file types, audio jacks and sampling rates, mass-produced components sourced from half a world away—another reverberation of the architectonic-sphere motif. These components are capable of being assembled because each one, down to the humblest screw, has been manufactured according to International Organization for Standardization specifications. The harmonies, even the dissonances that inevitably creep out of the massed playback, reflect a world ordered and regulated. Even when immersed in the Bach *Sphere,* you become aware that the surrounding gallery abides by fire and safety regulations, and that the installation is tuned to the 120 volts and 60 hertz of the U.S. electricity supply (a system distinct from that of Europe), which depends upon the industry that underpins it. Once you start to investigate a network, it is difficult to stop it from connecting, across space and time, via the logistics and politics of global standards and local accommodations.

This is the lesson of the fugue as formal system. Bloch was incorrect when he implied that Bach's aesthetic was an escape from either brute reality or the doctrines of sacerdotal feudalism.[2] Bach's Protestantism never led him into direct confrontation with his aristocratic and church patrons, and his music was a poor medium for political critique. But to the extent that he was a precursor to Systems Art, he was grappling with the intrinsically mathematical logic of Scholasticism, Gothic architecture, and ecclesiastical hierarchies as they returned, unresolved, both in the Baroque and in the evolutions of pentatonic and diatonic scales. We can ask whether there would be music as we know it without Bach, but it is clear that there would be no Bach without music as he knew it—very particularly the intricate geometry of the medieval canons and fugues he drew on for inspiration.

The parallel challenge for artists, who must confront the networks that provide their materials, shape the techniques they use to work on them, and underpin the institutions where they make a living, is to negotiate a relation to the system. Some artists reject, some embrace, and some ignore this situation. Perhaps disregarding the conditions that make artwork possible is the only honest way. Rejection would have to be premised on there being raw materials to use, but "raw data is an oxymoron,"[3] and the

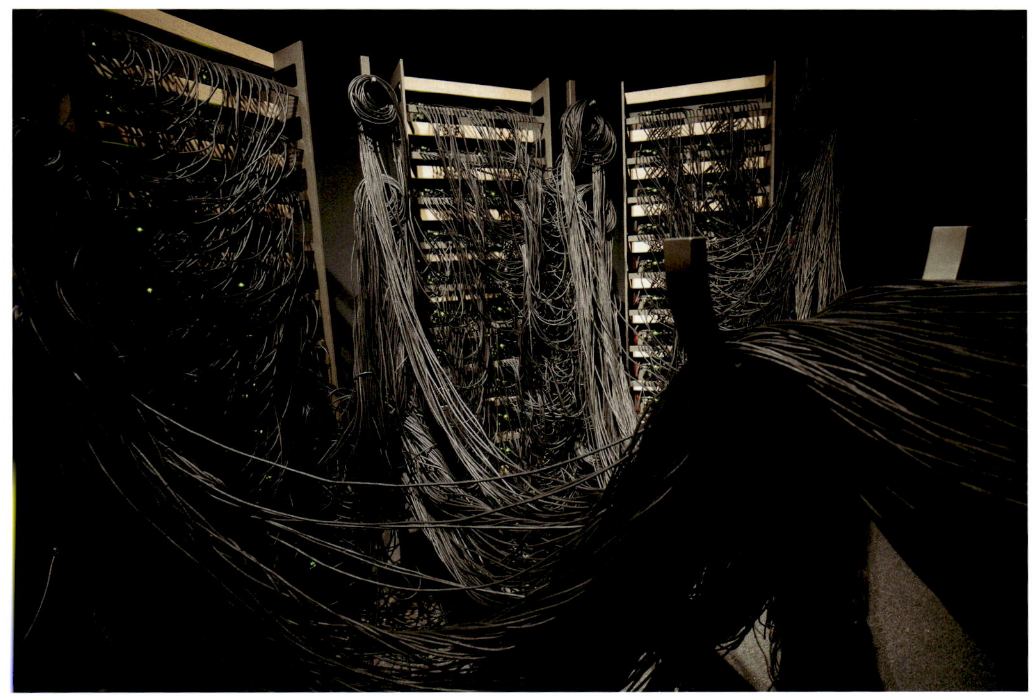

same is true of raw material. Materials are always already "cooked," or at least scrubbed, peeled, and sliced, not least in the artist's studio, and not just since the invention of tubes to hold ready-prepared paints. Someone had to mine the lapis, sail it to Renaissance Italy, and arrange for its sale before Michelangelo could grind it down and blend it with oil for the Virgin's robe. We do not expect Lozano-Hemmer to blow his own light bulbs, and we should expect that the custom software so often developed for his works stands on the shoulders of existing operating systems and coding practices. To embrace the network condition demands an understanding of such systems, of the labor of art, and of the circumstances that make an encounter between works and systems possible.

The encounter in Lozano-Hemmer's art unravels what it means to represent. Our dominant mode of representation is no longer pictures but statistics and diagrams. In *Pan-Anthem* (2014; see page 106), speakers playing national anthems are ordered according to statistical analyses of simple features, such as the year each country claimed independence, or more complex categories, like the Gini coefficient (the distribution of income levels across nations) or the Human Development Index (calculated from per capita income, life expectancy, and levels of education). The allocation of the speakers "represents" differences as being reducible to numbers. What does it mean to present a nation, or the relation between nations, on the basis of numbers? Does it matter how those numbers are converted into perceptible visualizations and sonifications? Since its emergence just over two hundred years ago, the visualization of data has become ubiquitous—in news reports, policy documents, and scientific papers—and highly standardized. Time's representation as a spatial dimension in clocks and calendars has become so pervasive that we no longer notice how deeply the harness has worn in. Lozano-Hemmer's works start from and dispute the normality of such visual and auditory regimes. The certainty and seriousness that data conveys become the material for a reconstruction of data that is as inventive, playful, and disorienting as Cubism was for perspective, and one that, in *Pan-Anthem*, can render relations between countries as harmonious or, more often, as dissonant and troubled.

Pulse Spiral (2008; see page 132) operates on the resistance of the self to a scientific imposition: the idea that the world is nothing but numbers and their relationships. An immense chandelier lights up and fades in sync with a participant's heart rate as they stand immediately below it. The Fermat spiral (defined by the equation $r2=a2\theta$) ordering the work's hanging lamps, like the Fibonacci sequence governing the seed heads of sunflowers, is pure geometry. The ancient realm of Platonic ideas has become the wholly contemporary belief that nature—and therefore human life—is organized by formulae. Fermat's formula hangs over the solo participant in *Pulse Spiral* like the sword of Damocles. Sociologist of science Bruno Latour says that reality "is what resists,"[4] but in data science (any science that relies on data), as in *Pulse Spiral*, what resists is the human being who finds herself at the focus of this ordered world. Of course the joyful animation of the lights makes you feel happy: the world responds to *me*. But there is, too, the awareness that what I illuminate is a structure that precedes everything that I am, logically and chronologically. The animating force is something I have little control over: my pulse, the passage of a life force beyond my will or knowledge. That animal spirit, this body operating below the threshold of consciousness, resists the formal organization of the spectacular chandelier the way Jackson Pollock's dripping defies the edges of his canvas.

In *Pulse Spiral*, as well as in *Volute 1: Au clair de la lune* (2016; see page 46) and *Vicious Circular Breathing* (2013; see page 78), pulse, breath, gestures, and eye movement—all signs of life—confront the technological apparatus, including its extended reach through supply chains and environmental imbrications, inseparable from the preordained and preordered natural world enumerated by science. The living body is both resistant to and a source of data, often overshadowed by the spectacular machinery the artist constructs, but it is a constant in Lozano-Hemmer's work, always there, always intrinsic to the work, always moving and acting, always somatic, but not necessarily consciously so. Our living bodies are no longer selves, but data subjects. Panofsky taught us how perspective placed the individual human, the universal singular "Man," at the center of the visual universe.[5] But what kind of spectator is constructed in the age of data visualization? Perspective had two vanishing points, one in the image and one in front of it. For Panofsky, it was clear which was the dominant: the one standing outside, for whom the pictured world was composed. Maps have a more one-sided aesthetic: you look down on the unfolded atlas with a god's-eye view. Data visualization is not as simple. A chart offers nowhere for the eye to rest, no central place on this side of the picture plane where it all makes sense. The only subject that can truly "see" what diagrams present is the machine behind them, the database itself. Pictures in perspective strive to re-present what a human observer might have seen; data visualizations strive to represent what a machine has sensed.

From the point of view of the databases that we interact with at every street crossing
and in every online encounter, we are not selves, not the complex, mortal mammals
we feel ourselves to be. Nor can we any longer identify with either the abstract gen-
dered Man, the rational One of the Enlightenment, nor even the collective knower of
Science. No longer autonomous individuals, nor actors deferring our seeing and know-
ing to collective or rational-yet-still-human abstractions, we have become behaviors.
The interface that interests Lozano-Hemmer is not the human-computer or graphic-
user interface. It is the interface between the social animal and the corporate cyborg;
between the sweating and emoting bodies and the calculations of a network intelligence harvesting and processing a world exclusively composed of data; between two
incompatible modes of representation—between the picture I have of myself and the
store of numbers I accumulate as I shop, travel, like, swipe, click, and tag.

One great difference between the artist's subjects and data is, quite simply, that the
sentient "I" breathes, where numbers do not. *Volute 1: Au clair de la lune,* which the
artist describes as "the world's first 3-D-printed speech bubble," portrays just such a
breath.[6] In the accompanying monitor, we can see a mouth exhaling as it speaks the
words of the title on a video loop, encoded through the MPEG video standard, con-
formed to the needs of mechanical storage and recall. The phrase *au clair de la lune*
derives from the oldest-known recording of a voice, which sings the line from the old
French song and was digitized after its rediscovery in 2008. Inventor Édouard-Léon
Scott de Martinville's 1860 phonautograph translated sound into a visual record;
Volute 1 rewrites the rescued audio in visual form through the 3-D print of the breath
of air that both the 1860 and 2008 versions exclude. The systems for transcribing from
the 150-year-old record and for playing it back are themselves bereft of the sense of
hearing and cannot know the aura of the speaking voice as we hear it in daily life
coming from the wet interior of the body, the most intimate of all expressions. Only in
this metal form mounted on the wall can we appreciate how subtle and ephemeral
our speaking is, and how precious it is to be able to hear the modulations of air we
perform so thoughtlessly, so innocently, so often.

A volute is a spiral form, like Fermat's parabolics. In *Volute 1,* the whorls of air dis-
turbed by speaking have been arrested in their tracks through laser tomography. In the
early twentieth century, Umberto Boccioni's futurist sculpture responded to the
emergence of cinema, which fuses a series of sequential images into a stilled summary
of action, as if instead of viewing the film frames one at a time, we looked at them all
at once in a backlit stack. The sculpture of action becomes a three-dimensional experience of time. Lozano-Hemmer's *Volute 1* responds similarly to the microsampling of
sound in digital recording, showing in the work's video component how a tomographic
sensor slices through the speaker's exhalation to build up a static volume in space, a
visible puff of air, the way 44.1 kHz sampling co-produces the illusory continuity of CD
playback. The word *volute* comes to us from the carved spirals on ancient monuments,
and was only later applied to mollusk shells, a rare instance of architectural ornament
preceding any natural source. It hangs in the space between the purity of ideas and
the spell of nature, between geometry and gesture. More like the grooves in shellac or

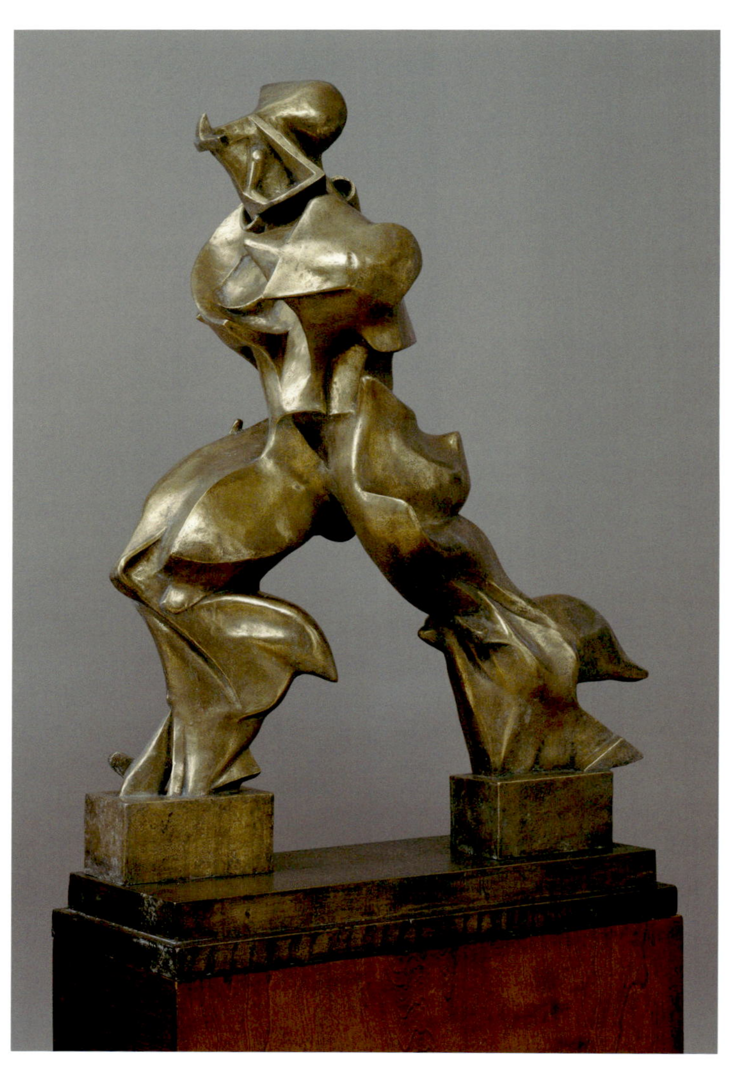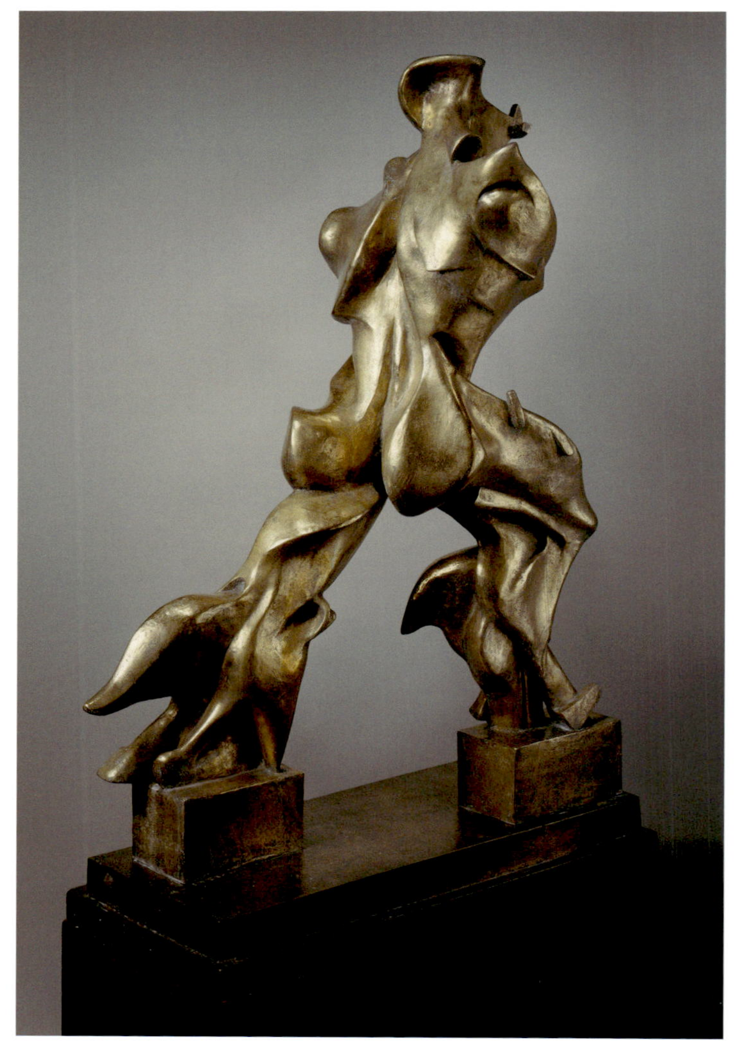

the spiral pitting of optical discs than the oriented magnetic particles of tape and hard drives, and most of all like Boccioni's *Unique Forms of Continuity in Space* (1913; figs. 14 and 15) a hundred years earlier, *Volute 1* is less concerned with the analog/digital divide than with the expression of sound in visual form. It is not a synesthetic experiment but an attempt to understand what sound is like for an intelligence that can audit nanoseconds but has no experience of time. This is what we "sound" like to a database—presented in a way only a human can contemplate.

Machines are finite, but humans are mortal. Every pulse, every breath struggles with entropy, where a machine only strives for stability. We are both ephemeral, but only machines can ignore that fact. The closed circulation of breath in *Vicious Circular Breathing* puts death in the room, requiring visitors to wager their lives on a device that threatens toxins and contagion. In this work, Lozano-Hemmer invites participants to enter a sealed glass booth and breathe the exhalations of their predecessors. Bellows as big as the ones on cathedral organs and sixty-one suspended brown paper bags fill and empty rhythmically across the gallery, imitating the lungs that participants contribute as components. Like Bach's baroque organ, *Vicious Circular Breathing* is a macro-scale reinvention of breathing, with its opening and closing door seals, pumps sucking in and pushing out, and inflating and deflating paper bags. All the machinery of song is here without the *vox humana*, reduced to the rhythm of resting respiration and the rustles and wheezing of indifferently mechanical or organic valves, the paper lungs crinkling and crackling, and stripping music of everything but the monotony of mechanical stability and mere timbre. The initial given of this fugue is breathing itself, and its permutations the breath's amplification as bellows and diminution as bags. Implicit and silent is the final reversal, the substrate of speech, deprived of the participants' words, which we outside observers cannot hear once they enter the apparatus.

It's already clear in *Vicious Circular Breathing* not only that there is no singular subject Man, but equally that humans have never lived solitary lives. Even the air we breathe is recycled, through humans, animals, plants, and ecosystems. Nonetheless, we insist on believing that we are distinct, and that we breathe *fresh* air. To which responds the maximalist environment of *Zoom Pavilion* (2015, with Krzysztof Wodiczko; see page 98), a four- or five-meter high room whose walls display a disorienting, immersive environment of magnified grayscale projections from surveillance cameras trained on the exhibition space, described in François LeTourneux's essay in this catalogue. *Zoom Pavilion*'s quasi-autonomous intelligence, constantly tracking faces and generating possible relations between them, trying and failing to understand, mirrors our human failure to apprehend the interactions between the people, places, and technologies that shape and link any social space. Thinking occurs *between*—in the fluster of language, or in *Zoom Pavilion*, in the constant evolution of an intelligence that cannot be pinned down to a single mind—or even to humanity—as abstraction, collective or aggregate. *Zoom Pavilion*'s failures of recognition teach us how to hear *Vicious Circular Breathing*. In its postmusical soundings we can hear the fugue returning, created in the mutual remediation of apparatus and participants, but

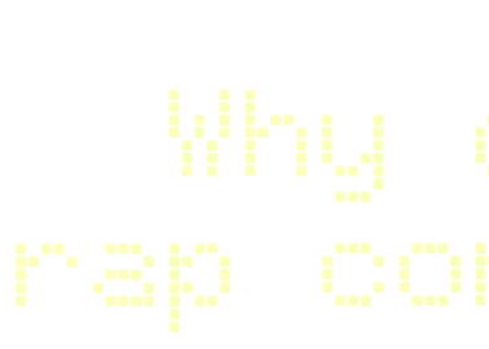

Figures 14 and 15
Umberto Boccioni, *Unique Forms of Continuity in Space*, 1913, cast 1950
Bronze
47 ¾ × 35 × 15 ¾ in. (121.3 × 88.9 × 40 cm)
Metropolitan Museum of Art, New York, bequest of Lydia Winston Malbin, 1989

this time as cacophony. And yet, just as dirt is "matter in the wrong place,"[7] cacophony is only sonic material that has not yet found its listener, still waiting to be born out of the interplay of ecology, technology, and the social forms of human life.

Lozano-Hemmer constantly toys with the human exception—its possibility, its frailty, and its transitions. This exception is a theme played in various voices, amplified, multiplied, reversed, stripped back and dispersed, and collated and articulated, in the end, with what is least human. The human element, whether the lone operator of *Pulse Spiral* or the projected crowd of *Zoom Pavilion*, is exceptional only if it is excepted from a context—in all of these pieces, all technological contexts, wherever language appears as symbol or seclusion that is technically mediated, where technologies participate in making the exception exceptional. Only in such mediations does anything like the social appear. Only on condition of technical mediation can we become human, in all the incomplete and therefore desiring forms we take as participants in Lozano-Hemmer's worlds. The failure of our autonomy is evidence of the autonomy of art, which even at the moment of its farthest escape from the human into the pure mathematics of the fugue, is grounded in the mutual dependence of humans and technologies. Each piece, and in their ensemble every piece, contributes statement and counterstatement, inversion and reversal, elaborating the endless choreography of freedom and dependence. It is up to the work of art—and the art of the fugue—to orchestrate the encounter of these forces, which are ontologically indistinguishable and sociologically irreconcilable. The second canto of Vicente Huidobro's *Altazor*, cited in the installation *Cardinal Directions* (2010; see page 150), ends with the line, "The stones knocking speak to you for me."[8] Like Huidobro's knocking stones, the clatter of equipment in the exhibition *Rafael Lozano-Hemmer: Unstable Presence* links us in dialogue, re-presents us to one another, and becomes partner in a conversation that continues long after its participants have left. To listen to the exhibition is to discover a history of the fugue that is in the process of becoming a critique of systems thinking and is building toward the invention of new systems. These sonic systems, even in silence, even in cacophony, resound and re-sound in the vast atmospheric, social, and technical cathedrals of our time. The designs, controls, and conviviality the artist has made possible are fugal pre-echoes of a human-natural-technical harmony we sense now as dissonance, but dissonance that is brimming with the utopian promise of resonance. Like Bach's forever-immanent paradise, even in the darkest hours of Western modernity, Lozano-Hemmer's work makes graceful and sensual the flux of matter in time.

Epigraph: Vicente Huidobro, *Altazor* (Santiago: Universidad de Chile / Biblioteca Virtual Universal, 2003), Canto II, line 23, https://www.biblioteca.org.ar/libros/8851.pdf. The artist's translation of Huidobro's poem (quoted here) appears in Rafael Lozano-Hemmer's work *Cardinal Directions* (2010; see page 150).

1. "In the chorale and fugue [of the Middle Ages], in the architectural staidness and in the spirit of the medieval *summa*, in these eminently ordered constellations, there are the attitude and the composure, the equanimity and the crystal clarity, there is the intended architectural style of an eternity. . . . Naturally there was still a pure reflection of class society that existed in these hierarchical works. As it passed away, so did the works—the Bach fugue was its last expression in Europe." Ernst Bloch, "Ideas as Transformed Material in Human Minds, or Problems of an Ideological Superstructure (Cultural Heritage) (1972)," in *The Utopian Function of Art and Literature: Selected Essays*, trans. Jack Zipes and Frank Mecklenburg (Cambridge, MA: MIT Press, 1988), 54.

2. Extracting Bach from the religious tradition, Bloch notes that, like Mozart and Beethoven, Bach benefits from the lack of a founding hypothesis of medieval sacred music: "This is the best for which the harmony of the spheres did serve and could serve: it wrested music from the mere inner light. . . . [F]rom the Gregorian chant onwards, music is applied to the tendency to moral order and to a harmony which sounds up—even without the myth of the spheres and the stars. Music therefore, historically and objectively, proves itself to be essentially Christian art, its harmony of the spheres breaks down and at the same time reveals itself: towards the wellspring sound of as yet unachieved selfshaping in the world." Ernst Bloch, *The Principle of Hope*, vol. 3, trans. Neville Plaice, Stephen Plaice, and Paul Knight (Cambridge, MA: MIT Press, 1986), 1,079–80

3. Lisa Gitelman, ed., *"Raw Data" Is an Oxymoron* (Cambridge, MA: MIT Press, 2013).

4. Bruno Latour, *Science in Action: How to Follow Scientists and Engineers through Society* (Cambridge, MA: Harvard University Press, 1987).

5. Erwin Panofsky, *Perspective as Symbolic Form*, trans. Christopher S. Wood (New York: Zone Books, 1991 [1924–25]).

6. Rafael Lozano-Hemmer, "Volute 1: Au clair de la lune," http://www.lozano-hemmer.com/volute_1_au_clair_de_la_lune.php, accessed May 10, 2019.

7. Mary Douglas, *Purity and Danger: An Analysis of Concepts of Pollution and Taboo* (London: Routledge, 1966).

8. "*Te hablan por mi las piedras aporreadas*." Huidobro, *Altazor*, Canto II, line 27.

VOICE ARRAY 2011

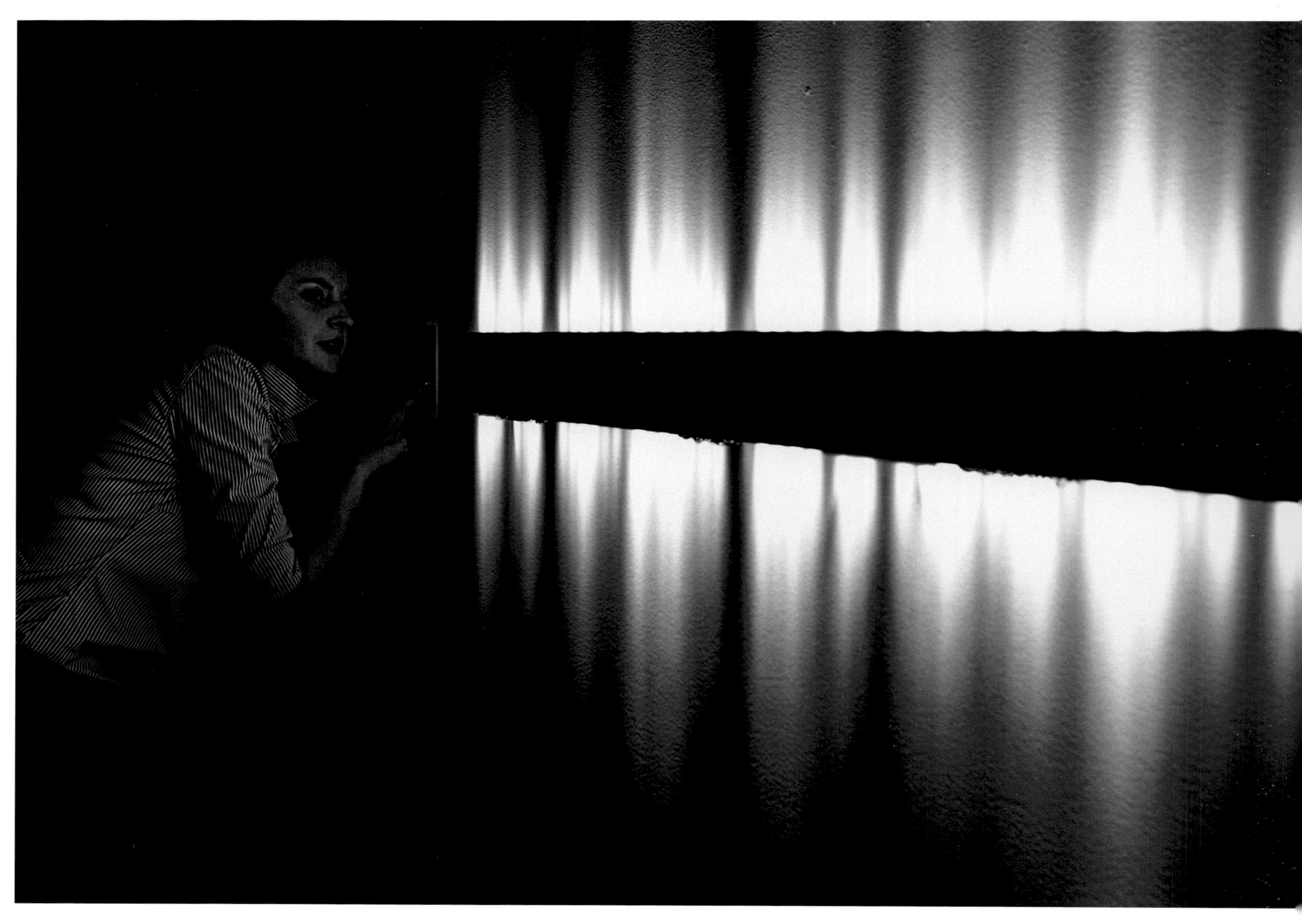

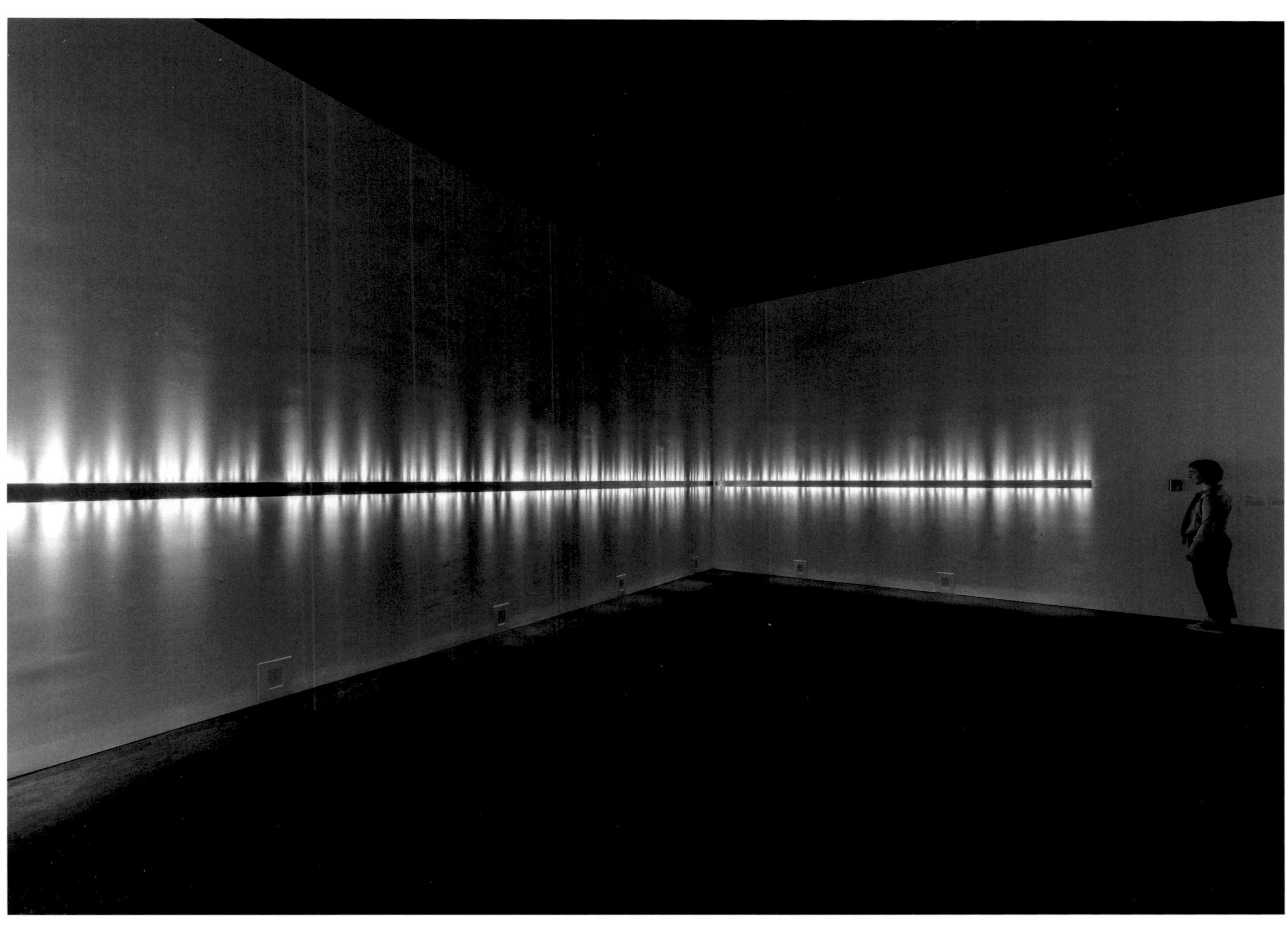

Installation views, Museum of Contemporary Art, Sydney, 2011 (left), and Musée d'a t contemporain de Montréal, 2018 (right)

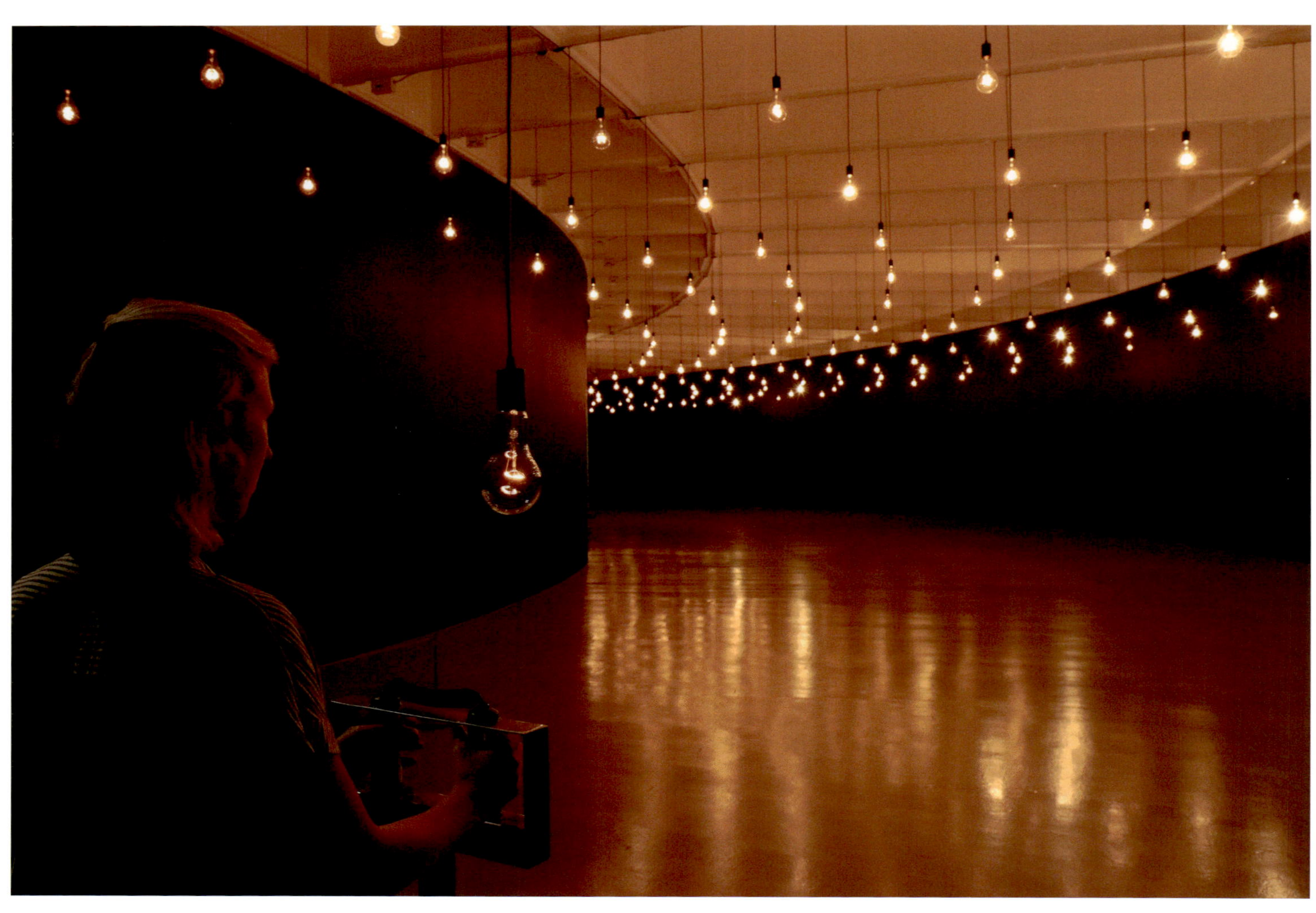

MERETE CARLSON AND ULRIK SCHMIDT

PULSE ON PULSE: MODULATION AND SIGNIFICATION

Rafael Lozano-Hemmer's *Pulse Room* (2006; opposite) is a large-scale installation featuring one hundred clear incandescent light bulbs suspended from the ceiling in a regular, grid-based structure. Each bulb flashes in an individual, repetitive rhythm. Together the bulbs compose a coherent event characterized by the tension between the grid-based order of the bulbs and the dazzling chaos of light generated by their random, nonsynchronized pulsations. *Pulse Room* presents a total spatio-temporal event under continuous variation, a pulsing "room" of light surrounding the visitor. In a dark corner of the gallery, however, one bulb stands out from the grid. It is suspended lower than the others (about 67 inches off the ground) and positioned in front of a metal sculpture-interface with two handles. When the visitor grips the two handles, the pulse is detected by a computer and sets off the single bulb in front of the interface.

This overall structure affects viewers' sense of space and time. Of greatest significance is the difference between visitors' experiences when positioned near the sculpture-interface in the dark corner of the room, and when situated in the flickering field. At the most basic level, the sculpture-interface experience is characterized by a subject–object relation to the static sculpture, with its firm handles and single bulb, isolated from the rest of the grid and synchronized to the visitor's own heartbeat, potentially producing a sense of localization in the room. In the total field of flickering light, however, th s sense of local subject–object relation will most likely dissolve into an ambient sense of the entire installation as a flickering surround. The spatial experience in *Pulse Room* is intricate, marked as it is by this tension between a relational subject-object interaction with the sculpture-interface and an ambient sensation of the work as a whole.

Pulse Room, 2006
Incandescent light bulbs, voltage controllers, heart rate sensors, computer, metal stand, speakers, and custom software written in Delphi
Dimensions variable
Collection of the Musée d'art contemporain de Montréal
Installation view, *Rafael Lozano-Hemmer: Pulse*, Hirshhorn Museum and Sculpture Garden, Washington, D.C., 2018

On the one hand, *Pulse Room* produces a chaotic light environment of pure, energetic modulation. At the same time, *Pulse Room* is strongly imbued with symbolic meaning. When biorhythms are transmitted from the energy of a visitor's beating heart to the flashing of the singular light bulb, it gives the individual a clear and unmistakable impression of being represented, directly and in real time, in the flickering display. This link between the body as living organism and the organic light patterns formed by the flashing bulbs further charges the installation with unambiguous metaphysical connotations. Apart from the a-signifying, modulatory repetition on a material level, the pulse in *Pulse Room* is articulated through a double representation: a subjective signification—with each light bulb representing an individual life—and through a symbolic reference to humanity in general, where the pulsations as a whole represent a fundamental rhythm of life. Thus, the visitors in *Pulse Room* are invited to take part in a complex event that continuously resonates between different layers of modulatory and signifying repetitions. At the same time, *Pulse Room* is profoundly subjectified as both a sign of life and a machinic generator of its own space-time.

The most evident symbolic meaning is associated with the singular sculpture-interface in the dark corner of *Pulse Room*. The visitor's relation to the work from this particular position begins as an encounter with the sculpture as physical structure (object), but evolves into a complex subject-interface situation, in which the visitor animates the light bulb and faces a visual representation of their pulse. This representation is heavily loaded with symbolic meaning: what you see in front of you is a copy of your own pulsing heart.

The relation established in the visitor's encounter with the sculpture is not itself temporally structured, but merely launches the registration process as an open interval in time, an empty moment, an experience of waiting for something (else) to happen. But as soon as the singular bulb in front of the visitor starts to pulse with light and the sculpture becomes an interface, a distinct and specific temporality is constituted. At this point, the visitor has a significant sense of having impact: your presence matters, you affect the room. A rhythmic structure, originally present latently in the body, has now started to resonate in the medium. The real-time effect produced here is thus relative, derived from and essentially defined by the physical presence of the visitor. The experience in front of the flashing "mirror bulb" is an experience not only of proximity (space) but also of simultaneity (time) between the visitor and their immediate surroundings, which intimately anchors the viewer in a local, particular time-space. *Now/here*, something is added to the piece, and the visitor enters the circuit, thereby articulating the situation as a specific place and a particular moment.

When a visitor releases the handles and triggers a transitory darkness, the subjective quality of the situation weakens, and another experience of time and space is initiated, one defined by a less subjectified and less organized time-space associated with the all-encompassing field of flickering light. The dominant effect of being situated in this environment is no longer that of signification or symbolic representation. It is a concrete, nonanthropomorphic sensation of the electronic medium in its fundamental appearance as energetic material pulsing in space and time. The complex modulation taking place here is an open process without beginning, climax, or end to define the formal structure of the actions and movements in the medium. It is fundamentally decentered, flowing, vibrating, and pulsing with no determinable cause—or by becoming its own cause (self-generation, emergence).

Hence, on the one hand, *Pulse Room* translates and transforms symbolic energy from a local situation to a broader one. On the other hand, the work as a whole produces its own energy as a continuous modulation of the real. This difference between signifying, symbolic aspects and a-signifying modulation persists as a fundamental tension during the visit to the work. The defining characteristic of *Pulse Room* is thus neither its profound symbolism nor its sensuous nonrepresentational ambience but the continuous interlacing and layering of the two into an ambiguous, multifaceted aesthetic situation: a pulse-on-pulse experience.

NOTE

Rafael Lozano-Hemmer's *Pulse* series, which started with *Pulse Room* (2006), generated multiple variations including *Pulse Spiral* (2008; see page 132), featured in this exhibition. Other works in the series are *Pulse Front* (2007), *Pulse Park* (2008), *Pulse Tank* (2008), *Pulse Index* (2010), and *Pulse Corniche* (2015; see fig. 4, page 27), some of them also belonging to the artist's series *Relational Architecture*. A version of this text, which examines *Pulse Room* specifically but offers insights that illuminate the entire series, was originally published as part of a longer essay: Merete Carlson and Ulrik Schmidt, "Pulse on Pulse: Modulation and Signification in Rafael Lozano-Hemmer's *Pulse Room*," *Journal of Aesthetics and Culture* 4, no. 1 (2012), DOI: 10.3402/jac v4io.18152.

PULSE SPIRAL ²⁰⁰⁸

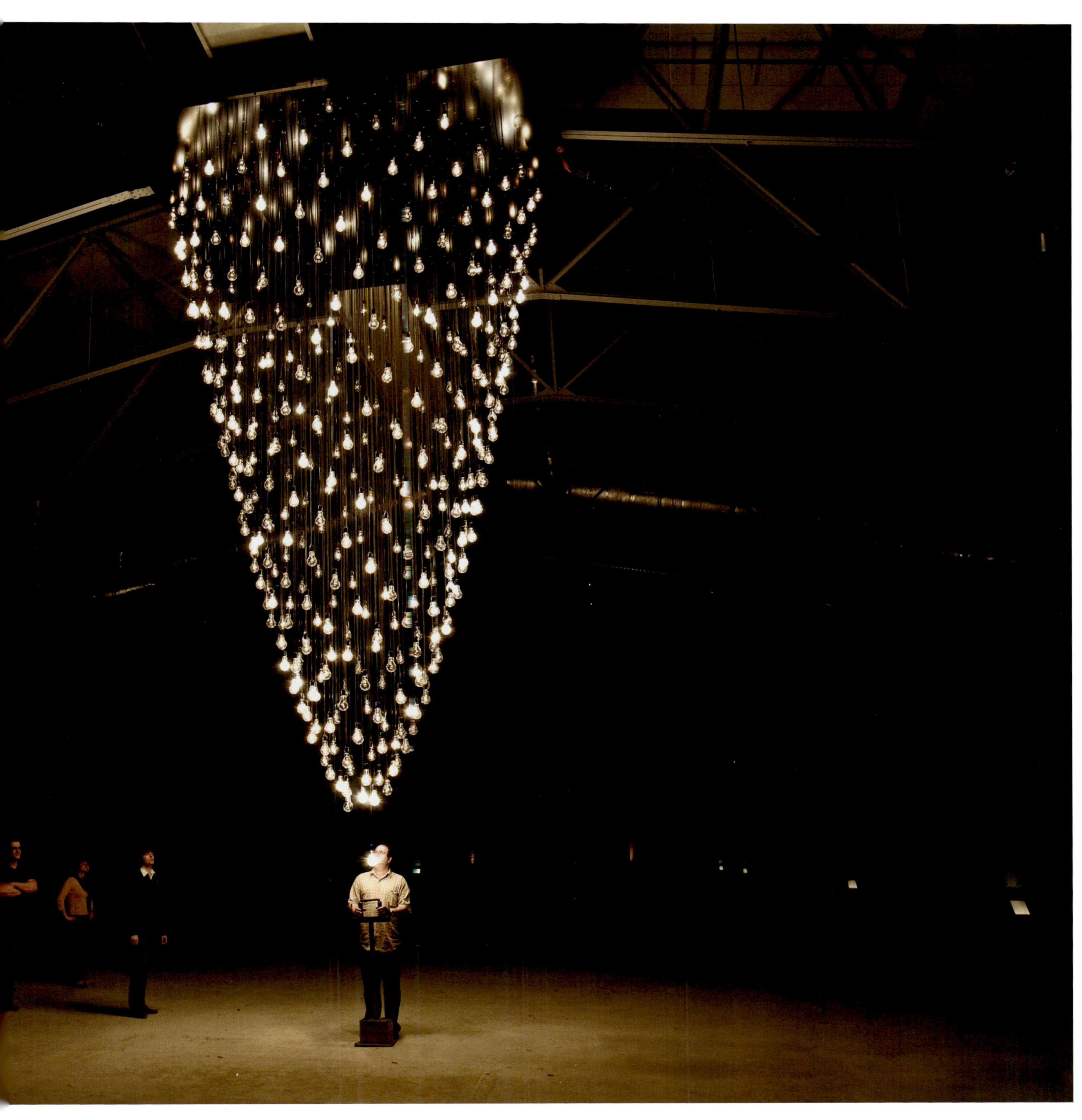

Installation view, Garage Center for Contemporary Culture (now Garage Museum of Contemporary Art), Moscow, 2008

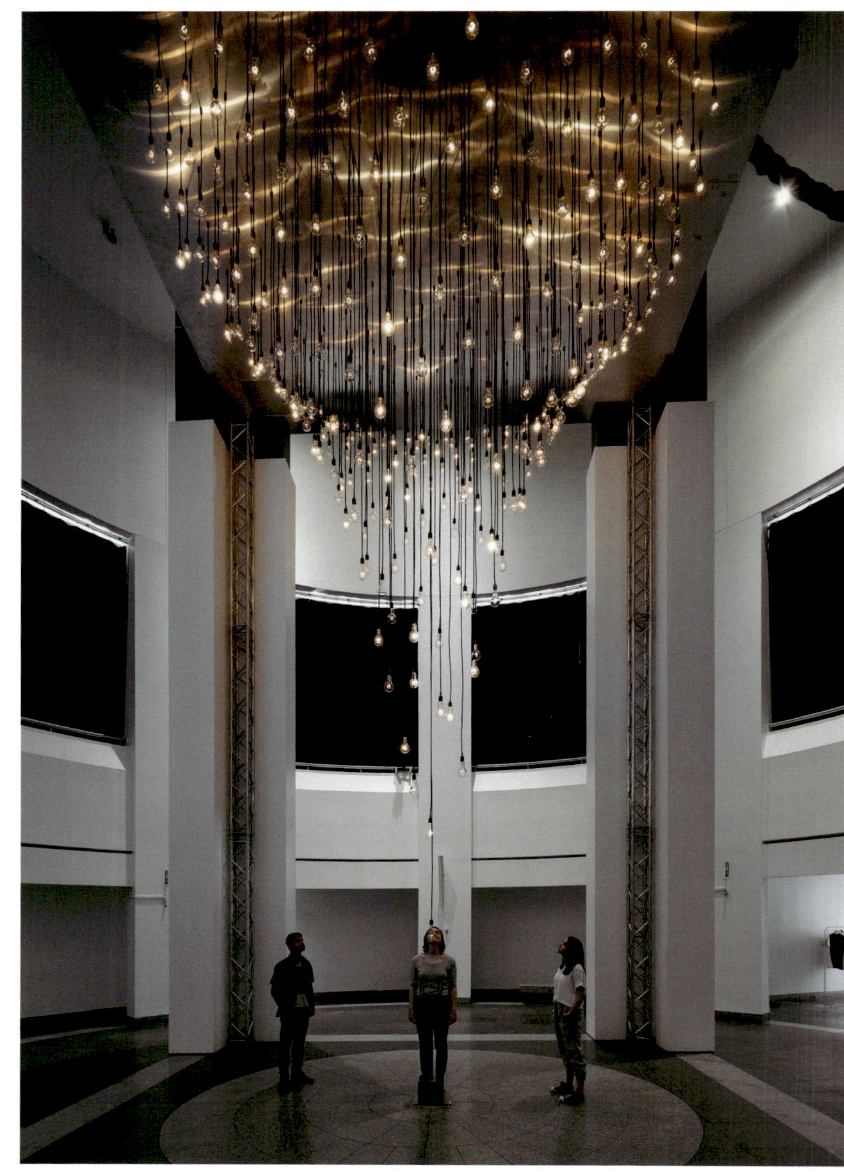

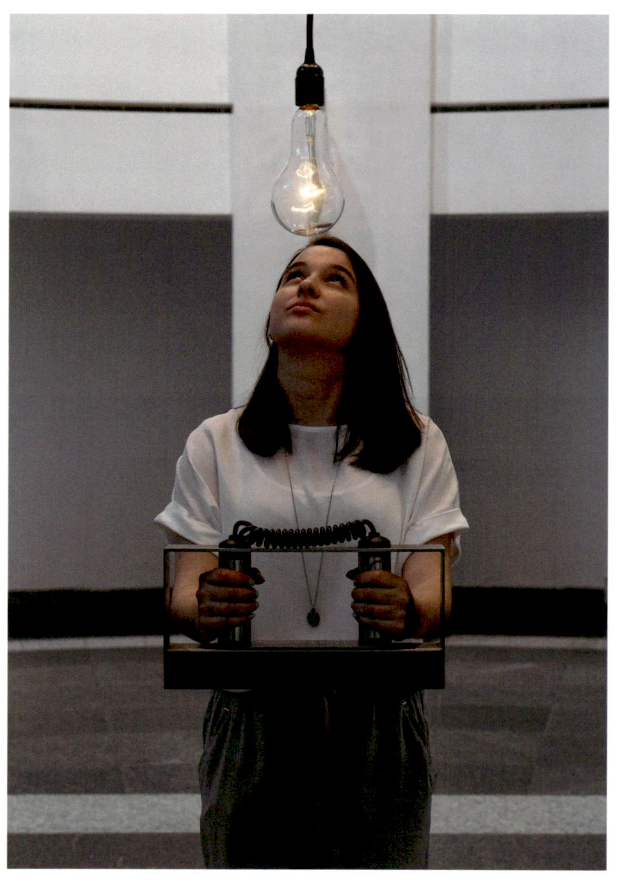

Installation views, Musée d'art contemporain de Montréal, 2018

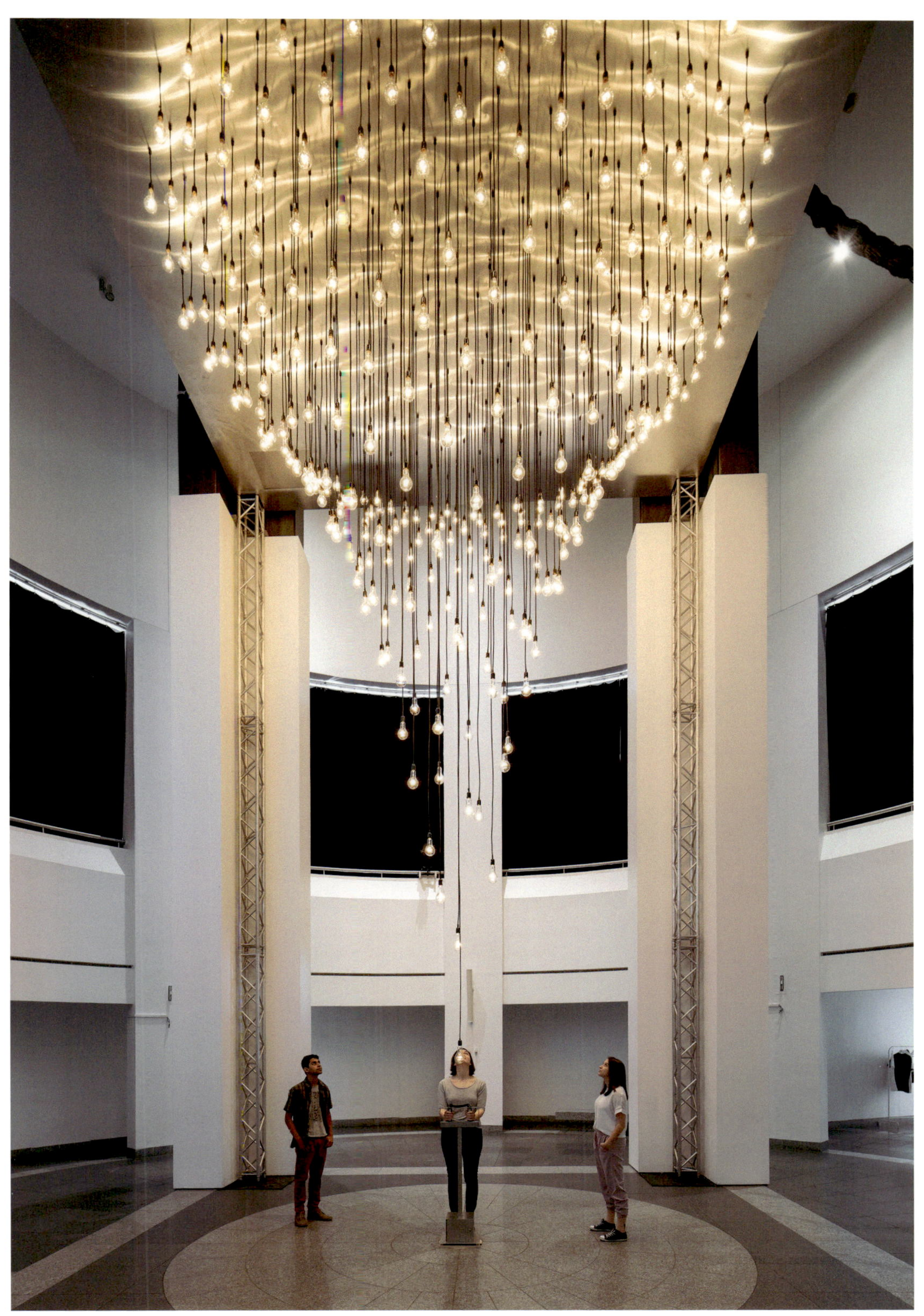

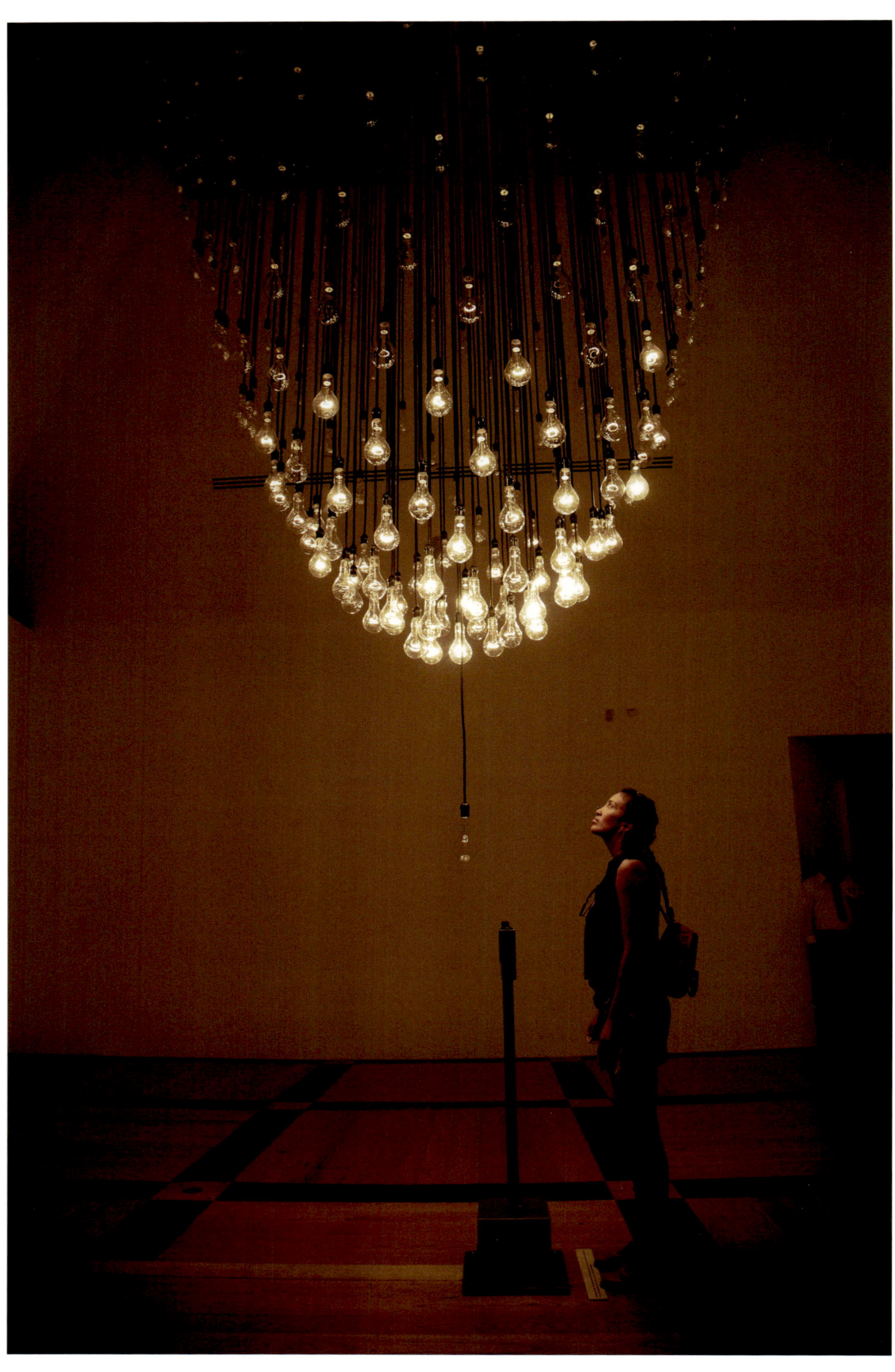

Installation views, Museo de Arte Contemporáneo de Monterrey, Mexico, 2019 (left), and Musée d'art contemporain de Montréal, 2018 (right)

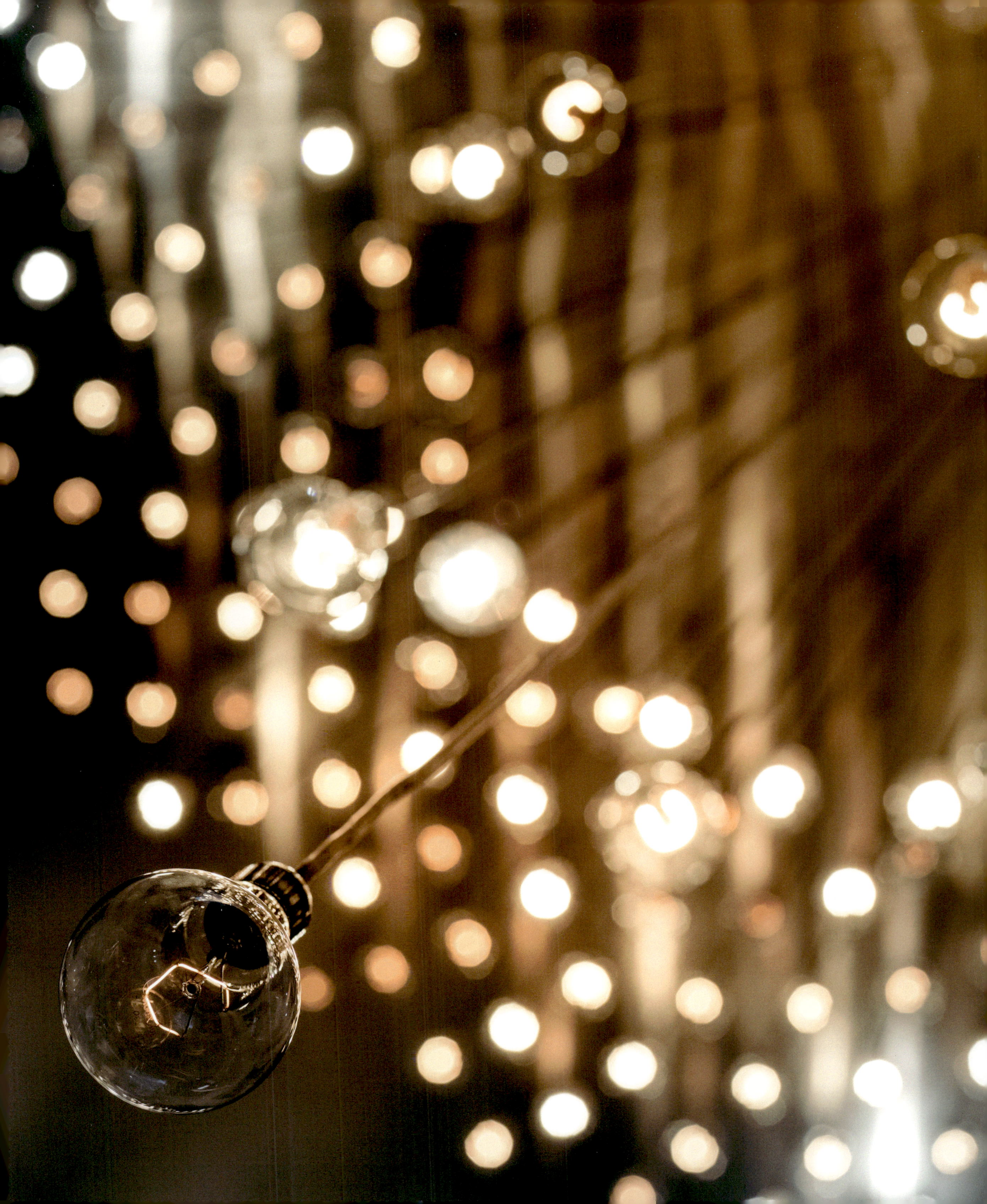

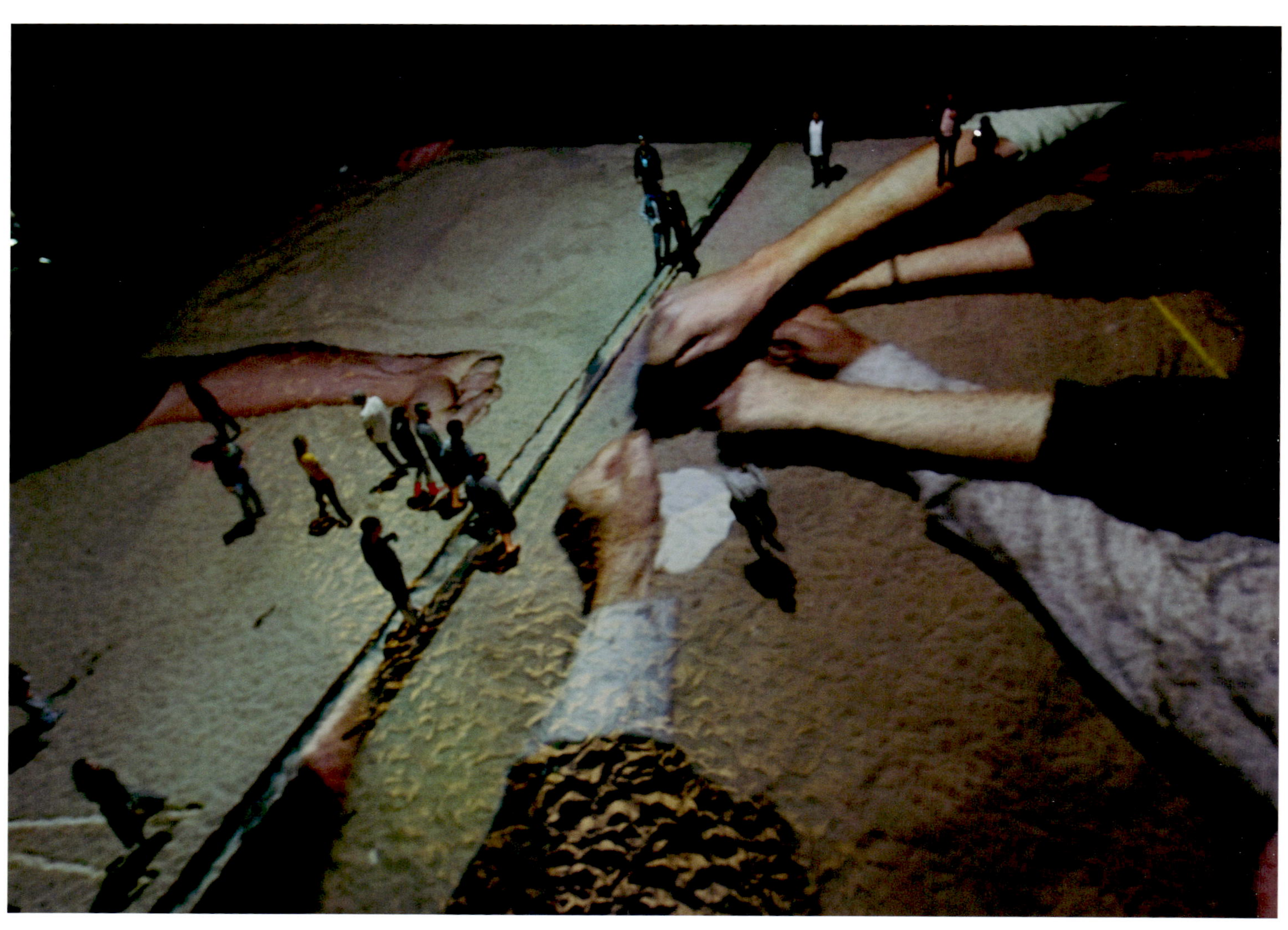

OLIVIER ASSELIN
TRANSLATED BY DONALD MCGRATH

SLOW MIRRORS AND BROKEN ECHOES: COMMUNITY IN LOZANO-HEMMER'S WORK

Most of Rafael Lozano-Hemmer's works can be considered portraits. With some, this is readily apparent: each work in the *Sphere Packing* series (2013–18; see page 110) is a "portrait" of a composer; *Pan-Anthem* (2014; see page 106) gives us an image of a nation and of the society of nations; and *Population Theater* (2016) visualizes the entire global population. But the artist's "portraits" generally do not represent absent people; rather, they show people present before the image. Since they are largely automated, these images may seem to have been produced by surveillance systems, but because they are also generally interactive, they give viewers a measure of control over their own images. Those being watched are aware of it—the apparatus is shown— and they are free to subject themselves to surveillance or to opt out; they can play with their image. Thus whatever has been written about them, these works are less about monitoring than they are about selfies, and group selfies at that.

SELFIES

Pulse Spiral (2008; see page 132), for example, combines a large chandelier and a heart rate sensor. When the viewer grips a set of handles, the chandelier bulbs switch on and off to the rhythm of his or her heartbeat, which is amplified over a sound system. *Voice Array* (2011; see page 126) connects an intercom, loudspeakers, and a set of lights lined up along the gallery wall. The viewer is invited to leave a voice message via the intercom—it can be in words or just sounds. The speaker's voice is converted into light flashes and a unique blinking pattern that is stored as a loop, circling through the array of lights. Then all the lights come on, one after another, to the

Sandbox, 2010
Infrared surveillance cameras, infrared illuminators, computers, DV cameras, video projection, sandboxes, *milagritos* (religious charms), and plastic rakes
Projection: 7,965 sq. ft. (740 sq. m); sandboxes, each: approx. 27 ⅛ × 36 ¼ in. (69 × 92 cm)
Installation view, *Glow*, Santa Monica, California, 2010

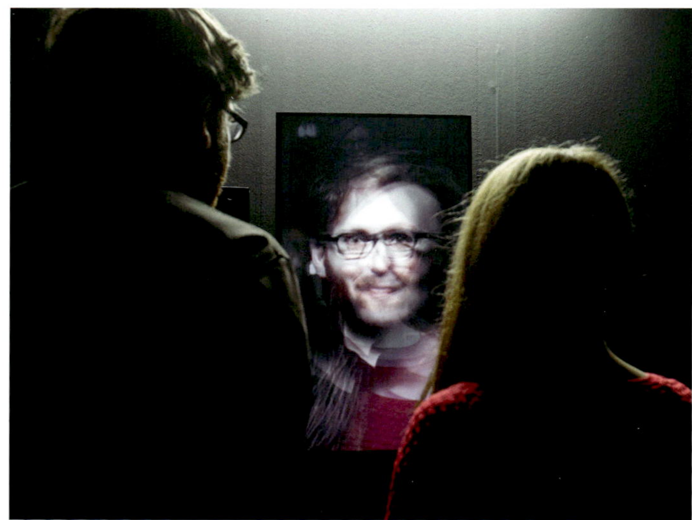

sound of other messages left by previous visitors. The room is filled with out-of-sync lights and cacophonous sounds that present a Babel-like image of all the visitors.

Vicious Circular Breathing (2013; see page 78) is a kind of artificial respirator, an enormous machine with motorized bellows that circulates air between a hermetically sealed glass chamber and sixty-one brown bags that inflate and empty like paper lungs. Visitors are invited to enter the chamber, sit down, and breathe the air for a moment—particularly the accumulated exhalations of previous participants (breathing in the remaining oxygen, breathing out carbon dioxide). With its discreet allusion to Marina Abramović and Ulay's celebrated performance *Breathing In / Breathing Out* (1977), Lozano-Hemmer's closed-circuit piece suggests allegory, but what it shows us is not so much the dependency in amorous relationships as ecological interdependency—as in a small-scale replica of the terrestrial ecosystem. Yet it remains, ultimately, a (chemical) portrait of viewers, as individuals and as a group.

Redundant Assembly (2015; fig. 16) and *Bilateral Time Slicer* (2016; fig. 17) function as mirrors that have been complicated by technology. In both pieces, cameras capture pictures of viewers, software analyzes these images and processes them in real time, and a large screen displays them instantly. In *Redundant Assembly*, which involves six cameras, the screen presents a composite image of the viewer's face seen from different angles. When two viewers appear before the "mirror" at the same time, the resulting image is a synthesis of their faces. In another version of the work, the image merges the face that is currently there and the face that appeared previously, which introduces a temporal dimension into the apparatus. In *Bilateral Time Slicer*, an image of the viewer is relayed live in a vertical strip at the center of a screen. But it is soon bisected along the axis of symmetry of the face and body, and archived on either side of the central band. A new live image then appears in the central band and is soon archived like its predecessor, and so on. The screen is quickly transformed into a

Figure 16
Redundant Assembly, 2015
Screen, computer, HD digital cameras, and custom software written in openFrameworks
Screen: 29 ½ × 25 ⅝ × 5 ⅞ in. (75 × 65 × 15 cm); computer: 6 ¾ × 6 ¾ × 9 ⅞ in. (17 × 17 × 25 cm)
Installation view, *Rafael Lozano-Hemmer: Preabsence*, Haus der elektronischen Künste Basel, Switzerland, 2016

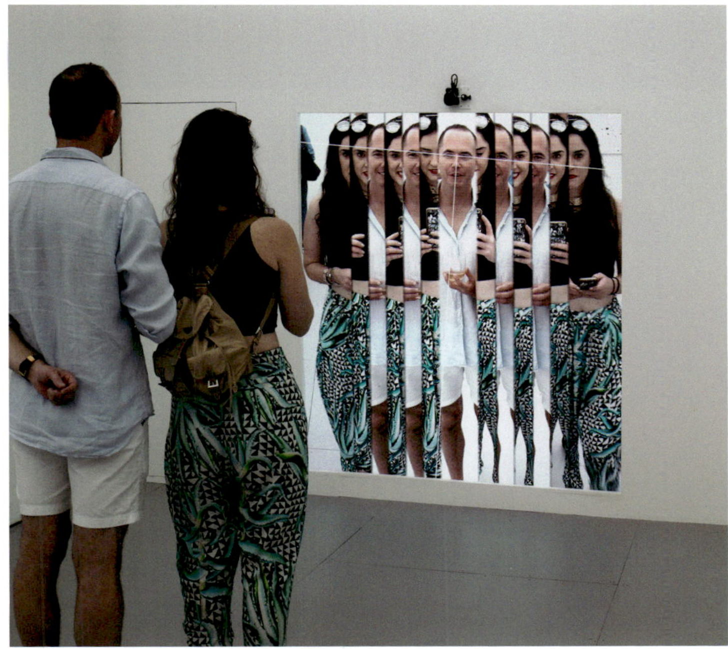

structure of laminated time slices that go from present to past and from center to periphery. When the next visitor stands before the camera, the mirror reflects not only an individual but an entire group.

MIRRORS

Many of Lozano-Hemmer's works privilege instant interactivity and feedback—on the model of light, shadows on a wall, and reflections in a mirror. They retain mainly visitors' physical characteristics: appearance, light, voices, movements, pulse, breath, and various other "biometric" measures.

Although these works employ digital technologies, they nonetheless privilege more traditional modes of representation: the icon (the resemblance or analogy between the sign and its referent) and the index (physical continuity, proximity, or contact between the sign and its referent). While the works generally involve programs that encode and decode data, converting it into digits and processing it by means of elaborate algorithms, this processing favors analogical relationships between light and sound, motion and sound, air and 3-D forms, etc. The data-collection process, for its part, privileges indexical relationships using optical, mechanical, chemical, electrical, and other types of sensors.

This live image surely contributes to the pleasure we experience when encountering Lozano-Hemmer's works. It reactivates the so-called "mirror stage," reconnecting us with the jubilation that children feel when playing with their reflections and controlling the image of bodies that they do not yet have complete control over physically. The works replay the moment when the self is first constituted, when the subject identifies with its likeness and opens itself up to the Other's gaze. But at the same time, even if they evoke what lies beyond the image—and the imaginary—these works

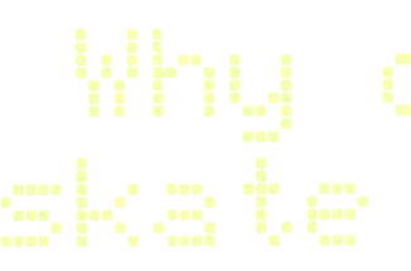

Figure 17
Bilateral Time Slicer, 2016
Custom software, 4K camera with digitizer, computer, and projector
Dimensions variable
Installation view, bitforms gallery, New York, at Untitled Art Fair, Miami Beach, 2016

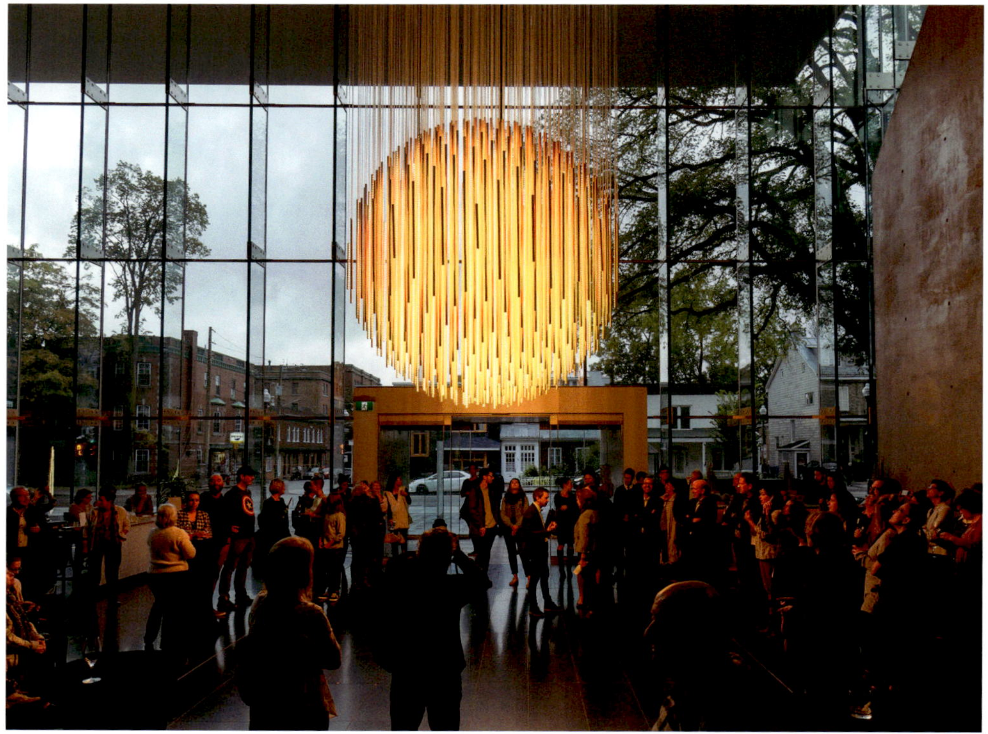

may seem to stop short of language—and the symbolic—even when words do appear: they remain on the threshold of signification, playing along the borders between matter, form, and sign; between air, noise, and speech; and between smoke, light, traces, and writing. To be convinced of this, we need only observe viewers of all ages interacting with the subtitles that are projected onto their bodies in *Subtitled Public* (2005; see page 148), or with their shadows, which dissolve the texts in *Airborne Newscast* (2013; see page 90).

NATURE

Lozano-Hemmer's "mirrors" often present the subjects they reflect and constitute (both individual and collective) as a localized and synchronous co-presence, in one and the same space and time, like a body and community of bodies, and sometimes even like an organism inscribed within the system of nature.

Pulse Corniche (2015; see fig. 4, page 27), for instance, uses ten automated projectors to cast light rays into the night sky. The intensity and direction of the rays vary in accordance with the viewers' heartbeats. This work evokes the childlike delight of projecting a private image of oneself onto the monumental scale of the public square and, indeed, of the entire city. It also has a social dimension, harmonizing the heartbeats of multiple viewers sharing a common space in order to form a community of bodies.

The artist's large-scale solar pieces inscribe this community of bodies within a broader ecosystem, existing on a galactic scale. *Volumetric Solar Equation* (2018; fig. 18) is an enormous chandelier consisting of 25,000 LED lights that simulate solar activity in almost real time, using algorithms and data provided by NASA. The work offers

Figure 18
Volumetric Solar Equation, 2018
LED batten lights, aluminum, wood, computer, custom software written in openFrameworks, and D3 programming
118 ⅛ in. (300 cm) diameter
Installation view, *Rafael Lozano-Hemmer: Solar Equation*, Musée national des beaux-arts du Québec, 2018

minimal interactivity: viewers can choose between various seasons in a solar cycle and select the type of behavior to be displayed. The work thus relates solar activity and a community of viewers, not only as if they were analogous—two complex systems—but as if they were physically connected within a single, interdependent, natural system.

AGORA AND DIASPORA

Configurations that use technology to link community, event, and locality should be understood within the broader context of recent transformations in the "media land-scape," and especially how mass media and the internet have reconfigured the public sphere.

Historically, the simultaneous presence of a number of people in the same time and place represented a constitutive condition of the public sphere. Of course, not all gatherings form a community or a public sphere apart from the number of individuals and the amount of time they are together, real community depends on how the group is structured and its members' awareness of sharing common goals, their relation-ships within the group, their actions, and the effects of these actions. The public sphere is intimately bound up with the opening up of the public square, a shared physical space in which people come together to meet and exchange ideas. Such were the Greek agora and the Roman forum. While the public square often presents top-down communication and control imposed by religious, political, or economic authori-ties, in certain circumstances, it becomes a forum for discussion, debate, and critique, a place where decisions are contested and alternatives proposed.

In the eighteenth century, the public sphere emerged from physical spaces—the literary salons and cafés, painting and sculpture salons, and theaters—and extended well beyond these into the media, epistolary relationships, and the political press. Interlocutors no longer needed to be present in the same time and space, as an as-sembly; it was enough, rather, for interrelationships to exist within a delocalized and desynchronized network of communication.

GLOBAL LIVE AUDIENCES

In the nineteenth and twentieth centuries, the mass media (wide-circulation daily newspapers and, especially, electronic media like radio and television that transmitted signals live and on a massive scale over broad areas) constituted a vast public sphere focused on current events, as well as a populous and widespread community that was delocalized but synchronized. In theory, electronic media favor two-way communica-tion. But in practice, they were soon transformed into a network of hierarchical, one-way communication constructed on the broadcast model.

The development of the Internet also led to a radical reconfiguration of the public sphere. In theory (because its software and hardware architectures are lattice-like, multinodal, and multidirectional, and because its transmission is instantaneous) the Internet fosters not only a delocalized and synchronized community but also an open, nonhierarchical public sphere that is egalitarian and accessible to all. But in practice, the Web is subject to the contrary forces of privatization and economic concentration, to audience segmentation, polarization, and "balkanization" (due to the combined effect of users, influencers, hackers, and algorithms) that have made it into a one-way means of communication, an instrument of influence, propaganda, surveillance, and control.

WEB LOCALITIES

The development of mass media and the Internet, media-based public spaces, and global communities may seem to make physical public spaces and local communities obsolete, as if the intangible world of the Internet had transformed the material world into an "Outernet"—a mere repository for infrastructures and bodies. But, paradoxically, new interest in collective experience is developing, in physical events and places, in synchronized and localized assemblies—like concerts, spontaneous commemorations, and political occupations of actual public squares.

The next phase of the digital revolution would turn this dialectic up a notch. With mobile platforms and giant stationary screens—all connected—new relationships have been established between the city and the Web, between objects in the world and databases, between physical communities (those of neighborhoods, public squares, and halls) and virtual communities (those of social networks). The communities that come together in this newly configured public sphere, with its "connected cities" and "net localities," are henceforth hybrid or mixed, simultaneously local and global, localized and delocalized, in situ and ex situ. They are often synchronized around a live event.

In this era of technologically mediated connections, Lozano-Hemmer's works—particularly his monumental pieces—feature experiences that are both localized and synchronized, live and site specific, and centered on a place and an event. The institutions that commission, produce, and host them—which are, for the most part, cultural and tourist institutions defined as specific physical places: this museum, this piece of architecture, this square, this neighborhood, this city—find ways to valorize their sites and to keep attracting new audiences through these works. And the public thereby has an opportunity to have a collective, live, and site-specific experience, something that the digital world has made less common, and more precious.

DISPLACEMENTS AND DELAYS

For all the ways they foster community, Lozano-Hemmer's "mirrors" are more complex than they appear. They often introduce a displacement of physical perspective and a delay in feedback, distance in proximity and the past within the present. Sometimes they divide the dominant point of view; they generate tension between the live image, like the mirror (an index *in presentia*), and the delayed or recorded image, like a photograph or echo, or image or sound recording (an index *in absentia*). Beyond the "capture" as such, they rely on inscription and, often, the creation of an archive that is constantly being remade.

Sandbox (2010; see page 138) set up a relationship between a broad stretch of beach and two small sandboxes using a crossover apparatus that combined image capture and live projection. A miniature image of everyone on the beach was projected onto the sandboxes; when people gathered around to "touch" these miniature figures by playing in the sandboxes, a camera relayed the images of their hands to two enormous, suspended projectors that, in turn, cast the images over a broad swath of the beach. This work divided the community of spectators into two proximate yet distinct places and invited them to interact. Despite the apparent symmetry within the apparatus, the respective images were on different scales, and their relationships reversed. On the one hand, the crowd around the sandboxes dominated the people on the beach, attempting to grab them, cover them in sand, crush them, and so on. On the other hand, the people on the beach, seemingly under the control of the sandbox people, tried to escape their clutches—as if in a game of cat and mouse. But these power relationships could be quickly reversed. The beach people were already taunting the sandbox people, attempting to step on their giant hands, or ignoring them, etc. The sandbox people had no real power over the beach people, who were, after all, only images. And finally, the relationships were physically reversible because participants from each side could change places—that is, move from the sandboxes to the beach, or vice versa—to experience the other point of view and position, like Gulliver traveling from Lilliput to Brobdingnag.

In *Zoom Pavilion* (2015, with Krzysztof Wodiczko; see page 98), infrared and robotic cameras linked to motion-detection and facial recognition software track viewers, zoom in on their faces, capture images of them, and then project them onto the pavilion walls. Here again, viewers can individually or collectively play with their images and thwart the cameras. But each of these viewers is also divided; every individual's point of view is decentered and multiplied, and the viewers see themselves not face-to-face, as if in a mirror, but from above and from different angles, as a surveillance system might show them. They are sometimes paired automatically with other people whom they may not know by means of straight lines superimposed on the image, which seem to represent elementary and, at times, arbitrary social connections. Moreover, certain images—close-ups of faces—are quickly paired, recorded, dated, and archived before being projected onto the room's back wall.

Lozano-Hemmer's works therefore reconstruct that inaugural moment of community formation when subjects identify with their fellow human beings and open themselves up to the Other's gaze. As noted above, the artist's pieces seem to cultivate communities of bodies that are perfectly localized and synchronized, here and now, live and in situ. But they also often introduce an absence into the very heart of this presence, a displacement of viewpoint and a delay in mirror feedback that provide opportunities for individual viewers to step outside themselves and put themselves in the Other's place, to begin to interact and coordinate their actions. The artist's works thereby break the imaginary unity of the community and show that it is never a given but always differed, displaced, and delayed, something that needs to be continually reconsidered and negotiated. In this way, they invite us to reflect on the political dimension of aesthetic communities.

AESTHETIC COMMUNITIES

In his *Critique of Practical Reason* (1788), German philosopher Immanuel Kant affirmed, in opposition to the "moral sense theory," that morality must not be based on feeling. While it may give rise to feelings (such as respect for the moral law), it must be grounded in reason (on the moral law itself, that is, on the universalization of the maxims of action). But in his *Critique of Judgment* (1790), Kant qualified this statement when he came up against the antinomy of taste, which is both subjective (it is grounded in feeling) and universal (it requires broad assent). For these reasons, he stated, taste could serve as a model for all other types of judgment.

At that point, Kant introduced a distinction between "empirical" feelings, which are more corporal in that they are produced directly by the senses, and "pure" feelings, which are more intellectual, being produced indirectly by the subject's reflection on his or her mental state, the "attunement of one's cognitive powers." Kant then attributed a fundamental role to pure feeling, not only in the judgment of taste but also in cognitive and practical judgment. In the final analysis, all reflective judgments— which adjudicate cases without reference to a rule, or a rule's applicability to a particular case—are pure aesthetic judgments based on feeling, indeed on the very feeling of their justness (of the attunement of the faculties). Finally, the judgment of taste, like all other forms of pure aesthetic judgment, lays claim to universal assent; it presupposes a subjective universality, a communicability of feelings and, by extension, a *sensus communis aestheticus* (an "aesthetic faculty of judgment")—in short, an aesthetic community.

The status of this aesthetic community (which is not, therefore, a physical community of bodies but a reflective community of consciences) remains problematic; and this is what accounts for the strength of Kant's contribution to reflection on "universal civil society." This aesthetic community is neither a reality (it has not yet been achieved) nor a certainty (nothing guarantees that it will be achieved some day); but it is a necessity, analogous to moral duty (it ought to be achieved). The aesthetic community is not something that one could experience in the strict sense of the term: it is, rather, both a presupposition and a requirement, a pragmatic principle and a practical imperative, both of which accompany all judgment. Here, the consensus is not material— natural, sensory, identity based, cultural, ethical, political, etc. (Kant is not Rousseau)— but formal; it pertains to the conditions of judgment, to the principles of discussion or the rules of play.

Lozano-Hemmer's works can be political, therefore, not because of their occasional political content or their rare political effects, but because they simulate, within the space of art, the basic conditions in which sociability, the community, and the public sphere are formed. Perhaps they could be considered within the tradition of the contractualist philosophers (like Kant) who, in order to better understand, found, or refound society, attempted to reconstruct the origins of social life in various *Gedankenexperimenten*, imaginary experiments or philosophical fictions—such as the "state of nature," the "original position," and the "ideal speech situation."

The community of viewers is at once a fragment and an image of society, while the "artistic contract" is at once a part and a scale model of the social contract. But the work of Lozano-Hemmer, like other exemplary relational work, extends far beyond metaphor and metonymy. While the social contract is never truly chosen (entry into society, like entry into the marketplace, is not optional—one is always already there; laws and norms are compulsory, infractions are punished, etc.), the artistic contract is optional (you can join in the game freely, and the rules are freely accepted and re-spected). Perhaps it is in a context such as this that true civility appears: it is not a matter of passing an obligation off as a choice but, rather, of presenting a choice as an obligation.

Lozano-Hemmer's works could very well encourage us to take part, within the separate space of art, in the continually renewed exercise of building the aesthetic community. In this time of flash mobs and Web tribes, the community, in the strict sense of the term, needs to be cultivated.

SUBTITLED PUBLIC 2005

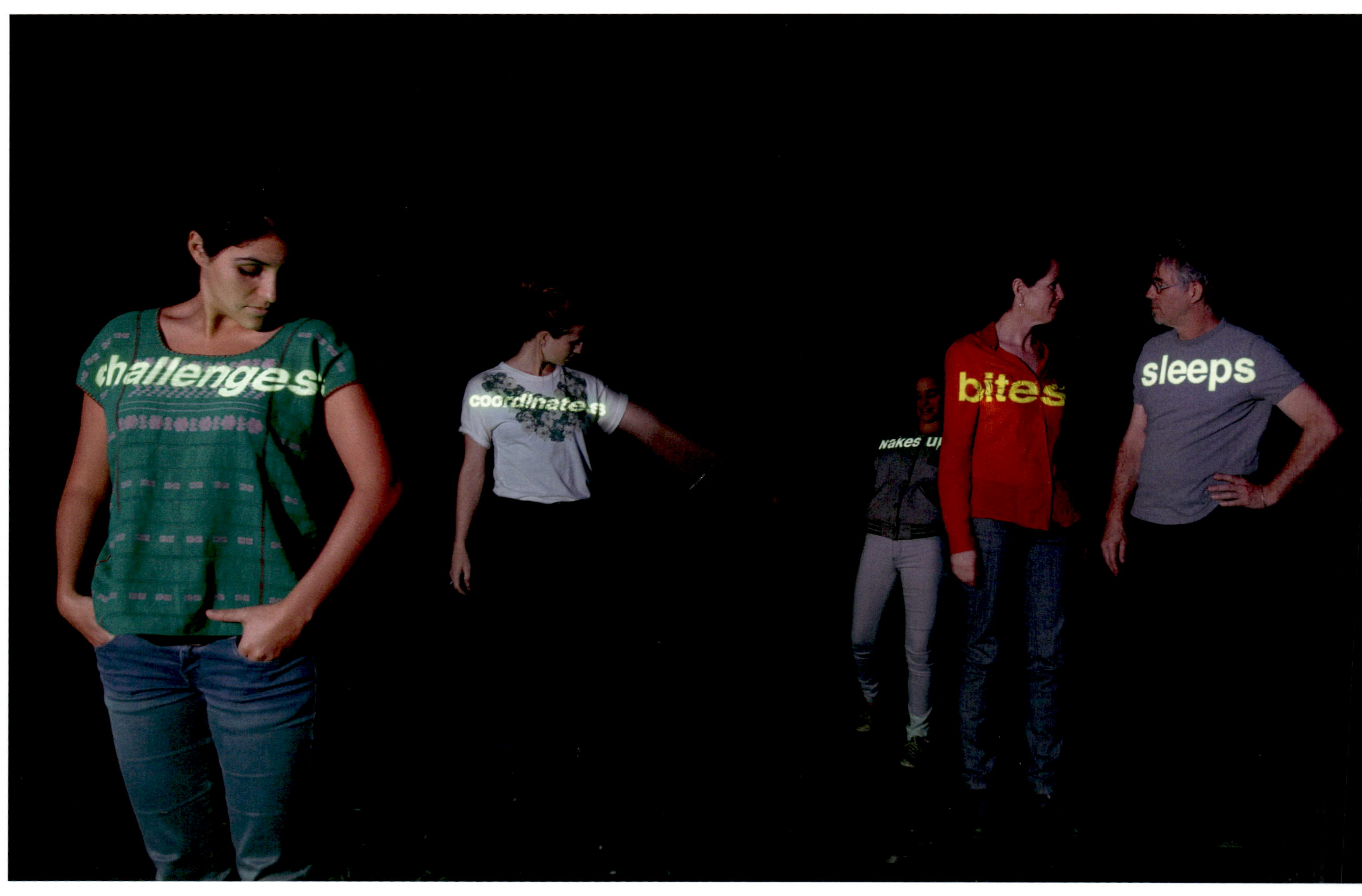

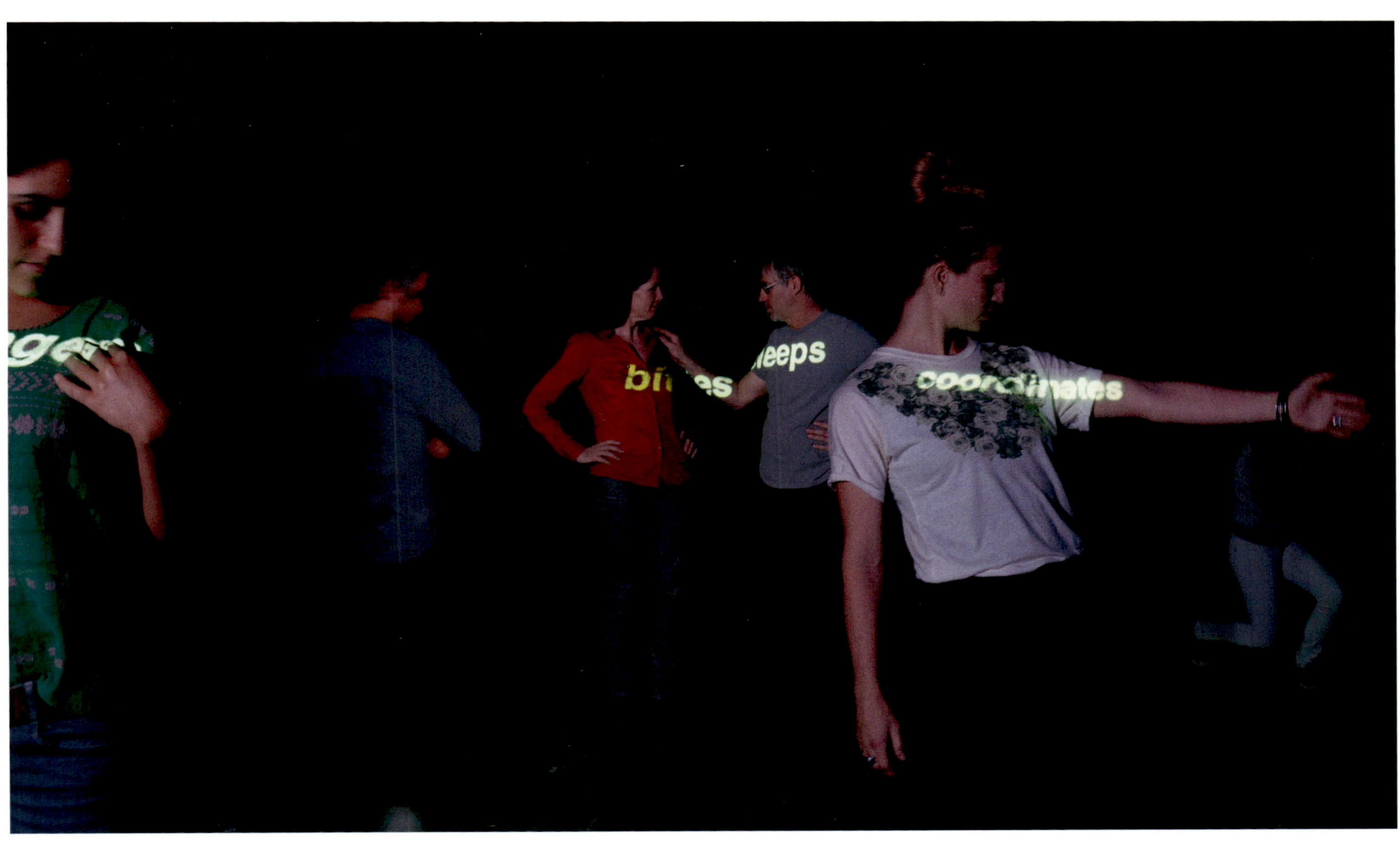

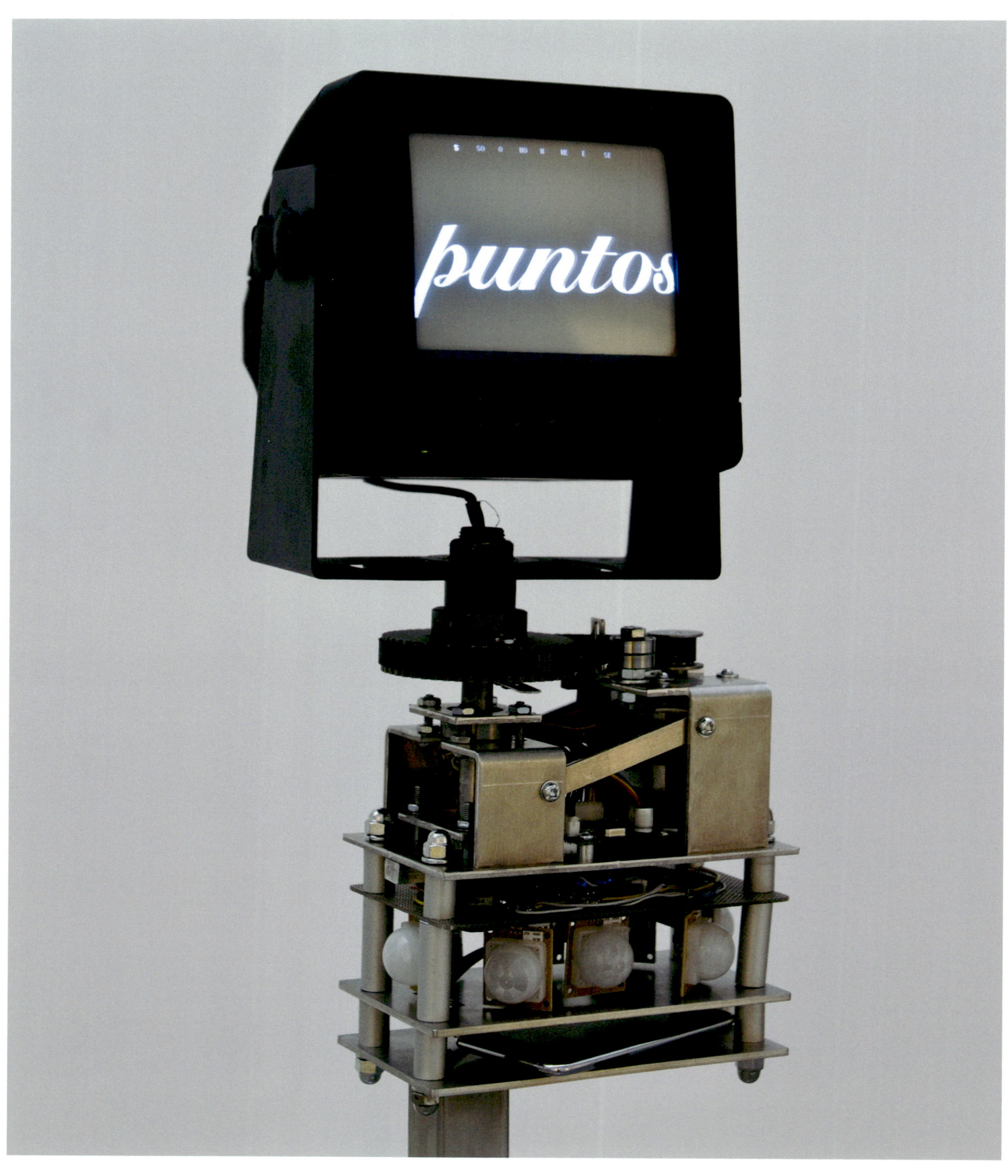
puntos

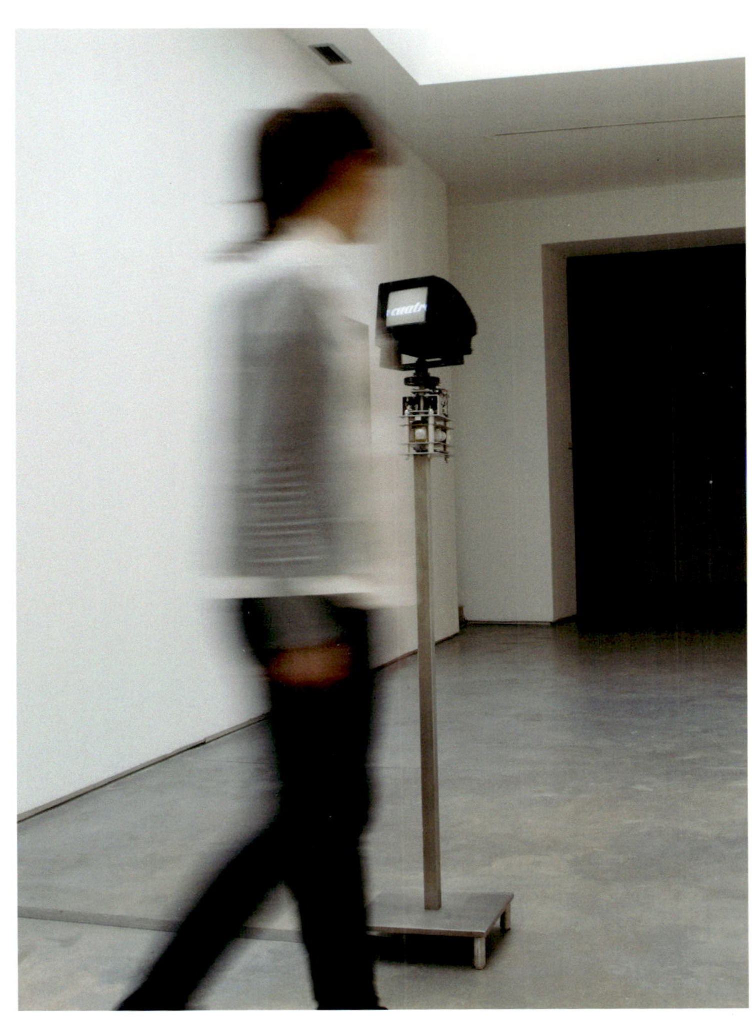

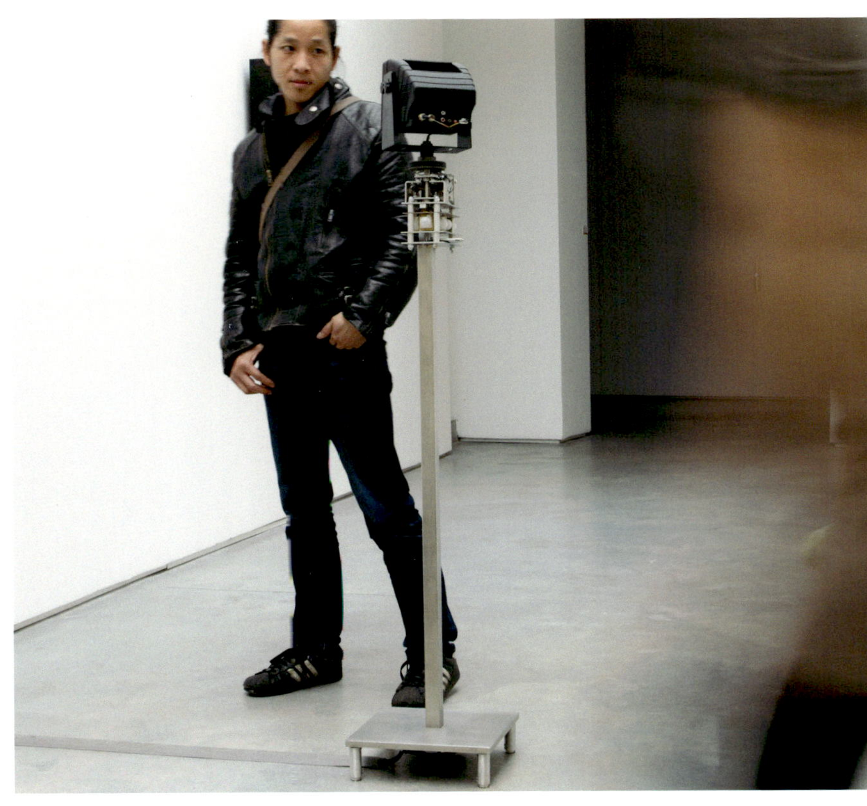

Installation views, Galeria Max Estrella, Madrid, 2010

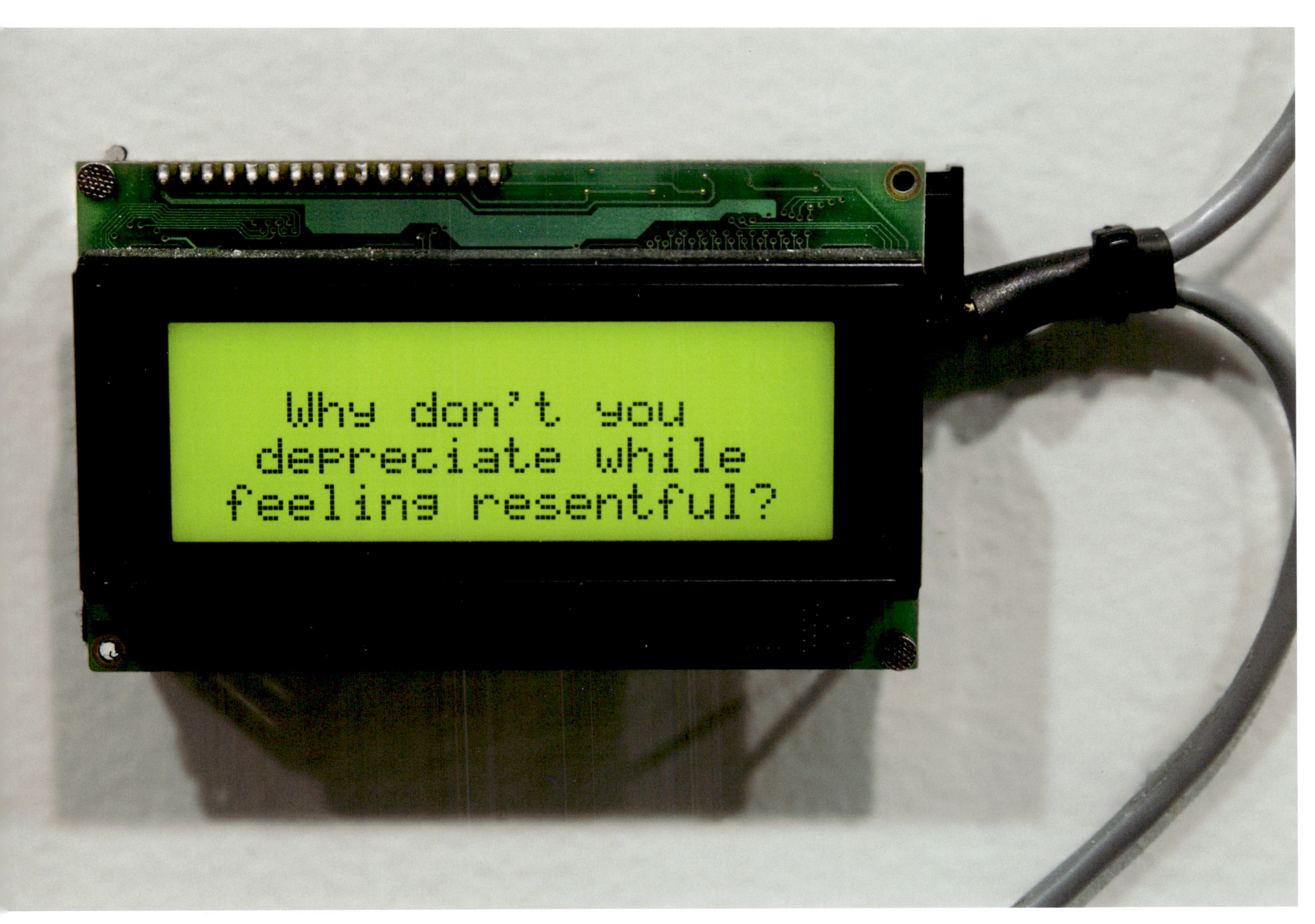
Why don't you
depreciate while
feeling resentful?

AIRBORNE NEWSCAST

2013

Projections, surveillance cameras, computers, and custom software

Dimensions variable

Airborne Newscast is an interactive shadowplay that projects live news feeds, covering a wall. The projectors are positioned so that an individual entering the space disrupts the projection. A set of surveillance cameras immediately identifies the visitor's presence and creates a "heat map" that generates "evaporations" of the projected news feeds. As visitors move in the space, the words over which their shadows pass dissolve into smoke-like patterns, making reading difficult. The *Airborne* series engages a variety of texts (literary, scientific, philosophical) that address entropy, complexity, chance, and nonlinear dynamics. *Airborne Newscast* projects live feeds from prominent international news outlets, such as Reuters, Agencia EFE, Notimex, AlterNet, and AP.

Pages 90–93

BABBAGE NANOPAMPHLETS

2015

Two million elemental gold leaflets, glass container, single-channel video, magnet, and LED light

Gold leaflets, each: 150 atoms thick; overall: dimensions variable

Lozano-Hemmer's nanopamphlets contain an excerpt from a treatise by English polymath and "father of the computer" Charles Babbage engraved at a microscopic scale on flakes of elemental gold. In this text, the author's *Ninth Bridgewater Treatise*, Babbage posits that the atmosphere is a vast repository of everything that has ever been said, and that we could potentially "rewind" the movement of every molecule of air to re-create the voices of everyone who has ever spoken. Lozano-Hemmer worked with Cornell University's NanoScale facility to print two million nano-pamphlets. Each gold leaflet is 150 atoms thick, each letter 250 nanometers wide. In this work, most of the nanopam-phlets are shown suspended in a crystal vial of water beside electron microscope images of the gold engraving and a first-edition copy of Babbage's text. Before the opening of the exhibition, the artist releases thousands of pamphlets into the museum's ventilation system so that they can potentially be inhaled by the public. Elemental gold is biologically inert, higher in purity than 24-karat gold, and poses no health risk as museum visitors carry Babbage's treatise with them into the world.

Pages 84–85

BIFURCATION

2012
Projection, tree branch, motion sensor, aluminum bracket,
motor, Arduino processor, computer, and custom software
written in openFrameworks
Dimensions variable
Collection of Pat Wilson, San Francisco

Birfucation pairs a small branch suspended from a thread
with a corresponding "shadow" projected on the wall
behind it. As the Y-shaped branch responds to drafts or
the directed breath of visitors, its rotations in space
are mirrored by its shadow. However, *Bifurcation* calls the
relationship between an object and its shadow into
question: the shadow represents not just the branch, but
the branch as it was within the tree in which it grew, one
small piece of a much larger bough. The entire tree branch
was generated using an L-system algorithm. As the small
branch moves, so does the larger tree, so that they are
always oriented in the same way. *Bifurcation* is the second
installation in the *Shadow Object* series of works inspired
by Mexican poet Octavio Paz and Argentine author Adolfo
Bioy Casares, among others, who insisted that absence
and presence are not opposites.

Pages 50–59

CALL ON WATER

2016
Aluminum and steel tank, ultrasonic atomizers, water,
computer, custom electronics, and custom software written
in openFrameworks
116 1/8 × 44 7/8 × 13 3/4 in. (295 × 114 × 35 cm)

Call on Water is a fountain from which words emerge as
plumes of ascending cold vapor. Fragment by fragment,
poems by Octavio Paz briefly materialize in the mist before
dissipating. The poems by Paz likewise meditate on the
power of ephemeral words: lines include, for example,
"My words watch me from the puddle of my memory," or
"Rippling shadows, flashes, echoes, the writing not of
songs but of murmurs." Hundreds of computer-controlled
ultrasonic atomizers under the reflecting water pool
produce the plumes of vapor.

Pages 10, 14, 86–89

<u>CARDINAL DIRECTIONS</u>
2010
Monitor, motor, portable media player, motion sensors,
custom electronics, and stainless-steel stand
12 × 12 × 45 in. (30.5 × 30.5 × 114.3 cm)

Cardinal Directions is a kinetic sculpture that interacts with
one visitor at a time using infrared sensors and a rotating
screen. At roughly human scale, a surveillance monitor
attached to the top of a pole turns to face viewers as they
move around it. The monitor displays text from an extract of
Vicente Huidobro's poem *Altazor* (1931), which refers to
the geography of the poet's native Chile: "The four cardinal
directions are three: North and South." The text of the
poem is "geolocated"—it always aligns itself to the cardinal
points ("North" always faces north; "South" always faces
south), and participants must walk around the piece in
order to read it, like a kind of periscope.

On view at SFMOMA

Pages 150–51

<u>LEVEL OF CONFIDENCE</u>
2015
Screen, webcam, computer, facial recognition algorithms,
and custom software written in openFrameworks
Dimensions variable

Level of Confidence commemorates the mass kidnapping of
forty-three students from the Ayotzinapa *normalista* school
in Iguala, Guerrero, Mexico. It was released on March 26,
2015, exactly six months after the kidnapping took place.
The project consists of a facial recognition camera that has
been trained to look relentlessly for the faces of the
disappeared students. As a visitor stands in front of the
camera, the system uses algorithms to find which student's
facial features most resemble the visitor's, providing a
percentage "level of confidence" of the accuracy of the
match. Biometric surveillance algorithms Eigen, Fisher, and
LBPH, which are typically used by military and police forces
to look for suspects, are here employed for locating victims.
The piece will likely fail to make a positive match, as the
students are presumed victims of a mass murder perpetrated
by the government in collaboration with police forces and
drug cartels.

The project's software is available for free download from
the artist's website so that any university, cultural center,
gallery, or museum can exhibit *Level of Confidence*.
Programmers can adapt the open-source code to make
their own versions based on a different set of individuals'
faces. The piece can also be acquired for art collections,
and all proceeds are directed to a fund to help the
affected community.

Pages 104–5

PAN-ANTHEM

2014
Steel plates, speakers, LED screens, ultrasonic proximity sensors, and custom electronics, with sound
Dimensions variable

Pan-Anthem is an interactive sound installation in which the national anthems of hundreds of countries play on individual speakers when the viewer approaches. The movable speakers are magnetically fixed on steel panels and arranged to represent a set of national statistics selected by the curator(s) of the given installation. For example, at the Musée d'art contemporain de Montréal, the speakers reflected the number of refugees given asylum in each country in 2016, as reported by the United Nations high commissioner for refugees in "Global Trends—Forced Displacement in 2016" (http://www.unhcr.org/globaltrends2016/). Turkey was thus on the far end of the wall, with the highest number of hosted refugees, closely followed by Pakistan and Lebanon. As visitors walk from panel to panel, they activate sensors placed beneath their feet, which trigger the speakers associated with that section of the statistical array. The overall effect is a positional panoramic playback of national anthems associated with concrete statistics.

On a side wall, a separate set of silent speakers hang. They represent countries that have ceased to exist—including Yugoslavia, the USSR, and Czechoslovakia—along with countries that may exist in the future, such as Quebec, Catalonia, and Scotland.

Pages 106–9

PULSE SPIRAL

2008
Incandescent light bulbs, heart rate sensor, voltage controllers, computer, custom electronics, and custom software written in openFrameworks
Dimensions variable
Courtesy of the artist and bitforms gallery, New York, with the generous contribution of the Musée d'art contemporain de Montréal

Pulse Spiral is a three-dimensional spiral paraboloid made up of hundreds of incandescent light bulbs hanging from the ceiling. The lights are arranged according to an equation by French mathematician Pierre de Fermat (1607–1665) describing an efficient spatial distribution along a surface that is found in phyllotaxis, the arrangement of leaves along a plant's stem. *Pulse Spiral* records and responds to the heart rate of a participant who holds a sensor installed beneath the light fixture. When a viewer grasps the sensor, their heartbeat is transformed into a flash of light in the lowest bulb. That flash, in turn, lights up the entire system, which flashes in unison, synchronized with the visitor's pulse. The individual's heartbeat then joins the recorded heartbeats of past participants, and the lights begin flashing in a constellation of individual rhythms.

Pages 132–37

<u>SEISMOSCOPES</u>

2009

XY-plotter, vibration sensor, ink, paper, stainless-steel stand, portable media player, custom electronics, and custom software written in Objective C
Plotter: 16 1/8 × 17 3/4 × 6 11/16 in. (41 × 45 × 17 cm); stand: 45 1/4 × 16 1/8 × 17 3/4 in. (115 × 41 × 45 cm); drawings, each: 17 × 11 in. (43.2 × 27.9 cm); overall: dimensions variable

A drawing device activated by vibrations it detects, *Seismoscopes* records nearby footsteps—or earthquakes—on paper using an automated XY-plotter, translating seismic activity into a portrait of one of twenty Skeptical philosophers. Thus far, Lozano-Hemmer has made eight *Seismoscopes*, each dedicated to its own philosopher. The first *Seismoscope* draws the portrait of Francisco Sanches (1550–1623), the Portuguese author of the seminal treatise *That Nothing Is Known*. Another depicts Pyrrho of Elis (360–270 BCE), a Greek proponent of Acatalepsy (the impossibility of comprehending a thing). In *Rafael Lozano-Hemmer: Unstable Presence*, the *Seismoscope* draws the portrait of Abū Hāmid Mohammed al-Ghazālī (1058–1111), Persian author of *The Incoherence of Philosophers*. The drawings generated by the device are different each time: the order of the lines is a random pattern, and the degree of intensity of any given line is dependent on the intensity of the corresponding seismic activity. A selection of completed drawings is presented on the wall behind the *Seismoscope*.

Pages 52–55

<u>SPHERE PACKING: BACH</u>

2018

1,128-channel audio, speakers, maple, aluminum, screen, computer, custom electronics, custom hardware, and custom software written in openFrameworks
118 1/8 in. (300 cm) diameter
Courtesy of Borusan Contemporary, Istanbul

<u>SPHERE PACKING: WAGNER</u>

2013

Porcelain 3-D print, 113-channel audio, and custom electronics
5 1/8 in. (13 cm) diameter

Sphere Packing: Bach supports 1,128 loudspeakers, each of which plays a different composition by Johann Sebastian Bach. Visitors can enter this sphere and immerse themselves in Bach's entire concentrated opuses. The speakers are programmed to play in waves: from time to time, all but one speaker are silenced and a single composition plays; at other moments, sounds from more and more speakers join the fray and the work reaches a cacophonous crescendo. Visitors can also follow the ebbs and flows of this polyvocal and complex sound environment visually via small amber LED lights that illuminate when a speaker is operating.

The piece includes a "backstage" where nearly seven miles of cables connect to a bespoke patch panel controlled by custom software that activates the speakers in sequences of geometrical eclipses. *Sphere Packing: Bach* is the culmination of the *Sphere Packing* series of sound sculptures Lozano-Hemmer has been making since 2013, each of which takes the form of a sphere proportional to the composer's musical output. For example, the earlier *Sphere Packing: Wagner* is a 3-D-printed porcelain sphere comprising 113 channels of sound. As the most prolific of the seventeen composers in the series, Bach required a room-like immersive environment to accommodate his vast body of work.

Sphere Packing: Wagner on view at MAC and MARCO

Pages 110–15, 119

STANDARDS AND DOUBLE STANDARDS

2004
Leather belts, stepper motors, computerized surveillance
camera, and tracking system
Dimensions variable

Standards and Double Standards consists of one to one
hundred fastened belts suspended at waist height from
stepper motors on the ceiling. Controlled by a computerized tracking system, the belts rotate automatically, turning
their buckles slowly to face visitors. When several people
are in the room, their presence affects the entire group
of belts, creating chaotic patterns of interference. Using
the belt as a symbol of patriarchal authority, the work turns
a condition of pure surveillance into an unpredictable
connective system. The presentation of this work at the
Musée d'art contemporain de Montréal featured a single belt
in a more intimate, one-on-one relationship with the viewer.

On view at MAC

Page 61

SUBTITLED PUBLIC

2005
Computers, projectors, tracking systems, infrared
illuminators, and custom software written in Delphi
Dimensions variable
Collection Tate: presented by Lombard Odier Darier
Hentsch 2007

When visitors enter the space of *Subtitled Public*, a
computerized surveillance system detects their presence,
generates a subtitle for each person, and projects it onto
them. The subtitle appears at random from a list of verbs
conjugated in the third person, such as *challenges*, *bites*,
sleeps, and *tastes*. The only way of getting rid of a subtitle
is to touch another person, which prompts the two
individuals' subtitles to transfer to one another. The project
exists in English, French, and Spanish versions.

On view at MAC

Pages 148–49

SYNAPTIC CAGUAMAS

2004
Glass bottles, wood table, motors, and custom software
written in Delphi
Collection of FEMSA, Monterrey

Synaptic Caguamas is a kinetic sculpture consisting of
a motorized Mexican "cantina" bar table with thirty
"caguama"-sized beer bottles (one liter each). The bottles
spin on the table with patterns generated by algorithms
that simulate the neuronal connections in the brain. Every
few minutes the bottles are reset automatically and seeded
with new initial conditions for the algorithm, so that the
movement patterns are never repeated. In this absurd way,
the sculpture makes tangible the mathematics of recollec-
tion and thought.

On view at MARCO and SFMOMA

Page 60

<u>TAPE RECORDERS</u>

2011

Measuring tapes, motors, surveillance tracking system, thermal printer, paper, computer, custom electronics, and custom software written in openFrameworks
Dimensions variable

Rows of motorized measuring tapes record the amount of time that visitors stay in the installation. When a person enters the space, a computerized tracking system detects their presence, triggering the tape measure closest to them. The tape slides up the gallery wall, rising steadily until the visitor moves away from it. When a single tape measure reaches its yield limit—around three meters—it succumbs to gravity and hinges out into the space, ultimately crashing to the floor. After a tape measure reaches the point of collapse, it recoils back and begins the process over again. At the end of each hour, the system prints the total number of minutes visitors spent in the gallery during that time.

On view at MAC

Pages 56–59

<u>VICIOUS CIRCULAR BREATHING</u>

2013

Glass room, automated sliding doors, motors, bellows, tubes, 61 brown paper bags, manifold valve system, carbon dioxide and oxygen sensors, and computer
Glass room: 95 ⅝ × 95 ⅝ × 95 ⅝ in. (243 × 243 × 243 cm); overall: dimensions variable
Courtesy of Borusan Contemporary, Istanbul

Vicious Circular Breathing is a large sculptural installation that collects and recirculates the breath of participants. The public is invited to enter a hermetically sealed chamber and to breathe the air that was previously breathed by visitors before them. Individuals can press a button on the outside of the glass room, step into the vestibule, and wait for it to be decompressed, then enter the main chamber to sit down and breathe the recycled air. Their breath is kept circulating and made perceptible by automatically inflating and deflating brown paper bags attached, via an electro-magnetic valve system, to respiratory tubes connected to a set of motorized bellows. The bags deflate and inflate around 10,000 times a day (the normal respiratory frequency for an adult at rest), with a noisy crumpling sound that fills the exhibition space. There are sixty-one bags, corresponding to the number of keys on a typical five-octave organ, the musical instrument that inspired the work's design.

The work warns would-be participants of the possibility of asphyxiation, contagion, and panic, and includes carbon dioxide and oxygen sensors as well as two emergency exits.

Pages 74, 78–83

<u>VOICE ARRAY</u>

2011
Intercom, LED batten lights, speakers, computer,
custom electronics, and custom software written in
openFrameworks
Dimensions variable

An interactive installation that spans the length of one or
several walls, *Voice Array* invites participants to speak into
an intercom. Their voices are then translated into flashes of
light, the unique blinking patterns of which are stored as a
loop in the first of a long row of lights in the array. Each
new recording pushes all previous recordings one position
down, and gradually the sound of the previous recordings
becomes audible. The oldest voices are pushed out of the
array one by one as new visitors record messages. Before
each recording disappears, it plays one last time while the
rest of the array is silenced, such that a wave of light
representing each individual voice travels the length of
the wall.

On view at MAC and MARCO

Pages 126–27

<u>VOLUTE 1: AU CLAIR DE LA LUNE</u>

2016
Aluminum cast from polymer 3-D print and single-channel
video (0:25 min.), silent
Aluminum: 25 ⅝ × 7 ½ × 8 ¼ in. (65 × 19 × 21 cm); overall:
dimensions variable
Collection of Giverny Capital

In 1860, Édouard-Léon Scott de Martinville recorded the
phrase *au clair de la lune*—the beginning of the eponymous
French folk song—on his phonoautograph, making the
first known recording of human speech. This sculpture
materializes that phrase in aluminum as the first 3-D-
printed speech bubble, using a method developed by the
artist's studio in conjunction with fluid dynamics scientists
from Georgia Institute of Technology, Auburn University,
and New York University. Breath exhaled while speaking
the given phrase is scanned by a custom-made laser
tomograph, a device that images the density of air in cross
sections. Through photogrammetry, a process that takes
measurements based on those images, the density map is
converted into a high-definition, 3-D-printed polymer form
and then cast in aluminum. *Au clair de la lune* is the first in
Lozano-Hemmer's series of *Volutes*, in which the artist
translates words, phrases, and songs into physical form.
The sculpture resembles a billowing cloud, as if the floating
phrase were concretized the minute it was spoken. The
work includes a video of the tomograph slices showing
the cloud in motion.

Pages 46–49

<u>VOZ ALTA AND PROTOTYPE</u>
2008
Searchlight, modified megaphone, FM radio recording,
transistor radio, computer, custom electronics, custom
software written in Objective C, and single-channel HD
video (16:09 min.), with sound
Dimensions variable
The Ella Fontanals-Cisneros Collection, Miami

Voz Alta (Out Loud) commemorates the fortieth anniversary
of the massacre of hundreds of students that occurred in
Tlatelolco, Mexico City, on October 2, 1968. Located on the
Plaza de las Tres Culturas where the massacre took place,
and in stark contrast to the traditional mode of historical
monuments, Lozano-Hemmer's site-specific anti-monument
invited participants to step up to a megaphone and speak
freely about the tragedy or anything else on their minds. A
10kW searchlight automatically visualized a participant's
voice as a sequence of flashes, its brightness determined
by the speaker's volume. The searchlight was trained on
the former Ministry of Foreign Affairs, now Centro Cultural
Tlatelolco, then relayed into the city by three additional
searchlights, making the project visible to millions. Anyone
in the city could tune into 96.1 FM Radio UNAM to listen
in live to the spoken messages. Participation included
statements from survivors of the student massacre, street
poetry, shout-outs, ad hoc art performances, marriage
proposals, calls for protest, and more. When no one
was participating, the three lights on the building were
synchronized with archival recordings of survivors,
interviews with intellectuals and politicians, music from
1968, and radio art pieces commissioned by Radio UNAM.
In this way, the memory of the tragedy in Tlatelolco was
mixed with live participation in *Voz Alta*.

In later installations, *Voz Alta* is represented by a functional
prototype shown with video documentation of the 2008
public artwork. For the prototype, Lozano-Hemmer modified
a megaphone, incorporating inside it a powerful xenon
searchlight that converts the voices of participants into
flashes of light. An FM radio transmitter relays the sounds
to which the light corresponds. An archival recording of the
memorial plays after a participant has finished speaking.

Pages 36, 40–45

<u>ZOOM PAVILION (WITH KRZYSZTOF WODICZKO)</u>
2015
Projections, infrared cameras, infrared illuminators,
speakers, computers, custom electronics, and custom
software written in openFrameworks, with sound
Dimensions variable

Zoom Pavilion is an immersive installation with interactive
projections on three walls fed by twelve computerized
surveillance systems trained on visitors. Using facial
recognition algorithms, the work detects the presence of
participants and records their spatial relationship to one
another within the exhibition space. Visitors' images
appear projected on the walls with a line measuring their
separation and accompanied by classifications such as
"potential," "interest," "remote," and "suspicious." The
back wall is an archive of the faces of past participants
organized in twos, specifying how long they were paired,
how far apart they remained, and when their assembly
happened.

Lozano-Hemmer's first collaboration with the artist
Krzysztof Wodiczko, *Zoom Pavilion* is at once an experimen-
tal platform for self-representation and a giant monitoring
system that tracks—and fosters—connections among the
public. Independent cameras zoom in to amplify the
images of participants up to thirty-five times. These
disorienting zoom sequences transform the entire
imagescape from easily recognizable wide shots of the
crowd to abstract close-ups of individuals. The entire
installation is fluid, as perpetual camera movement
highlights particular visitors' relationships through
constantly shifting projections.

Pages 96, 98–103

<u>**33 QUESTIONS PER MINUTE**</u>

2000

21 LCD screens, computer, custom electronics, and custom
software written in Delphi

Dimensions variable

Employing grammatical algorithms that draw from a list
that includes most words in the dictionary, *33 Questions
per Minute* generates unique questions in random
combinations that never repeat. Tiny LCD screens display
the questions at a rate of thirty-three per minute, a pace
calibrated to the threshold of legibility. Readers have just
enough time to decipher the words, but not enough to
reflect or absorb their meaning. The often-absurd nature of
the questions is further destabilizing: Will you bleed in an
orderly fashion? Is the creator always being born? Do I snip
the marriage bed without rhyme or reason? Occasionally,
questions have serendipitous meaning within the context
in which they are exhibited: Who bribes the artist? Why did
computers become so self-congratulatory? The system is
capable of generating 4.7 trillion questions in four languages
(English, French, German, and Spanish); it would take
3,000 years to ask all of them.

In addition to displaying the questions on LCD screens
mounted in the exhibition space, they can also be
projected at a larger scale, as they were at MARCO. If the
personal computer used to run the algorithm has an
Internet connection, the texts can simultaneously be
mirrored on a website for remote viewing.

Pages 18–21, 153

<u>**218 POLYGONS PER SECOND**</u>

2015

Single-channel video (1:14 min.)

In this short video, Lozano-Hemmer quickly draws cross-
hatching lines with a pencil, automatically forming dozens
of small polygons. The activity pits the artist's hand against
the production capability of contemporary computer graphic
cards that can render billions of polygons per second. After
multiple attempts, Lozano-Hemmer found he could create a
maximum of around 218 polygons per second.

Born in Mexico City in 1967, Rafael Lozano-Hemmer spent his early years surrounded by musicians, artists, and dancers, as his parents owned nightclubs in Mexico City's disco, drag, and salsa scenes. The artist's ongoing interest in poetry and science was influenced by family figures, notably his father's cousin, Octavio Paz (whose work is featured in *Call on Water*, 2016), and his maternal grandfather, amateur chemist Carlos Hemmer Torres (who, according to the artist, invented Bakelite plastic thirty years after it had already been invented).

After living in Mexico and Spain, Lozano-Hemmer attended the University of Victoria, British Columbia, and then earned a bachelor of science in physical chemistry (1989) from Concordia University in Montreal. During his studies, Lozano-Hemmer cofounded the PoMo CoMo collective (1988–91), which created technological performances, including radio and radio art. After spending time at the Banff Center for the Arts, where he befriended artists such as Dick Higgins, Trimpin, and Gordon Monahan, he began making works to be presented in visual art contexts. Returning to Madrid in 1992, Lozano-Hemmer founded the Transition State Theory group with his life partner, choreographer Susie Ramsay, and collaborator Will Bauer. Using Bauer's pioneering 3-D-wireless sensor technology, Lozano-Hemmer created *Surface Tension* (1992), an interactive installation composed of a giant projected eye that followed a dancer around a stage. After the performances, members of the public were invited to participate in the installation, to see that the Orwellian eye tracked them effectively.

Public space and participation became the central focus of Lozano-Hemmer's *Relational Architecture* series over the following decades. Early projects like *Displaced Emperors* (Linz, 1997), *Re:Positioning Fear* (Graz, 1997), *Vectorial Elevation* (Mexico City, 1999), and *Body Movies* (Rotterdam, 2001) used projection, shadows, telerobotics, and lights to activate and amplify the presence of participants, encouraging individuals to personalize public space.

Since then, Lozano-Hemmer's large-scale installations have been commissioned for events such as the United Nations World Summit of Cities in Lyon (2003), the opening of the Yamaguchi Center for Arts and Media in Japan (2003), the expansion of the European Union in Dublin (2004), the memorial for the Tlatelolco Student Massacre in Mexico City (2008), the Winter Olympics in Vancouver (2010), the pre-opening of the Guggenheim Museum in Abu Dhabi (2015), and the activation of the Augusta Raurica Roman Theatre in Basel (2018). Recently, Lozano-Hemmer has produced large-scale permanent art commissions, including *Fiducial Voice Beacons* (Science Museum, London, 2014), *Colorimeter* (Maison Manuvie, Montreal, 2017), *Metrónomos* (Museum of Memory and Tolerance, Mexico City, 2019), *Speaking Willow* (Planet Word Museum of Language, Washington, D.C., 2020), *Voice Canopy* (Peace Plaza, Rochester, MN, 2020), and *Reflejo Peatonal* (Puerta Polanco, Mexico City, 2020).

In 2003, Lozano-Hemmer and Ramsay founded Antimodular Research, a Montreal-based studio that currently comprises fifteen full-time developers (programmers, architects, designers, writers, and musicians) and an extended team of collaborators from around the world. Lozano-Hemmer sees his practice as closer to the performing arts than the visual arts; he directs various interconnecting disciplines and the work of specialists who are credited in each production. The studio runs according to established approaches to the conservation of media art; Lozano-Hemmer has particularly adhered to the practice of releasing open-source software code and schematics for collectors and other artists.

Lozano-Hemmer's artworks are featured in museum collections including the Museum of Modern Art, Guggenheim Museum, and Museo del Barrio, all in New York; the San Francisco Museum of Modern Art (SFMOMA), the Hirshhorn Museum and Sculpture Garden in Washington, D.C., Tate London, the Singapore Art Museum, the Museo Universitario Arte Contemporáneo (MUAC) in Mexico City, the Museum of Old and New Art in Hobart, Tasmania, and the 21st-Century Museum of Contemporary Art in Kanazawa, Japan. His works have also been the focus of group and solo exhibitions, including solo shows at SFMOMA, MUAC, the Museum of Contemporary Art in Sydney, the Amorepacific Museum of Art in Seoul, the Musée d'art contemporain de Montréal, and the Museo de Arte Contemporáneo de Monterrey, Mexico.

While Lozano-Hemmer has experimented within technological spheres, social praxis has remained a vital crux of his
work. Most recently, *Border Tuner* (2019) created bridges of
light and communication channels to join participants in
the cities of El Paso, Texas, and Ciudad Juárez, Mexico, on
both sides of the U.S.-Mexico border. Lozano-Hemmer's
exhibition-performance hybrid project *Atmospheric Memory*
launched at the Manchester International Festival in 2019.
The project includes *Zoom Pavilion* (2015); *Vocal Folds*
(2019), a series of endoscopic videos showing the larynxes
of actors reading a treatise on the atmosphere; and *Cloud
Display* (2019), an interactive voice-recognition fountain
that converts words into clouds of cold-water vapor.

Rafael Lozano-Hemmer is represented by bitforms gallery
(New York), Max Estrella (Madrid), Wilde (Geneva and
Basel), and Pace (worldwide).

BIBLIOGRAPHY

MONOGRAPHS

Alonso, Rodrigo. *Rafael Lozano-Hemmer: Detectores*, exh. cat. Buenos Aires: Fundación Telefónica, 2012.

Barrios, José Luis, Kathleen Forde, Alejandra Labastida, Rafael Lozano-Hemmer, Scott McQuire, and Jaime Urrutia Fucugauchi. *Rafael Lozano-Hemmer: Pseudomatismos/ Pseudomatisms*, exh. cat. Edited by Ekaterina Álvarez Romero. Mexico City: Museo Universitario Arte Contemporáneo, 2015.

Barrios, José Luis, Manuel DeLanda, Barbara London, Príamo Lozada, Cuauhtémoc Medina, Bárbara Peréa, and Victoria Stoichita. *Rafael Lozano-Hemmer: Some Things Happen More Often Than All of the Time*, exh. cat. Edited by Príamo Lozado. Mexican Pavilion, 52nd Venice Biennale. New York: Turner, 2007.

Forde, Kathleen, John G. Hanhardt, and Rafael Lozano-Hemmer. *Rafael Lozano-Hemmer: Vicious Circular Breathing*, exh. cat. Edited by Kathleen Forde. Istanbul: Borusan Contemporary, 2013.

Hanhardt, John. *Mad. Sq. Art 2008—Rafael Lozano-Hemmer—Pulse Park*, exh. cat. New York: Madison Square Park Conservancy, 2008.

Kim, Kyoungran, Hye Jin Mun, Timothy Druckrey, Rodrigo Alonso, and Manuel DeLanda. *Rafael Lozano-Hemmer: Decision Forest*, exh. cat. Edited by Kyoungran Kim. Seoul: Amorepacific Museum of Art, 2018.

Lozano-Hemmer, Rafael, and David Hill, eds. *Under Scan*, exh. cat. Nottingham and Montreal: EMDA and Antimodular, 2007.

Lozano-Hemmer, Rafael, ed. *Vectorial Elevation: Relational Architecture No. 4*. Mexico City: Conaculta, 2000.

Stevenson, Moira, Rafael Lozano-Hemmer, Timothy Druckrey, Cecilia Fajardo-Hill, Beryl Graham, and Jacinta Laurent. *Rafael Lozano-Hemmer: Recorders*, exh. cat. Manchester: Manchester Art Gallery, 2010.

SELECTED ARTICLES, ESSAYS, AND GENERAL REFERENCE

Adrieensens, Alex, and Joke Brouwer. "Alien Relationships from Public Space: A Winding Dialog with Rafael Lozano-Hemmer." In *TransUrbanism*, by Joke Brouwer, Philip Brookman, and Arjen Mulder. Rotterdam: NAI Publishers, 2002.

Austen, Kat. "*Level of Confidence*: Open-Source Art Memorial to the Missing." *New Scientist*, August 5, 2015. http://www.newscientist.com/article/dn28007-level-of-confidence-open-source-art-memorial-to-the-missing.

Balmisa, Alberto Sanchez. "Out of Control: Interview with Rafael Lozano-Hemmer." In *Practicable: From Participation to Interaction in Contemporary Art*, by Samuel Bianchini and Erik Verhagen. Cambridge, MA: MIT Press, 2016.

Bock, Anja. "The Crossover of New Media Immersion and Site-Specificity: Contemporary Art and Spatial Experience." PhD diss., Concordia University, 2009.

Boucher, Marie-Pier, and Patrick Harrop. "Alien Media." *Inflexions* 5 "Simondon: Milieu, Techniques, Aesthetics" (March 2012): 148–59.

Brown, Kathryn. "Computer Art and Cosmopolitan Imagination." In *Interactive Contemporary Art: Participation in Practice*. London: I. B. Tauris, 2014.

Brunner, Christoph, and Jonas Fritsch. "Beyond the Network: Experiential Fields and Urban Media Ecologies." In *Mediacities*, edited by Jordan Geiger. Buffalo, NY: University of Buffalo, 2013.

Bullivant, Lucy. "Responsive Artworks." In *Responsive Environments—Architecture, Art and Design*. London: V&A Contemporary, 2006.

Canogar, Daniel. "Illuminating Public Space—Light Shows in Contemporary Art." *Public Art Review. Light* 15, no. 30 (Spring/Summer 2004): 9–13.

Castres, Mathilde. "Rafael Lozano-Hemmer: Une révolution techno-poétique." *Inferno*, February 3, 2016. http://inferno-magazine.com/2016/02/03/rafael-lozano-hemmer-une-revolution-techno-poetique.

Cecchetto, David. *Humanesis: Sound and Technological Posthumanism*. Minneapolis: University of Minnesota Press, 2013.

Cubitt, Sean. *The Practice of Light: A Genealogy of Visual Technologies from Prints to Pixels*. Cambridge, MA: MIT Press, 2014.

Daniell, Thomas. "Exposure Time: Two Media Art Installations." *Archis*, no. 1 (2004): 106–7.

De Kerckhove, Derrick. *The Architecture of Intelligence*. Basel: Birkhâuser, 2001.

Dewdney, Andrew, and Peter Ride, "Vectorial Elevation—Public Arts Project: Rafael Lozano-Hemmer." In *The New Media Handbook*. New York: Routledge, 2006.

Druckrey, Timothy. "Relational Architecture: The Work of Rafael Lozano-Hemmer." In *Debates & Credits, Media / Art / Public Domain*, edited by Tat'jana Gorjučeva and Eric Kluitenberg. Amsterdam: Centre for Culture and Politics, 2003.

Ekman, Ulrik. "Of the Untouchability of Embodiment I: Rafael Lozano-Hemmer's Relational Architectures," *CTheory* (June 2012). http://ctheory.net/ctheory_wp/of-the-untouchability-of-embodiment-i-rafael-lozano-hemmers-relational-architectures/.

Fernandez, Maria. "Illumination Embodiment: Rafael Lozano-Hemmer's Relational Architecture." *Architectural Design* (August–July 2007): 78–87.

———. "Postcolonial Media Theory." *Art Journal*, no. 58 (1999): 58–73.

Flores, Tatiana. "The Historical (Self-) Consciousness." *Art Nexus* 7, no. 71 (2009): 66–71.

Gladman, Randy. "Body Movies: A Linz Ars Electronica Festival Award Winner on the State of Interactive Art." *Canadian Art* 19, no. 4 (Winter 2002): 57–61.

Hesselberth, Pepita. "Between Infinity and Ubiquity: Perspectives in/on Rafael Lozano-Hemmer's Body Movies." *Continuum: Journal of Media & Cultural Studies* 27, no. 4 (2013): 585–99.

Johung, Jennifer. "Network Dependencies: Rafael Lozano-Hemmer's Relational Architecture." In *Replacing Home: From Primordial Hut to Digital Network in Contemporary Art*. Minneapolis: University of Minnesota Press, 2012.

Laurenson, Pip. "Rafael Lozano-Hemmer: Interview by Pip Laurenson." In *The Fifth Floor: Ideas Taking Space*, edited by Peter Goschluter. London: Tate, in association with Liverpool University Press, 2009.

Lovink, Geert. "Real and Virtual Light of Relational Architecture: Interview with Rafael Lozano-Hemmer." In *Computer Music Journal* 28, no. 2 (Summer 2004): 86–88.

Lozano-Hemmer, Rafael, and Krzysztof Wodiczko. "Zoom Pavilion." In *The Participatory Condition in the Digital Age*, edited by Darin Barney et al. Minneapolis: University of Minnesota Press, 2016.

Massumi, Brian. "Flash in Japan: Brian Massumi on Rafael Lozano-Hemmer's *Amodal Suspension*." *Artforum* 43, no. 2 (November 2003): 37.

———. "Relational Architecture: Rafael Lozano-Hemmer." In *Architectures of the Unforeseen: Essays in the Occurrent Arts*. Minneapolis: University of Minnesota Press, 2019.

Massumi, Brian, and Rafael Lozano-Hemmer. "HUge and MObile (HUMO)." In *Making Art of Databases*, edited by Lev Manovich, Arjen Mulder, and Joke Brouwer. Rotterdam: V2/ NaI, 2003.

Oswald, John. "Disembodied Presence: Rafael Lozano-Hemmer Interview." *Neural: Disturbing the System*, no. 26 (Winter 2006): 40–43.

Ozog, Maciej. "Surveilling the Surveillance Society: The Case of Rafael Lozano-Hemmer's Installations." In *Conspiracy Dwelling: Surveillance in Contemporary Art*, edited by Outi Remes and Pam Skelton. Newcastle-upon-Tyne: Cambridge Scholars Publishing, 2011.

Ravetto-Biagoli, Kriss. "Shadowed by Images: Rafael Lozano-Hemmer and the Art of Surveillance." *Representations* 111, no. 1 (Summer 2010): 121–43.

Stern, Nathaniel. "Flesh-Spaces." In *Interactive Art and Embodiment: The Implicit Body as Performance*. Canterbury: Gylphi Limited, 2013.

Susik, Abigail. "The Perpetration of the Cultural Act: Interview with Rafael Lozano-Hemmer." *Media-N Journal of the NMC* (Fall 2014): 111–13.

Waelder, Paul. "Rafael Lozano-Hemmer: Fragments of a Source Code," *Art.es*, Spain, 48–49 (2012): 78–99.

EXHIBITION HISTORY

SELECTED SOLO EXHIBITIONS

2020

Rafael Lozano-Hemmer: Unstable Presence, San Francisco Museum of Modern Art

2019

Atmospheric Memory, Manchester International Festival, Manchester, England

Rafael Lozano-Hemmer: Presencia Inestable, Museo de Arte Contemporáneo de Monterrey, Mexico

Sintonizador Fronterizo / Border Tuner, Chamizal Park, Ciudad Juárez, Mexico / El Paso, California

2018

Rafael Lozano-Hemmer: Decision Forest, Amorepacific Museum of Art, Seoul

Rafael Lozano-Hemmer: Pulse, Hirshhorn Museum and Sculpture Garden, Washington, D.C.

Rafael Lozano-Hemmer: Solar Equation, Musée national des beaux-arts du Québec, Quebec City

Rafael Lozano-Hemmer: Unstable Presence, Musée d'art contemporain de Montréal

Rafael Lozano-Hemmer: Voice Array, Mexican Cultural Institute of Washington, D.C.

Rafael Lozano-Hemmer: Voice Theatre, Haus der elektronischen Künste Basel—Augusta Raurica, Switzerland

2017

Rafael Lozano-Hemmer: Wavefunction, Subsculpture 9, University of Michigan Museum of Art, Ann Arbor

2016

Rafael Lozano-Hemmer: Preabsence, Haus der elektronischen Künste Basel, Switzerland

Rafael Lozano-Hemmer: Transition States, Gund Gallery, Gambier, Ohio

2015

Rafael Lozano-Hemmer: Pseudomatisms/ Pseudomatismos, Museo Universitario Arte Contemporáneo, Mexico City

Solar Equation, Ulm Cathedral, Ulm, Germany

2014

Rafael Lozano-Hemmer: A Draft of Shadows, Bildmuseet, Umeå, Sweden

Rafael Lozano-Hemmer: Abstracción Biométrica, Fundación Telefónica, Madrid

Rafael Lozano-Hemmer: Pulse Spiral, Exploratorium, San Francisco

Rafael Lozano-Hemmer: Signos e Índices, NC-arte, Bogotá

Rafael Lozano-Hemmer: The Year's Midnight, Canada Council for the Arts, Ottawa

2013

Solar Equation, Lumiere Festival, Durham University, England

Pulse Room, Foundation IZOLYATSIA Platform for Cultural Initiatives, Donetsk, Ukraine

Rafael Lozano-Hemmer: Vicious Circular Breathing, Borusan Contemporary, Istanbul, Turkey

Voice Array, Casa Daros Rio, Rio de Janeiro

Voice Tunnel, Park Avenue Tunnel, DOT Summer Streets, New York

2012

Rafael Lozano-Hemmer: Frequency and Volume, San Francisco Museum of Modern Art

Open Air, Philadelphia Live Arts

Rafael Lozano-Hemmer: Trackers, Fundación Telefónica, Buenos Aires

2011

Pulse Spiral, Pei Ling Chan Gallery, Savannah College of Art and Design

Rafael Lozano-Hemmer: Recorders, Museum of Contemporary Art, Sydney

Rafael Lozano-Hemmer: Trackers, La Gaîté Lyrique, Paris

2010

Pulse Show, Beall Center, University of California, Irvine

Rafael Lozano-Hemmer: Recorders, Manchester Art Gallery, England

Solar Equation, Light in Winter Festival, Federation Square, Melbourne, Australia

Vectorial Elevation, Cultural Olympiad, English Bay, Vancouver

2009

Levels of Nothingness, Guggenheim Museum, New York

Pulse Glow, Glow Festival, City Hall, Eindhoven, Netherlands

2008

Body Movies, Te Papa Museum, Wellington, New Zealand

Body Movies, Fête du 400e anniversaire de Québec, Parc de la Cétière, Quebec City

Frequency and Volume, The Curve, Barbican Centre, London. Commissioned by Kate Rich

Pulse Park, Madison Square Park, New York

Pulse Spiral, Garage Center for Contemporary Culture, Moscow

Rafael Lozano-Hemmer: Recorders, Edith Russ Haus für Medienkunst, Oldenburg, Germany

Under Scan, Trafalgar Square, London

Voz Alta, Memorial for the Tlatelolco student massacre, Mexico City

Wavefunction, Kulczyk Foundation, Poznań, Poland

2007

Pulse Front, Power Plant, Harbourfront, Toronto

Some Things Happen More Often Than All of the Time, Mexican Pavilion, 52nd Venice Biennale

2006

Body Movies, Hong Kong Museum of Art, Hong Kong Arts Development Council

Under Scan, East Midlands Development Agency, Castle Wharf, Nottingham, United Kingdom

Under Scan, East Midlands Development Agency, Market Square, Derby, United Kingdom

Under Scan, East Midlands Development Agency, Humberstone Gate West, Leicester, United Kingdom

2005

33 Questions per Minute, SPOTS Media Façade by Realities:United, Postdamer Platz 10, Berlin

Subtitled Public, Sala de Arte Público Siqueiros, Mexico City

Under Scan, East Midlands Development Agency, Brayford University Campus, Lincoln, United Kingdom

2004

Vectorial Elevation, European Union Day of Welcomes, O'Connell Street, Dublin

2003

Amodal Suspension, Yamaguchi Center for Art and Media, Japan. Access pods and terminals for the piece were installed at: MACBA in Barcelona; MARS Lab in Bonn, Germany; C3 in Budapest; Fundación Telefónica in Buenos Aires; MIT MediaLab in Cambridge, Massachusetts; Bauhaus in Dessau, Germany; ZKM in Karlsruhe, Germany; Kyoto Art Center, Japan; FACT in Liverpool, United Kingdom; Science Museum in London; Ojo Atómico in Madrid; Laboratorio Arte Alameda in Mexico City; SAT in Montreal; Sarai in New Delhi; Eyebeam in New York; IAMAS in Ogaki, Japan; Wood Street Galleries in Pittsburgh; V2_Organisatie in Rotterdam, Netherlands; Itaú Cultural Center in São Paulo; Sendai Mediatheque in Sendai, Japan; Art Center Nabi in Seoul; NTT-ICC in Tokyo; MeSci in Tokyo; Ontario Science Centre in Toronto; Emily Carr in Vancouver; WRO Center in Wrocław, Poland; and Multimedia Institute in Zagreb, Croatia

Body Movies, Duisburg Akzente, Duisburg, Germany

Relational Architectures, Laboratorio Arte Alameda, Mexico City

Vectorial Elevation, Fête des Lumières, Place Bellecour, Lyon, France

2002

Body Movies, Liverpool Biennial, Williamson Square, United Kingdom

Two Origins, Le Printemps de septembre, Place du Capitole, Toulouse, France

Vectorial Elevation, Opening project of Artium, Basque Contemporary Art Museum, Vitoria-Gasteiz, Spain

2001

Airport Cluster, Foto/Graphik Galerie Käthe Kollwitz, Berlin

Body Movies, Cultural Capital of Europe Festival, V2 Grounding, Rotterdam, Netherlands

SELECTED GROUP EXHIBITIONS

2018

Art in the Age of the Internet, 1989 to Today, The Institute of Contemporary Art Boston

I Was Raised on the Internet, Museum of Contemporary Art Chicago

You Are Here: Light, Color, and Sound Experiences, North Carolina Museum of Art, Raleigh

2017

Drawn from a Score, Beall Center, Irvine, California

Electronic Superhighway (1966–2016), Museum of Art, Architecture, and Technology, Lisbon

From Selfie to Self-Expression, Saatchi Gallery, London

Future Energy: Solutions for Tackling Humankind's Greatest Challenge, Art Pavilion at Expo 2017, Astana (now Nur-Sultan), Kazakhstan

Future Shock, Site Santa Fe

Lección de Arte, Museo Thyssen-Bornemisza, Madrid

NGV Triennale, National Gallery of Victoria, Melbourne, Australia

Soundtracks, San Francisco Museum of Modern Art

Unsettled, Nevada Museum of Art, Reno

Wavefunction, University of Michigan Museum of Art, Ann Arbor

2016

Electronic Superhighway, Whitechapel Gallery, London

From Ferron to BGL, Musée national des beaux-arts du Québec, Québec City

Mouse in the Machine: Nature in the Age of Digital Art, Thoma Foundation–Art House, Santa Fe

2015

Big Bang Data, Somerset House, London

DarkMOFO Festival, Detached, Hobart, Australia

Global Control and Censorship, Zentrum für Kunst und Medientechnologie, Karlsruhe, Germany

Luminous Flux v2.0, Thoma Foundation—Art House, Santa Fe

Meta, Narrativas Digitales, Galería Andrea Pozzo–Universidad Iberoamericana, Mexico City

Poetics and Politics of Data, Haus der Elektronischen Künste Basel, Switzerland

Seeing Now, 21C Museum, Durham, North Carolina

Seeing through Light, Guggenheim Abu Dhabi, United Arab Emirates

2014

//the_ART_of_DATA, Boulder Museum of Contemporary Art, Colorado

1+2: Coleccion Jumex in Dialogue with the Lowe Art Museum, Lowe Art Museum, Miami

DarkMOFO Festival, Museum of Old and New Art, Hobart, Tasmania, Australia

Digital Revolution, Barbican Centre, London

Kochi-Muziris Biennale, Kochi, India

Limited Visibility, Contemporary Art Museum, Raleigh, North Carolina

Permanent Collection Presentations of Contemporary International Art Exhibition, National Gallery of Victoria, Melbourne, Australia

Permission to Be Global, Museum of Fine Arts, Boston

Seeing Now, 21C Museum, Louisville, Kentucky

2013

0 to 60: The Experience of Time through Contemporary Art, Pratt Manhattan Gallery, New York

5000 Moving Parts, Massachusetts Institute of Technology Museum, Cambridge, Massachusetts

Modern Contemporary Permanent Collection, North Carolina Museum of Art, Raleigh

Permission to Be Global, The Cisneros Fontanals Foundation, Miami

The Red Queen, MONA Museum, Hobart, Tasmania, Australia

2012

11th Bienal de la Habana, Havana

Field Conditions, San Francisco Museum of Modern Art

Migration, ARNDT Gallery, Sydney

Son et Lumière, 21st Century Museum of Contemporary Art, Kanazawa, Japan

Time-Lapse, Site Santa Fe

2011

Interconexiones 2000–2009: Arte contemporáneo en la Colección FEMSA, Colección FEMSA, Pinacoteca Diego Rivera, Xalapa, Mexico

Non-site, Centre for Contemporary Art, Ujazdowski Castle, Warsaw

Open House, Singapore Biennale 2011, Singapore Art Museum

Rewriting Worlds: The 4th Moscow Biennale

The Spring Party, Madison Square Park Conservancy, New York

2010

Intensif-Station, K21 Ständehaus, Kunstsammlung Nordrhein-Westfalen, Düsseldorf

Decode: Digital Design Sensations, Central Academy of Fine Arts Museum, Beijing

Hyperlinks: Architecture and Design, Art Institute of Chicago

Trayectos: paisaje y memoria. Arte contemporáneo en la Colección FEMSA, Centro Cultural de Chiapas Jaime Sabines, Tuxtla Gutiérrez, Mexico

2009

Art & Electronic Media, bitforms gallery, New York

Decode: Digital Design Sensations, Victoria and Albert Museum, London

Emergentes, Fundación Telefónica, Santiago

Enter Action-Digital Art Now, ARoS Aarhus Kunstmuseum, Aarhus, Denmark

One Hundred Stories about Love, 21st Century Museum of Contemporary Art, Kanazawa, Japan

The World Is Yours, Louisiana Museum, Copenhagen

2008

The Art of Participation: 1950 to Now, San Francisco Museum of Modern Art

Emergentes, Espacio Fundación Telefónica, Buenos Aires

Maquinas y Almas—Souls and Machines, Museo Nacional Reina Sofía, Madrid

Prospect.1, New Orleans Biennial, New Orleans Museum of Art

Synthetic Times—Media Art China, A Beijing Olympics Cultural Project, National Art Museum of China, Beijing

Turn and Widen, 5th Seoul International Media Art Bienniale, Seoul Museum of Art

YOUniverse, 3rd International Biennial of Contemporary Art of Seville, Centro Andaluz de Arte Contemporáneo de Sevilla, Spain

2007

E-art, Musée des beaux-arts de Montréal

2006

Pre-Emptive, Kunsthalle Bern, Switzerland

Zones of Contact, Biennale of Sydney, Art Gallery of New South Wales

2005

Algorithmic Revolution, Zentrum für Kunst und Medientechnologie, Karlsruhe, Germany

Art Meets Media, NTT InterCommunication Center (ICC), Tokyo

2004

Digital Gallery, Los Angeles Museum of Contemporary Art

Navigator Exhibition, National Taiwan Museum of Fine Arts, Taichung

Techniques of the Visible, Shanghai Biennial, Shanghai Art Museum

2003

Ill Communication, Dundee Contemporary Art, Dundee, United Kingdom

2002

Ars Electronica Festival, OK Centrum, Linz, Austria

Cibervisión 2, Conde Duque, Madrid

Egofugal, 7th International Istanbul Biennial

2001

Interactiva '00, Museo de Arte Contemporáneo, Mérida, Mexico

Istanbul Biennial

2000

Centro de Arte Contemporáneo Wifredo Lam, 7th Bienal de la Habana, Havana

Yo y mi Circunstancia, Musée des beaux-arts de Montréal

Olivier Asselin is professor in the department of art history and film studies at the Université de Montréal.

Merete Carlson is an educational consultant for the Center for Educational Resources at University College Capital in Copenhagen, Denmark.

Sean Cubitt is professor of screen studies, School of Culture and Communication, University of Melbourne.

Tatiana Flores is associate professor of Latin American, Latino, and Caribbean contemporary art at Rutgers, the State University of New Jersey.

Rudolf Frieling is curator of media arts at the San Francisco Museum of Contemporary Art.

Robin Adèle Greeley is associate professor of art history at the University of Connecticut and affiliate faculty in the department of architecture at Massachusetts Institute of Technology.

Lesley Johnstone is curator and head of exhibitions and education at the Musée d'art contemporain de Montréal (MAC).

François LeTourneux is associate curator at MAC.

Ulrik Schmidt is associate professor in performance design and visual culture at Roskilde University in Denmark.

Gloria Sutton is associate professor of contemporary art history and new media at Northeastern University.

Unless otherwise noted, all works by Rafael Lozano-Hemmer appear courtesy of the artist; bitforms gallery (New York); Max Estrella (Madrid); Wilde (Geneva and Basel); and Pace (worldwide).

All works by Rafael Lozano-Hemmer are © 2019 Rafael Lozano-Hemmer / Artists Rights Society (ARS), New York / VEGAP, Spain.

Additional copyright credits are provided below, listed by page number.

Page 27 (right): © 2019 Artists Rights Society (ARS), New York / SOMAAP, Mexico City. Page 37: © Krzysztof Wodiczko, courtesy of Galerie LeLong & Co., New York. Page 66: © 2019 Jenny Holzer, member Artists Rights Society (ARS), New York. Page 70: © Marta Minujín.

Additional photography credits are provided below, listed by page number.

Pages 10, 14, 20, 45, 50, 51, 74, 79, 81 (top), 84 (left), 89, 91, 99, 100, 102, 107, 111, 112 (bottom), 114, 119 (left), 136: Mariana Yañez. Pages 18, 27 (left), 34, 40–43, 52, 56, 59, 60, 62, 64, 65 (left), 80, 81 (bottom), 82, 85, 104, 105, 112 (top), 115, 126, 133, 138, 140, 141, 148, 149, 150, 151, 153: Antimodular Research. Pages 19, 44, 46, 57, 86, 88, 92, 94, 113, 127, 134, 135: Guy L'Heureux, courtesy of Musée d'art contemporain de Montréal. Page 21: Peter Mallet. Pages 22, 24: César Flores. Pages 25, 26: Martin Vargas. Page 27 (right): Pablo Esteva, courtesy of Museo Casa Estudio Diego Rivera y Frida Kahlo / INBA, Mexico City. Page 30: James Ewing. Pages 37, 128: Cathy Carver, Hirshhorn Museum and Sculpture Garden. Page 47: Miguel Legault. Pages 48, 49: Devesh Ranjan, Stephen Johnston, Dan Fries, Jessica Imgrund, and Enrico Fonda, School of Mechanical Engineering, Georgia Institute of Technology, Atlanta. Pages 52, 53, 57: Alex Davies. Pages 54, 84 (right), 93, 101 (left), 103: Roberto Ortiz Giacomán, courtesy of Museo de Arte Contemporáneo de Monterrey (MARCO). Pages 58, 101 (right), 137: François Maisonneuve, courtesy of Musée d'art contemporain de Montréal. Page 61: Peter Hauck. Page 65 (right): Jon Rawlinson. Page 66: Lisa Kahane, courtesy Jenny Holzer / Art Resource, NY. Page 70: © Marta Minujín

Archives. Pages 83, 108 (bottom), 109, 116: Oliver Santana. Page 108 (top): Courtesy Museo Universitario Arte Contemporáneo, Mexico City. Page 115: Sébastien Roy, courtesy Musée d'art contemporain de Montréal. Page 142: Idra Labrie.

Exhibition titles for installation views are provided below, listed by page number.

Pages 10, 14, 20, 45, 50, 51, 54, 74, 79, 81 (top), 84, 89, 93, 99, 100, 101 (left), 102, 103, 107, 111, 112 (bottom), 114, 119, 136: *Rafael Lozano-Hemmer: Presencia Inestable*. Pages 18, 21, 52, 53, 56, 57, 59, 126, 153: *Rafael Lozano-Hemmer: Recorders*. Pages 19, 44, 46, 57, 58, 86, 88, 92, 94, 101 (right), 113, 115, 127, 134, 135, 137: *Rafael Lozano-Hemmer: Unstable Presence*. Page 47: *Rafael Lozano-Hemmer: Decision Forest*. Pages 80, 81 (bottom): *Rafael Lozano-Hemmer: Abstracción Biométrica*. Page 82: *Rafael Lozano-Hemmer: Vicious Circular Breathing*. Pages 83, 85, 91, 108, 109, 116: *Rafael Lozano-Hemmer: Pseudomatismos*. Pages 150, 151: *Materialized Surveillance*.

This book is published on the occasion of the exhibition *Rafael Lozano-Hemmer: Unstable Presence*, curated by Rudolf Frieling and Lesley Johnstone with François LeTourneux and co-organized by the Musée d'art contemporain de Montréal and the San Francisco Museum of Modern Art.

Musée d'art contemporain de Montréal
May 24 to September 9, 2018

Museo de Arte Contemporáneo de Monterrey, Mexico
August 22, 2019, to March 1, 2020

San Francisco Museum of Modern Art
April 25 to November 1, 2020

Generous support for *Rafael Lozano-Hemmer: Unstable Presence* is provided by Debbie and Andy Rachleff and Carlie Wilmans.

San Francisco Museum of Modern Art
151 Third Street
San Francisco, CA 94103
sfmoma.org

Published in association with DelMonico Books · Prestel
DelMonico Books, an imprint of Prestel Publishing, a member of Verlagsgruppe Random House GmbH

Prestel Verlag
Neumarkter Strasse 28
81673 Munich

Prestel Publishing Ltd.
14–17 Wells Street
London WIT 3PD

Prestel Publishing
900 Broadway, Suite 603
New York, NY 10003

prestel.com

This book was produced by the publications department at the San Francisco Museum of Modern Art (Kari Dahlgren, director of publications; Amanda Glesmann, senior editor; Lucy Medrich, editor; Brianna Nelson and Jessica Ruiz DeCamp, publications associates).

Project Editor: Kari Dahlgren
Designer: James Brendan Williams
Copy Editor: Kristin Swan
Editorial Assistant and Image Coordinator: Brianna Nelson
Proofreader: Laura Lesswing

Production management by
Lucia|Marquand, Seattle
luciamarquand.com

Color separation by iocolor, Seattle
Printed in China by Artron Art Group
Typeset in Covik Sans, Meta, and Rational TW Text by
     James Brendan Williams and Tina Henderson
Printed on 157 gsm Chinese OJI matte art paper

Library of Congress Control Number: 2019951802

ISBN: 978-3-7913-5911-3

Title pages and page 176: Rafael Lozano-Hemmer, *Call on Water*, 2016 (details). Installation views, *Rafael Lozano-Hemmer: Presencia Inestable*, Museo de Arte Contemporáneo de Monterrey, Mexico, 2019. Photo: Mariana Yañez.